TARTAN

The Highland Textile

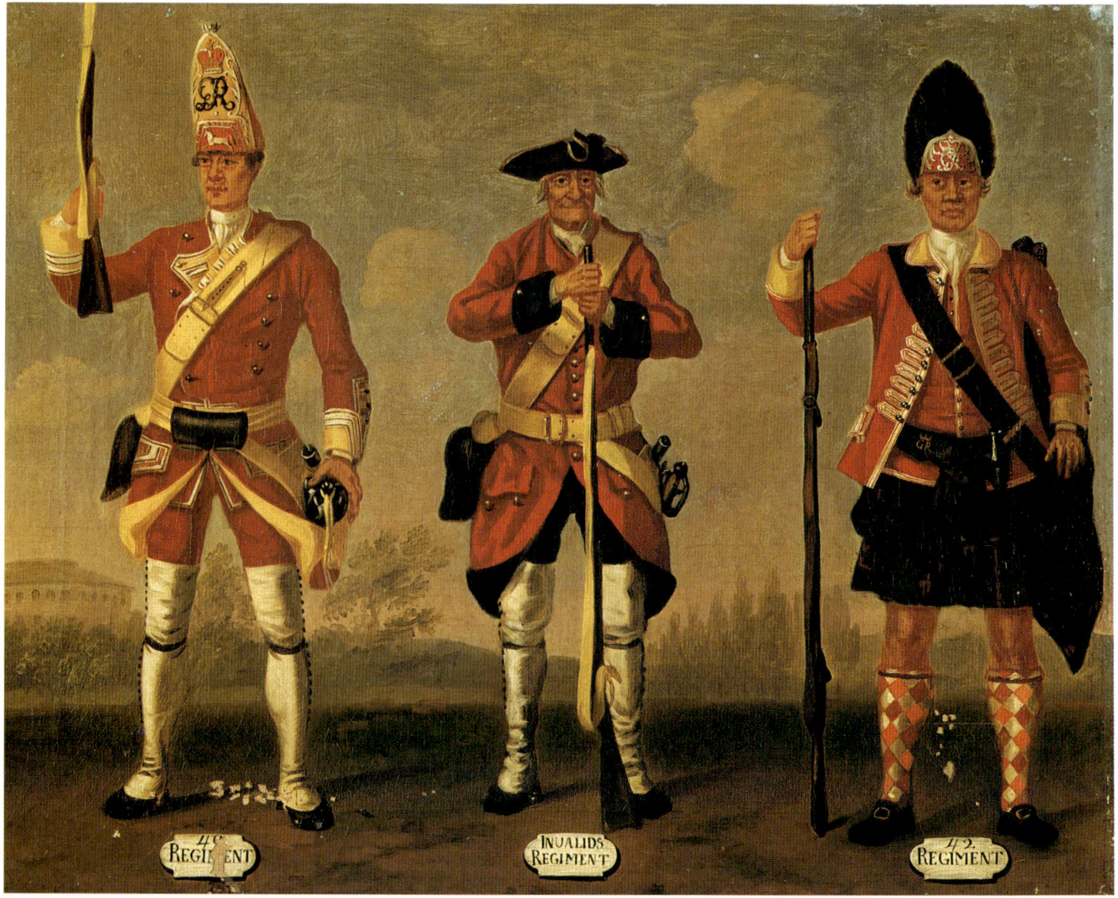

David Morier's painting showing a Grenadier of the 42nd Regiment *(By gracious permission of Her Majesty the Queen)*

TARTAN

The Highland Textile

JAMES D. SCARLETT

SHEPHEARD-WALWYN (PUBLISHERS) LTD

First published in 1990 by Shepheard-Walwyn (Publishers) Ltd
26 Charing Cross Road (Suite 34)
London WC2H 0DH

British Library Cataloguing in Publication Data

Scarlett, James D.
Tartan: the Highland textile.
1. Scotland. Tartans
I. Title
929.9

ISBN 0-85683-120-4

The publisher acknowledges subsidy from the Scottish Arts Council towards the publication of this volume

Typesetting by Alacrity Phototypesetters,
Banwell Castle, Weston-super-Mare, Avon
Printed in Great Britain by
Billing & Sons Ltd, Worcester

Contents

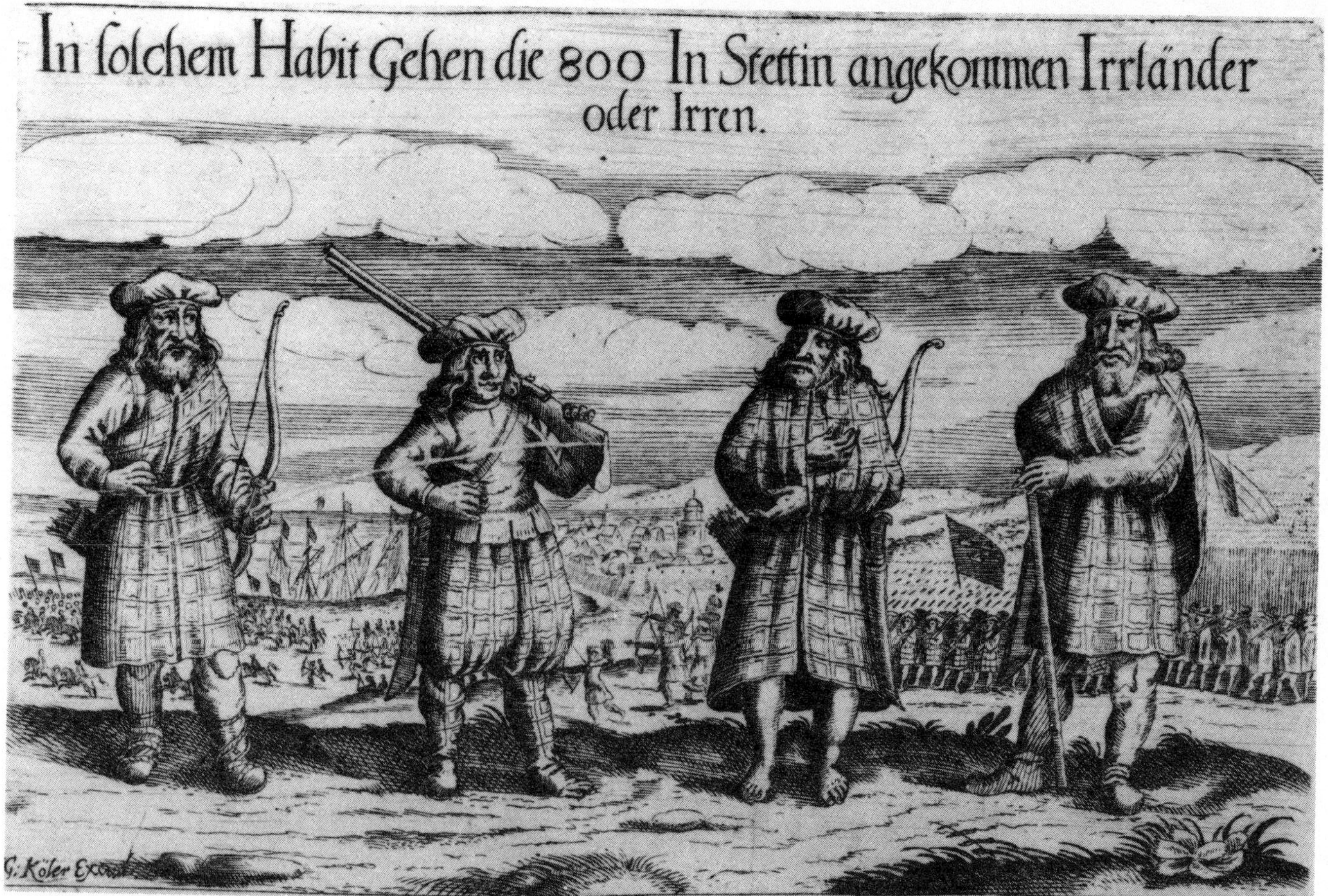

Highland soldiers in the army of Gustavus Adolphus, *c.*1631 *(By courtesy of the Trustees of the British Museum)*

List of Plates

(*See over*)

The tartans for the facsimile plates were all specially woven by the author and with the exception of plates 6 (a) and (b), 7 (a), 8 (a) and (b) and 9 (a) the yarn used was 2/16s worsted dyed to match closely actual early nineteenth-century specimens. The tartans for plates 6 (a) and (b), 7 (a), 8 (a) and (b) and 9 (a) were woven from 2/16s worsted in commercial colours of the present day.

There are no 'standard' colours for tartan, the choice of shade being a matter for the individual weaver who, in the past, sought to achieve a harmonious effect with the colours at his disposal. Shades varied widely from dye-lot to dye-lot and the fact that a colour has been matched to a given specimen does not mean that it will match another, or indeed any other. Therefore, with the exceptions already referred to, no attempt has been made to standardize the colours used for the facsimiles: they are simply the *kind* of colours found in early trade specimens and show the range of shades to be expected.

Preface

'Something of a doubtful mist still hangs over these Highland traditions, nor can it be entirely dispelled by the most ingenious researches of modern criticism . . .'

When D.C. Stewart chose these as the opening words of the Preface to the first edition of *The Setts of the Scottish Tartans*, he had no inkling of the part he was to play, so far as tartan was concerned, in rolling away those mists.

The Setts was born out of a dissatisfaction with the existing tartan books which, although lavishly illustrated, told nothing of the tartans depicted and left the reader to assume that they had been worn by the respective clans from time immemorial. The idea which came to the author in 1942, on a train journey between Inverness and Watford, where he worked as a process engraver, did not become a published book until 1950, by which time he had retired to a cottage in Devonshire; it seemed that when he had dealt with the correspondence engendered by the book there would be little to occupy his declining years. However, early in 1963 a Stirling schoolmaster, Stuart Davidson, had the happy inspiration to found a society for the purpose of studying tartan and Highland dress and invited 'D.C.', among others, to join its Advisory Panel. The Scottish Tartans Information Centre was officially inaugurated by Sir Thomas Innes of Learney, Lord Lyon King of Arms, in July of that year, prospered, and soon became the Scottish Tartans Society. From the beginning D.C. was among the Society's most active workers and what had promised to be a lonely old age became a new life. By the time of his death in 1977 *The Setts* had run to a successful second edition and he left behind a host of friends, a sound basis for future research (including the 'Sindex' filing system) and at least one grateful pupil. This book is an attempt to repay the debt of gratitude and to carry the work of the master a trifle further.

I believe that tartan is a Highland art form and that, like the Highland dress of which it is a part, it is of Pictish or earlier origin. Evidence is scanty, but an extant fragment of cloth shows that the chequered pattern and the 2/2 twill weave that is characteristic of tartan were known in the third century A.D. I find it totally illogical that the ankle-length linen garment, pleated and quilted and 'manifoldly sewed' — the *Leine chroich* or saffron shirt — brought by the invading Scots to Argyll should have somehow developed, as we are sometimes expected to believe, into the large sheet of chequer-patterned woollen cloth that was the belted plaid. Nor do I believe that the Picts went into battle clad only in tattoo marks; they are reputed to have been a hot-blooded race, but surely not as hot as that. The probability that I see is that when the Scots arrived wet and shivering, to face a far harsher climate than their own, they were only too glad to adopt the dress of the natives — that same belted plaid.

Some authorities consider that the tattoo marks of the Picts were tribal marks and it would not be surprising if this were so; here, deeply embedded in Highland folk-memory, might be the reason for the extraordinary spread of the Clan Tartan Idea in the nineteenth century.

It is only comparatively recently that tartan came to the Lowlands, first as a political badge, then as the trademark of everything Scottish and finally to be debased into a tourist souvenir. It is my aim to replace it where it belongs in the framework of Highland social history.

It cannot be said of tartan that truth is stranger than fiction for it is everywhere apparent that the more fantastic the story the more readily it is believed but, long ago, I found that the truth, and the search for it, are far more interesting than all the myths and fantasies. I hope that others will find it so and follow me along the path of discovery.

MILTON OF MOY
MOY
INVERNESS
April 1989

Acknowledgements

Many people have helped me in this work, often unsuspecting, for the chance word or glimmer of an idea can spark off a line of thought that will end who knows where. If anyone sees his hand in what I have done he may assume my gratitude.

More specifically, The Mackintosh gave me free access, as on numerous other occasions, to the Moy Hall tartan collection and to the piece of Prince Charles' plaid there: Mr Brian Nodes, Administrator at Blair Castle, was equally helpful towards my examination of a further fragment of the plaid preserved at Blair.

Ruairidh MacLeod supplied the threadcount for the 'snuff-box' tartan and also gave me a transparency of the Lord Loudoun's Highlanders' tartan.

Mr. Arnold Kennedy, of Oakville, Ontario, Canada gave me the details of the two fragments from the Royal Museum of Ontario described on page 173, and Mr. Robin Maclaren, Kinrara, kindly allowed me to inspect his Bhutanese tartans.

Hugh Cheape, Assistant Keeper at the Royal Museum of Scotland, Queen Street, Edinburgh, smoothed my way towards sundry Wilson papers, particularly their notes concerning *The Scottish Gaël.*

Peter Reynolds, as Reference Librarian at Inverness, and his successor Michele Williams were helpful beyond the strict call of duty in obtaining rare reference books for me and in finding books on their shelves when the Dewey system defeated me.

Gordon Richardson read the main text and by his always-to-the-point and never-carping criticism caused me to put in several things I had not thought of and so to make a better book.

My wife fed me and helped in many ways, especially in unravelling many of the statements that seemed clear enough to me: my publisher has been patient.

My thanks to all of them.

I must pay tribute here to Stuart Davidson, Founder of the Scottish Tartans Society. We were friends for many years and his ready ear for my thoughts and willing sharing of his knowledge have been of inestimable help on many occasions. His death in October 1988 broke my last link with the early days of the Society.

Part One

TEXTILE AND ART FORM

The Textile

The earliest references to tartan speak of 'Helande tertane' and it is in the 'Helande' context that it has to be considered for, centuries before it was adopted in the Lowlands, first as an anti-Union symbol, then as a sign of Jacobite sympathies and finally as the trademark of Scotland, tartan was the indigenous woollen cloth of the Highlands. Then, except in the cattle-trysting towns on the fringe of the Highlands, the sight of a flurry of tartan was more likely to send Lowlanders scurrying behind barred doors and shuttered windows than to bring them out to cheer. Then, too, tartan was an art form, in which the artist-weaver manipulated a limited range of colours to produce designs of squares and rectangles that would appeal to the Celtic eye of his customers. Some weavers were innovators who designed, as it were, from scratch, and some of their designs can be traced among the few genuinely old patterns that have come down to us, but most, it seems, were content to copy from the masters, making small changes, perhaps adding a line here and there to make the new patterns their own.

As nearly as it is possible to be certain of such things, the word tartan derives from the French *tiretaine*[1] by way of the *tertane* aforementioned. James Logan[2], whose ingenuity in finding derivations from the Gaelic often outstrips his skill, attempted to equate it with *tarsuinn*, meaning transverse or across, in allusion to both the pattern and the weaving process. Logan's argument would carry more weight if the Highlanders themselves had ever called tartan anything but *breacan*[3] or if *tarsuinn* occurred among Gaelic weaving words; as things stand, it is unconvincing.

Writers of the romantic school have conjured up a pretty picture of tartan manufacture in the Highland clachans, telling how the fleece was plucked from the sheep; carded and spun by the light of the peat fire; dyed with extracts of local plants used in accordance with jealously guarded recipes handed down from generation to generation; woven with loving care and incantations by the womenfolk for their men and finally shrunk to a dense cloth by being laid out wet on a table made from a door removed and supported on trestles and beaten, thumped and twisted to the accompaniment of much singing and merriment. However, a great deal is left untold which, if revealed, would spoil the idyllic picture.

The native British sheep was a small animal with a fine and somewhat scanty fleece. It came in shades from cream through various browns to black and the fleece was removed by plucking just before the moult, when it was on the point of being pushed out by the new growth. In England in Roman times there was an improved breed of sheep which was probably imported, probably white, probably crossed with native breeds and probably clipped[4]. The improved breed and its crosses would have been of less interest to those dwelling in the fringe areas of Britain, whose prime concern was the getting of clothes for themselves, than to those in the south of England with an export business to the Continent to think of, but knowledge of such developments travels fast. White or near-white fleece is a prerequisite if bright colours are to be dyed and clearly this was available to the Highlanders by the time the art of dyeing had advanced far enough to make tartan possible.

The 'Saxony' type of spinning wheel, with its continuous twist-and-wind mechanism, was a late-comer to the Highlands, its introduction due mainly to attempts made about the end of the eighteenth century to start a linen industry. Prior to that the less sophisticated but in some ways more efficient 'Big' wheel[5] was used but both these machines are static and have to be got out and sat at to be used. It is probably less from Highland conservatism than from its own peculiar suitability that the spindle continued to be used until a late date[6]. For largely pastoral people this little instrument has the advantage that it can be carried about by the spinster who can use it in spare moments or even concurrently with other domestic tasks. This, and the fact that it is simple to make and easy to use, so that there could be many spinsters working at once, probably made up for the spindle's much lower rate of yarn production.

'Carding' the fleece before spinning lays the fibres at random and the thread that results is hairy and aerated thus having excellent qualities of heat insulation and water absorption, the latter, incidentally, causing the generation of heat. Tartan, however, was a hard, smooth cloth nearly proof against wind and water. Such a material is made from a yarn of the worsted type in which the fibres are laid parallel, and for this the fleece is prepared by combing.

Although it is generally assumed that the yarn was dyed after spinning it is known that the alternative of scouring and dying the fleece was also employed. For various reasons the latter method is preferable, but some lubrication of the fleece is necessary for spinning and so it can be employed only if suitable oil is available to replace the natural grease removed by scouring. Among the few natural oils available to the Highland weavers whale oil and fish oil are both suitable for this purpose and it is therefore likely that it was in coastal areas and the Islands that they dyed before spinning, inland areas having to make the best of spinning in the natural grease.

Though there are indications that local variations of shade existed it is clear that dyers all over the Highlands were able, within a limited range, to obtain whatever colours they wanted in clear, bright shades and without great difficulty. Although their secrets have been kept successfully from *us*, their methods cannot have been very secret at the time. There is little information available concerning the ways in which the old time dyers went about their business. Beginning with Logan, various writers have published lists of Highland dye plants with the colours that they are supposed to give but these are often somewhat imaginative and, since few if any working details are quoted and almost all plants will yield a dye of some kind, are of little value. The methods employed by Highland dyers *must* have been dictated to some extent by conditions — slow stewing over peat, in non-stainless vessels — and the social historian may perhaps be better fitted to reproduce them than the earnest craft worker. That such an enterprise would have surprises as well as successes is already known.

Undoubtedly there were women who wove. The mother of the notorious 'Black Officer' of Ballachroan in Badenoch came of the 'line of the female weaver' but the very fact that a female weaver was noteworthy indicates some scarcity. In fact weaving was a full-time professional occupation requiring special apparatus and a long apprenticeship; Highland women already had several full-time occupations and would not have found it convenient to add weaving to them.

The '*luadhadh*' or waulking of the finished web was noted by most of the early tourists from Pennant[7] onwards and subsequently made into a tourist attraction but its practical use is by no means universal. A yarn spun from dyed fleece will shrink if immersed in very hot water, but one that has been dyed after spinning is pre-shrunk, and only a very little further shrinkage will take place when it is soaked. It may be assumed then that tartan was waulked only in those areas where the fleece was dyed before it was spun into yarn. Elsewhere the only finishing process necessary would have been to soak the cloth and wind it firmly round a wooden roller, rewinding from alternate ends every few days until nearly dry. Light pressing with a flat-iron could follow but such niceties may not always have been employed.

Popular descriptions of tartan manufacture in the Highlands before 1745 have drawn too much on imagination but an imaginative reconstruction is the only way open to us in seeking to find out how it was really done. Two clues, one largely disregarded and the other long misread, are there to guide us.

At the period under discussion life did not allow for leisure. The men and boys earned a living and the women and girls looked after the domestic side and so it may fairly be assumed that John Smith would normally have been found working at the forge. The same rule would apply to other "trade" names and in cloth-making we have Shepherd, Dyer, Weaver (and Webber and Webster) and Fuller (and Walker) and their Gaelic equivalents to tell us that these trades were carried on by different people as separate businesses. Significantly, Spinster and Warper do not figure in the list of surnames, but Martin Martin's *A Description of the Western Islands of Scotland*[8], first published in 1703, throws some feeble light. Unusually for his time, Martin has much to say about tartan, which would be of great value if his meaning were ever plain. As it is, what he has to say is entirely open to wishful interpretation and the opening has been fully exploited.

On making tartan, Martin wrote "... and there is a great deal of Ingenuity requir'd in sorting the Colours, so as to be agreeable to the nicest Fancy. *For this reason the Women are at great pains, first to give an exact Pattern of the Plad upon a small rod, having the number of every Thred of the Stripe on it.*"* As written, this means little and its meaning was made no clearer by the change from 'small rod' to 'piece of Wood' in the second edition, but Logan quoted the original form adding, by way of explanation, "... the pattern of the web was not left to the weaver's fancy. He received his instructions by means of a small stick, round which the exact number of threads in every bar was shewn, *a practice in use to this very day.*"* We do not know what it was that Logan saw; possibly it was the back stick of a loom with the cut off thrums hanging from it, but the Sobieski brothers[9] seized upon it and re-wrote Logan's description in their own variety of Old Scots to make it appear that the practice had been in use as early as 1571, the supposed date of their Douai Ms. Their version read "... yt wes vsit to lay vp wt in ylk hovse aine litel wande, quharvpon wes twinit wollin thridis to ye samen nonbre and couloris as thai svld be wowen to ye ylk set in ye lom, and quhen yt onie walds haue tartanis of newe, thai send the wande vntil ye wabster wt sae meikle yarne as yai had neede ..." Thus did the Pattern Stick pass into tartan lore.

Even with such modern aids as quick-drying glue and double sided sticky tape, pattern sticks are difficult to make and soon come unravelled. They tell the weaver less than would a strip of the cloth that they are

* Author's italics.

supposed to define and give no indication of the final pattern. Diligent enquiries over a number of years have failed to discover even one of them and their existence must be regarded as another of the myths about tartan.

Martin has been accused of knowing too little of the outside world to know what would interest it and much of his reporting lacks explicitness. However, he clearly meant to convey some information and we have to find a better interpretation than Logan's of what he intended. 'An exact pattern upon a piece of wood' gives little to build on but D. C. Stewart realized that the two could be separated, the 'exact pattern' being the warp made up for the loom and the 'piece of wood' or 'small rod' the carrying stick on which it was wound in Logan's day and for long after, to be taken to the weaver. This shows a different picture from the popular one, making the women no longer customers giving instructions to the weaver but sub-contractors working under his orders. In this capacity they would certainly be 'at great pains' for a badly made warp is one of the worst things that can happen to a weaver and their employer would be unlikely to tolerate inferior workmanship on the part of his warp-makers. Support is given to Stewart's theory by contemporary accounts of warps being made at home and taken to the weaver and by an eighteenth century picture[10] of a woman winding a warp from a warping mill on to a spool.

Recognizing that some of the people in the cloth-making chain worked as direct sub-contractors while others plied their own trades independently, we can now see the Highland village weaver in a position somewhat analogous to that of the English 'clothier' of the day, who bought fleece and sold it to spinners, bought yarn and sold it to weavers, bought woven webs and sold them to dyers and finishers and finally, having financed the whole process of production, sold the finished cloth to merchants or exporters.

In England, cloth-making was a major industry while in the Highlands it was a small-scale activity supplying mainly local needs; because of this we may suppose that the manufacture of tartan was less rigidly planned than that of West of England Broadcloth. Nevertheless, the available evidence does not refute the proposition that the same principles of organisation applied, rather than that it was a domestic free-for-all.

The cloth that came from Highland looms was hard and harsh, of great durability and often extremely finely woven. The colours were clear, bright and soft, altogether unlike the eye-searing brilliance or washed-out dullness of modern tartans and the patterns too, tended to be bolder and more clearly defined. The result was a harmonious blend of colour and pattern worthy to be looked upon as an art form in its own right.

NOTES

1 LAROUSSE: *Nouveau Dictionnaire Encyclopédique* 56th ed. 1910.
Tiretaine: Nom de plusieurs étoffes anciennes en laine pure ou mélangée.

2 *The Scottish Gaël.* James Logan was born in Aberdeen about the year 1794 and, after attendance at the grammar school there, entered Marischal College to study law. After a near-fatal accident he gave up his studies and took to art, at which he appears to have excelled, but he gave this up in its turn and took to writing which gave him a precarious living until he died in 1872. His greatest work was *The Scottish Gaël*, published in 1831, in which was included a set of tables giving accurate descriptions of fifty-four tartan patterns by the simple process of listing the stripes in order and stating the width of each in units of one eighth of an inch, the first attempt to describe the tartan pattern in layman's terms.

3 *Breacan* derives from *breac* which is applied to anything which is not plain-coloured: spotted, speckled, piebald, chequered or pockmarked.

4 J. P. Wild. *Textile Manufacture in the Northern Roman Provinces.* Cambridge University Press. 1970.

5 Peter Teal. *Hand Woolcombing and Spinning.* Blandford Press. 1976.

6 I. F. Grant. *Highland Folkways.* Routledge and Kegan Paul. 1961.

7 Thomas Pennant. *Tour in Scotland.* 1771.

8 Second edition 'very much corrected' 1716.
Facsimile reprint of second edition by The Mercat Press, Edinburgh, 1970.

9 *Vestiarium Scoticum.* 1842.

10 Keith Dawson. *The Industrial Revolution.* Pan Books. 1972.

Tartan in History

Historical references to tartan, real and imaginary, are not uncommon; their significance, however, has been greatly distorted by over-eager interpretation. Workers in the field of tartan have too often sought to assert the great antiquity or relative modernity of tartan, and especially 'clan' tartans, rather than seek diligently for the truth and, since the available evidence is quite inadequate to prove *anything* the deficiency has been made good by a strange kind of 'wishful proving'. Wishful proofs are found in profusion in the literature of tartan, early and late, and consist of stating an opinion as a fact and adding some more or less relevant historical reference in support, either implying or stating that this proves the point. That it probably proves nothing at all is neither here nor there, so long as the manner of the presentation is sufficiently authoritative; given this treatment the wildest theory will be accepted, copied from one book to the next and so pass into tartan lore. It is almost axiomatic that the wilder the theory the more acceptable it will be, disbelief being reserved for the more scrupulous workers who try to make the truth known.

It therefore behoves us to consider some selected examples of historical mentions and the conclusions that have been drawn from them, with a view to exposing some of the fallacies and underlining the necessity of tracing supposed facts back to their sources before accepting them as genuine. The subject cannot be dealt with exhaustively, the opportunities for wild surmise being seemingly inexhaustible; the intention is to give enough examples to convince the reader of the dangers of accepting apparently authoritative pronouncements without question.

The earliest reports cover the period from the time of the Roman Empire to about 1300 A.D. and are characterized by a simplicity of expression that has been a gift to the school of wishful proof; many are in Latin, some poetic and some just not very good Latin, and this makes any clear meaning difficult to determine. From them we learn of the ancient Celts delighting in bright colours in their dress and, later, of the dress of the Highlanders being 'striped' (sometimes 'striped across'), 'marled', 'variegated', or 'of divers colours'. Virgil has it that '*Virgatis lucent sagalis*'[1] which is usually translated as 'Their cloaks are striped and shining'.

Virgatis is related to *virga*, a streak or stripe of colour on clothes, *lucent* to *luceo,* to be bright, and *sagalis* is perhaps *sagulis,* a short military cloak, so that 'Their cloaks are striped with bright colours' might be considered a better translation. Nearer to the other end of our time scale, a letter written to King Malcolm by the Archbishop of St Andrews about the middle of the eleventh century tells of '*diversis coloribus vestes*', which seems to indicate parti-coloured clothes.

Although it appears to have been possible to say 'chequered' in Latin, there was not at this time nor, indeed, for long after, any word that could adequately describe a tartan type of pattern. Before there could be one, 'tiretaine' had to evolve and change its form to 'tartan', and tartan had to change its meaning from being a type of cloth to being a type of pattern. It has therefore been taken for granted that if one of these early writers wished to describe the tartan pattern 'striped' or 'variegated' would be about the closest he could get. This is reasonable. What is not reasonable is the ready assumption by many modern authors that every time one of these words, or something like it, was used, tartan was intended. In several of the popular tartan picture-books we can read something to the effect that the ancient Celts wore tartan and that their way of describing it was to call it striped or mottled; a very few steps along this path have the Ancient Britons facing Caesar's army in clan regiments, each distinguished by its own tartan.

Among the near-apocrypha of the early days, Logan[2] tells of a certain Achy Edgathach, who introduced the Laws of colours to the ancient Irish. Under these laws, which were also followed by the Caledonians, a person's social status was indicated by the number of colours in his cloak, a king or chief being allowed seven colours, a druid six, nobles four and, by implication, so on down to the peasantry, who had garments of a single colour. Considering the period and the people it is difficult to allow such a tale any credibility and it seems far more likely that if there ever was an Achy Edgathach his 'Law' was no more than a report of an existing state of affairs, namely that finery was for those who could afford it.

Frank Adam[1] goes further and, quoting one MacGregor, recounts that an officiating priest of the early Scotic church wore a robe of *eight* colours, to show that his office placed him above the king. Adam goes on to quote the *Leabhar Breac* and gives the eight colours as yellow, blue, white, green, brown, red, black and purple. Leabhar breac means literally 'a speckled (or piebald or variegated) book' but what it really was or, indeed, if it was just another figment of the Sobieski imagination, appears to be unknown.

Close to the end of the period[3] we come upon various Church ordinances which decreed that ecclesiastics should *eschew* 'all kynd of light and variant hewes in cloathing, as red, blew, yellow and sicklyke, quhilk declares the lightness of the mynd', from which it would appear that there had been a change of heart over the intervening centuries. Logan[2] gives a scale for a 'Clergy' tartan in black, white and grey (Plate 1 (a)), leaving us to infer that it is of ancient origin, but the design has enough in common with a post-1820 'fancy' pattern by Wilsons' of Bannockburn, which they named 'Priest' (Plate 1 (b)), to suggest that it may be either a developed version or an inaccurate rendering of that. Adam[1] makes reference to a *Breacan nan Chleireach* in blue, black and white, but his illustration is a faulty rendering of 'Priest', as are most of the illustrations of the Clergy tartan published subsequently. It is not only the printed word that leads us astray; failure of the colour-printer to register accurately the successive blocks of a four-colour reproduction will often introduce a spurious overcheck and the well-meant efforts of the process engraver, aimed at improving the colour rendering, can suppress detail just as effectively.

Adam also quotes from a list of expenses of John, Lord of the Isles, dated 1355; among the items listed are '*unus caligularium braccatarum de tiretatana*', which he translates as 'one pair of tartan truis'; *caligularium braccatarum* certainly seems to imply trews but *tiretatana* (which I suspect of having gathered an extra syllable in continued repetition) can only be cognate with the Spanish *tiretaña* and the French *tiretaine*, neither of which is patterned.

The earliest unambiguous reference to tartan in English (or, more properly, Scots) occurs in those oft-repeated accounts of King James V's treasurer in 1538: "for iij elnes of Helande Tertane to be hoiss to the Kingis Grace ..." This is 'tertane' and it is 'Helande' and there can be no argument about it. The comment added by a modern author of great authority that "this would have been the bright Royal tartan" can safely be ignored, as there is no indication that the Royal Stuart tartan was named as such much before the end of the eighteenth century and the use of the word 'tartan' to describe a type of cloth not necessarily having any pattern at all persisted until at least 1825, when a merchant ordered a quantity of "plain green coloured tartan without pattern" from Wilsons' of Bannockburn[4].

From now on references occur with greater frequency and, in general, have greater significance. In 1582, George Buchanan wrote in *Rerum Scoticorum Historia* "They delight in variegated garments, especially striped, and their favourite colours are purple and blue. Their ancestors wore plaids of many different colours and numbers still retain this custom, but the majority, now, in their dress, prefer a dark brown, imitating nearly the leaves of the heather, that when lying upon the heath in the day, they may not be discovered by the appearance of their clothes ...". James

Logan[2] derived 'caddis', another type of cloth, from the Gaelic *cath dath* which he translated as 'battle colour', assuming that the Highlander went to war in clothing different from his daily wear, but an even more ingenious etymologist worked out that *cath dath* meant 'strife of colours' i.e., tartan! There was no strife between the colours of the old tartans, which though bright, were soft and gentle. When the violent colour clashes of the early aniline dyes came along the seed planted by Buchanan germinated into the 'hunting' tartan.

When John Taylor, Thames Waterman and self-styled 'King's Water Poet' visited the Braes of Mar during his *Pennylesse Pilgrimage* of 1618 he remarked not only upon the Highland dress "of a warm stuffe of divers colours, which they call Tartane" but also that "any man of what degree soever that comes amongst them, must not disdaine to wear it;" this has been supposed to indicate a strong possessive pride in their dress and their Clan tartans but it is perhaps equally indicative of their awareness of the need to dress for the country and the climate, and their unwillingness to turn their guest loose in the equivalent of jeans and T-shirt. There is no suggestion that Taylor's host had a dress of the Taylor tartan handy.

About the same time as the Water Poet was travelling in the Highlands, a German artist made a woodcut depicting Highland soldiers in the army of Gustavus Adolphus. Their garments are strange and underline the difficulty of the medium (and the difficulty that artists experienced in depicting Highland dress in easier media) but the pattern of the cloth, although only in outline, is clearly a tartan (page vi).

There is a suggestion that tartan had achieved some significance as a mark of identity at the beginning of the eighteenth century in the words of Martin Martin[5]: "Every Isle differs from each other in their Fancy of making Plads, as to the Stripes in Breadth and Colours. This Humour is as different thro the main Land of the Highlands, in-so-far that they who have seen those Places, are able, at the first View of a Man's Plad, to guess the Place of his residence . . .". This has been taken to prove the existence of a fully organised system of District tartans at that time.

Patterns which were recorded soon after the Proscription was raised in 1782 — and which may therefore be regarded as likely to have been in existence before the ban was imposed — indicate that a single basic pattern can serve a wide area, passing from weaver to weaver, each one making some small change according to his fancy. The red Mackintosh tartan can be traced from Moy to and along the Great Glen and south through the hill passes into Badenoch and Perthshire and other, less extensive, groups can be found, though the old patterns available are too few in number to permit a detailed study of such pattern distributions. On present knowledge, Martin was probably stretching the point, but he did say 'guess'.

In 1691, James Philip composed a somewhat turgid epic poem, in Latin, describing the campaigns of Viscount Dundee in the earliest days of Jacobitism. In its Victorian translation[6] this tells of Glengarry's men wearing tartan "woven with Phrygian skill in triple stripe" and of his brother having "a hundred men all clothed in garments interwoven with the red stripe"; two MacLean brothers both wore "the flowing plaid with yellow stripe". These descriptions, poetic licence and all, have provided fuel for many a fiery argument and there have even been some who would have had us believe that the tartans described were the same as the present-day tartans that bear those names. However, there is a clear indication of group-identity, though this would not be very surprising in armies kitted out by their Chiefs who, for reasons of cheapness and personal prestige, would want their men to be in uniform dress.

In July 1703 the Laird of Grant ordered six hundred of his men to turn out "in arms, in good order, with Tartan Coats all of one colour and fashion" for a "match of Hunting" and in the following year the whole of his able-bodied tenantry was "ordained to have readie tartan short coates trewes and short hose of red and grein set dyce all broad springed" and to be ready to turn out for "hosting or hunteing" at 48 hours notice on pain of a fine of five pounds sterling. Here we see a definite beginning of the Clan Tartan Idea, though it is fair to argue that, had the men of Strathspey been accustomed to wearing uniform tartans it would not have been necessary to order them to do so. It is perhaps not without significance that the Lairds of Grant at this time were rather military-minded, to the extent that one of them tried to make all his men grow moustaches and laid down regulations for the same.

We are now coming close to the period of the major Jacobite efforts and to the time when portraits of tartan-clad sitters were painted with increasing frequency, showing a material not very different from what we have to-day: a fine cloth woven in twill, and an approximately square pattern in which the warp and weft, if not actually identical, at least bear some resemblance to each other. Up to and beyond The '45 it is to portraits that we have to look to follow the development of tartan and these portraits have one thing in common: in no case does the tartan shown bear any close resemblance to the modern 'Clan' tartan. Even in the fine series of Grant portraits painted by Richard Waitt there is no suggestion of any general tartan uniformity. As may be expected, vigorous efforts have been made to explain this away in the 'Clan' tartan context; perhaps the most likely explanation is that, if tartan *had* reached a group-identifying stage of its development it had not become sufficiently important to supplant the sitters' best clothes for special occasions.

The written records of The '45 tell of a young Highlander apprehended in the debacle at Culloden. Claiming to be a Campbell, he had no bonnet and hence no black, Hanoverian, cockade to prove his loyalty. His captor explains that these cockades (black for Government troops and white for Jacobites) were the only positive means of identification and this has been cited as proof that Clan tartans did not exist in 1745. What it really tells us is that tartan was not a certain means of identification as indeed it could not be in a battle in which even brothers were fighting on opposing sides.

Another account tells of a group of Jacobite MacDonalds who were concerned lest they might come up against their 'bretheren and nighbours' the MacDonalds of Skye "seeing we were both Highlanders and both wore heather in our bonnets, only our white cockades made some distinction". D. W. Stewart[7] commented "The inference from the passage is, that the opposing battalions being of the same great family, the sole remaining difference between them was the cockade." John Telfer Dunbar[8] remarks "If all the MacDonalds wore the same tartan, surely the writer would have mentioned this rather than the heather which they all wore in their bonnets".

Inconclusive though the arguments about Clan tartans now are, the Government of the day, perhaps remembering the 'Hunting Matches' of 1703 and 1704, seemed to think there was something dangerous about tartan for it included in its measures to break the power of the Clans, and thus to prevent further Jacobite outbreaks, an absolute prohibition on the wearing of tartan or Highland dress in Scotland by any but soldiers. There are signs that this ban soon ceased to be rigidly enforced[9] and apart from the loss of many old patterns, which simply fell into disuse and disappeared, the important result of the ban was that manufacture of tartan left the Highland villages and became concentrated in factory villages on the Highland fringes, where the material was made in great quantity for the Army and for export to the Colonies where, being bright, cheap and durable, it was popular for dressing slaves. These large concerns could make a much wider range of patterns than could any village weaver and when the ban was lifted, in 1782, the demand was for 'latest patterns and bright colours'; Clan tartans still did not count for much. However, by 1815, Stewart of Garth and Robertson of Struan were writing to each other about preserving the old Clan setts before they were entirely lost and at about the same time the Highland Society of London set up its own collection of Clan tartans certified as such by the Chiefs.

Then Sir Walter Scott came on the scene. With all the romantic ardour he employed in bringing history back to life — and improving on it — there could have been no better publicist for the Clan Tartan Idea, and when he, with Garth, stage-managed the King's visit to Edinburgh in 1822, 'Clan' tartans were seen to have arrived. Never mind that some of them had suddenly changed from being numbered patterns on some manufacturer's list to being the ancient and traditional MacSomething tartan. The King wore the kilt. Tartan was no longer the dress of northern barbarians or political dissidents; it had become respectable and the garb of loyal subjects. Patterns that had been made by local weavers and bought by the local people because there were no others available had become identified with the people and recognised as a badge of clanship. Later, under the influence of romantic exaggeration, a tartan cult was to develop but that story will be told in its place.

NOTES

1 *The Clans, Septs and Regiments of the Scottish Highlands.* W. & A. K. Johnston, 1908. Revised 1934. Largely re-written 1955.
2 *The Scottish Gaël.*
3 13th cent.
4 Copy in the author's possession.
5 *A Description of the Western Islands of Scotland.*
6 Scottish History Society. 1888.
7 *Old & Rare Scottish Tartans.* 1893.
8 *History of Highland Dress.* Oliver & Boyd, 1962.
9 *Statistical Account of Scotland.* c.1792. Although this was not published until some years after the raising of the Proscription the wording of the various Ministers' Accounts of their parishes leaves little doubt that in some places the Highland dress had never been laid aside. In Petty, '... the tartan kilt and hose ... are still the ordinary dress ...". In Moy, "The tartan plaid and kilt ... are still in general use". A minister on Skye said that it would take more than an Act of Parliament to make his people give up the old dress.

Tartan in Books

Since tartan first became interesting books have been written in which it has figured extensively if not always informatively. Many came into being to cope with the tartan-hunger that has been abroad from late Victorian times to the present day and many touch so lightly upon the subject as to be of little or no value to the serious enquirer. To deal with all would require superhuman knowledge and more space than is available. What has been attempted is to review briefly the most important, to tell of their faults and virtues and to make some assessment of their individual contributions to our story.

Tartan books come in two kinds. First there are those consisting principally of short histories of the Clans accompanied by pictures of their tartans, with introductory essays on tartan, Highland dress and other kindred subjects and lists of affiliated septs; and second, those much less common, that are actually about tartan. Some attempts have been made to combine the two but the markets are too different for a compromise to be successful.

It is rare for books of the first kind to have anything useful to say about tartan and their value to the student is as an 'instant' collection of tartans for reference. Since there is inevitably some overlap between the products of different publishers there is room for two or three of these volumes in most libraries. Although the type has developed into a tourist's handbook some of the early productions are important source-works and collectors pieces. One such, an Edwardian version of W. & A.K. Johnstons' *The Scottish Tartans* was issued as a catalogue by the Edinburgh firm of Cranston & Elliot; the illustrations of the Clan tartans and Arms are supplemented by sketches of Highland dress worn after the manner of the time and after the supposed manner of earlier times. Elegant gentlemen shoot, fish or contemplate the landscape while their ladies, in long tartan skirts and brightly coloured bonnets, play golf or just look on from a safe distance; fighting clansmen stand arrayed for battle in full evening dress. Additional to the standard edition are half-a-dozen plates showing 'National Sports'; my favourite is of an elegant athlete putting the shot, stripped to his kilt and long-sleeved woolly vest.

The first book with anything of consequence to say about tartan was James Logan's *The Scottish Gaël*, published in 1831. Logan was born in Aberdeen about 1794, attended grammar school there and entered Marischal College with the intention of studying law. His studies were brought to a premature end when he received a severe blow on the head either from a carelessly thrown quoit in the College quadrangle or from a badly aimed hammer thrown during an athletics meeting.This incident almost cost him his life and when he eventually recovered he became a gatherer of historical, archaeological and antiquarian lore. *The Gaël*, which he sold outright to the publisher for one hundred guineas, was the outcome of a tour of the Highlands that he made about 1826 and thereafter for some years he earned a livelihood writing for magazines. In later life the results of his accident became apparent in a quick-tempered and quarrelsome nature which caused him frequently to fall out with his benefactors. In 1866, after he was 'rusticated' from Charterhouse, where he had been found what had promised to be a permanent and comfortable home, friends took care of him until his death in 1872.

Logan was a reasonably accurate reporter of what he saw but suffered from a fault, common in his day, of an over-romantic approach to history; in particular, he liked to present the Gaelic culture as something that was inherited, ready-made, from ancient times, rather than as something that developed gradually over some centuries. His deductions have therefore to be treated with caution, but this does not matter a great deal for his importance to us is that he was the first to attempt to record the patterns of tartans; he did this by means of tables in which "Commencing at the edge of the cloth, the depth of the colours is stated throughout a square, on which the scale must be reversed or gone through again to the commencement." The unit of measurement was one eight of an inch and the intention was that the figures given should be repeated back and forth to fill the width of the web, the same pattern then being woven in the weft; tables are given for fifty-four tartans. There is inevitable distortion at the edge of a web and it is far more difficult to measure the width of a stripe than to count the number of threads, so this is not a highly accurate method of setting down a pattern. Moreover, Logan was somewhat inconsistent in the application of his own rules, making the translation of his tables not always a simple matter, but he laid the foundations for others to build upon.

All in all, *The Gaël* is a valuable reference book though less so to those who take its pronouncements without question.

In 1842, the brothers John Sobieski Stuart and Charles Edward Stuart published their masterpiece, *Vestiarium Scoticum: from the Manuscript formerly in the Library of the Scots College at Douay; with an Introduction and Notes.*

These two young men, originally named John and Charles Allen, had made their appearance in the Highlands about 1825. Widely supposed to have been the legitimate grandsons of Prince Charles Edward, they were quickly accepted into society and before long were letting it be known that they had a manuscript dated 1721, a copy of another, written before 1571 and in the possession of their father in London, which gave details of some seventy-five Clan tartans that had been current at that time. Later, another copy, said to have been made before 1608, came into the picture. Beginning by handing out patterns to their friends, they finally produced the edited version of the original document, supplemented by information contained in the two copies; the artwork was by brother Charles and the tartans were illustrated by means of the 'Machine Painting' process invented by William and Andrew Smith, of Mauchline. Since the descriptions of the tartans are by no means as explicit as was claimed — "Mackfarlan of ye Arroquhar hath thre stryppis quhite vpon ane blak fyeld" is fairly typical — the detailed design of these tartans must also be laid at Charles' door. The brothers had a great supporter in Sir Thomas Dick Lauder, who championed their cause in argument with Sir Walter Scott, and he was allowed to make a copy of the 1721 document which Charles "with very great politeness, agreed to illuminate for me with drawings of all the Tartans . . . by which labour he has made me a most beautiful book." There is in the Royal Library, at Windsor Castle, 'a most beautiful book' which goes by the name of the Lauder Transcript though there are some features which suggest that it may have been entirely the work of Charles, perhaps the prototype of the eventual book.

On publication, the *Vestiarium* was largely accepted for what it claimed to be and it was not until some years later that any public controversy developed concerning its authenticity; by that time, many of these 're-discovered' tartans had become recognised, on the flimsiest of evidence, as the 'true and ancient' tartans of the Clans and Lowland tartans, previously unknown, had become established[1].

James Logan puts in another appearance in the years 1845 to 1847, collaborating with the artist R. R. McIan in *The Clans of the Scottish Highlands*. The two volumes were issued in loose sections over the two-year period and Logan states in his Introduction some of the intentions behind the work; "Accurate data will be furnished on the clan tartans." "Those will be given which are acknowledged by the present chiefs and clans . . ." "Some of the sketches will represent individuals who have in any way distinguished themselves, when authentic portraits can be procured."

And so on. The intentions were clearly good and some notes on dress and tartan were included in respect of most of the sketches. McIan does not enjoy a high reputation for accuracy and his sketches, representing Highlanders, male and female, from all walks of life and periods of history, vary from fanciful to incredible in their composition but, in general, he did not do too badly with the tartans, faults, where they occur, being traceable to the method of reproduction employed. This involved the lithographing of the outlines, which were then handed out to hack artists for colouring; differences were therefore likely to occur between two plates of the same sketch and if the checking of the finished plates was done carelessly spurious tartans could, and did, result. In the excellent modern reprint the tartan shown on the Buchanan figure bears no resemblance to the familiar asymmetrical Buchanan tartan though the pocket edition of the 1890s shows it quite clearly. The 'Shaw' plate, painted from a 'scarce old portrait' depicts Farquhar Shaw — shot in the Tower of London for his part in the Black Watch mutiny of 1743 — clad in the regimental tartan. Logan describes this[2] as "blue, black and green" but "a red stripe in the middle of the former is often introduced" to distinguish the philabeg from the belted plaid. It was a weakening of the colour in the body of the black stripe that caused it to be interpreted as two black bars on a blue ground and gave us an entirely baseless 'Shaw' tartan that lasted until 1969, when the Chief, Shaw of Tordarroch, had a new and more historically correct tartan designed.

The Clans of the Scottish Highlands was reprinted as one volume in 1980[3]. Presumably, publishers who issue such reprints do so primarily as a commercial venture, but the service they do for the student in putting important source-works within his reach is inestimable.

William and Andrew Smith used the 'Machine Painting' process to illustrate their own book, *Authenticated Tartans of the Clans and Families of Scotland* which appeared in 1850, the year in which Thomas Smibert's *The Clans of the Highlands of Scotland* was published. Both books set out to record and illustrate genuine tartans and to authenticate their use as far as possible. This last was not an easy task, for the Clan Chiefs of the time appear to have been singularly lacking in knowledge of the tartans that they and their forbears should have been wearing since the Celtic mists parted — at least in what was fast becoming the popular imagination. Smibert says, "The Highland chiefs themselves have of late thrown the most serious obstacles in the way, seeing that they have been too ready to adopt changes at the mere dictation of fancy, with a view to improving, no doubt, the look of their family setts" and Robertson of Struan, in his correspondence with Stewart of Garth, previously mentioned, concerning the preservation of the old Clan setts, tells that, in his efforts to discover the correct Robertson tartan he had consulted several old men of the Clan who claimed to know and all had given him different answers.

Smibert illustrated fifty-five tartans, mostly specimens obtained from Wilsons' of Bannockburn, by colouring-in the squares of finely ruled graph paper, an effective if inartistic method, making up for those shortcomings by making his Clan histories very long and detailed. The Smiths, on the other hand, had histories of only a few lines but the illustrations of sixty-nine tartans, culled from various trade sources and private collections are works of art. In brief, the 'machine' which executed the 'painting' consisted of a bank of ruling pens mounted to slide on a guide-rail so that a series of parallel lines could be drawn in opaque colour on a piece of black paper affixed to a turntable. Pens that were not needed could be lifted clear of the paper and the whole bank could be adjusted laterally, so that although the pens were mounted about a quarter of an inch apart, a number of strokes with small adjustments between them would result in a band of colour made up of fine lines corresponding to the 'warp' of the picture. The 'weft' was put in by rotating the turntable through ninety degrees and repeating the process. These operations were gone through for each colour of the tartan in order, the lightest first, and resulted in a surprisingly realistic representation of a piece of plain-woven fabric.

Nearly forty years were to elapse before the next major work, James Grant's *Tartans of the Clans of Scotland* made its appearance in 1886. Despite its size — 15″ × 12″ × 1½″ thick — this is the prototype of the majority of the pocket-sized tartan picture-books that fill the bookshops in tourist areas of Scotland to-day, and while it is a classic and a collectors' piece, it has as little to say about tartan as any of them.

Last of the major picture-books was the handsome two-volume 'Library Edition' of *The Tartans of the Clans and Septs of Scotland* published by W. & A.K. Johnston in 1906. Many tartans made their first appearance in this, including 'Stewart, black and white', but there is no information as to their origins. Otherwise, it is the mixture as before.

Donald William Stewart was a partner in the Edinburgh firm of Romanes and Paterson and well-known in Edinburgh antiquarian circles when his *Old & Rare Scottish Tartans* was published in 1893, an entirely new departure in tartan books, for it was *about* tartan and about very little else, Highland dress and the *Vestiarium Scoticum* being taken in only as ancillaries to the main subject. The greater part of the book is taken up with an introductory essay on the history of tartan and Highland dress which includes an account of the origin of the *Vestiarium*, based on unpublished records; this is followed by descriptions and illustrations of forty-five tartans, chosen for their particular interest by reason of age, rarity or inaccessibility. The problem of illustrating tartan in colour was overcome by the use of mounted specimens of fabric hand-woven in silk. The credit for this idea was claimed by the tartan manufacturers William Cross & Co., of Glasgow, in their advertisements in *The Celtic Monthly* but the pieces of silk were mounted by Mrs. Stewart and her sister! 'D.W.' made much of the care taken to match the colours of the silk samples exactly to the originals but fell far enough short of accuracy in the case of MacDonald of Kingsburgh to cast doubt on several of his other examples; these will be dealt with when the tartans in question come under discussion.

In 'D.W.'s son, Donald Calder Stewart, born in the same year as *Old and Rare*, the tartan bug lay dormant for many years until, returning to the south from Inverness in 1942 and looking for something to read on the train, he picked up one of the current tartan picture-books at the station bookstall. By the time he reached his home at Watford he had decided how books about tartan should be written and began to put his energy to work in writing one. Owing to war-time exigencies it was not until 1950 that *The Setts of the Scottish Tartans* was published[4], a fitting successor to *Old and Rare*. Covering much the same field of history *The Setts* also dealt with tartan design and offered weavers, for the first time, a comprehensive collection of thread counts, a total of two hundred and sixty-six covering most of the well-known tartans and many less well known as well as a number of patterns of historical interest. *The Setts* also broke new ground in the matter of illustrations, using 'colour strips' to show the stripes of the warp as they would appear on the loom. Revised and reprinted in 1974 *The Setts*[5], the first modern book about tartan, has remained a work of prime importance on the subject. Its author has a just claim to be considered the founder of serious tartan research.

NOTES

1 *Scotland's Forged Tartans.* Paul Harris Publishing. 1980.
2 *The Scottish Gaël.*
3 By Webb and Bower (Publishers) Ltd., Exeter.
4 By Oliver & Boyd, Edinburgh
5 By Shepheard-Walwyn, London

Tartan in Paintings

Family portraits, which began to become popular in the Highlands early in the eighteenth century, have been a fruitful source of tartan setts and some beautiful old patterns have been preserved in them. It is a mistake, however, to assume that paintings are necessarily faithful reproductions of the tartans worn by the sitters for, however fervently an artist may be eulogised for the accuracy of his work he is unlikely to have achieved a photographic standard in this respect and probably did not wish to do so.

The portrait painter has the capability of falsifying the true record to a very large extent and, although it is not to be supposed that any would deliberately set out to do so, an individual's skill must have some effect and he would not be an artist if he took no account of his own impressions of the sitter, the sitter's impression of himself, and even of the purpose of the picture and the place where it is to be hung, in making his composition. The famous portraits by Richard Waitt of the Grant 'Piper' and 'Champion' hung on either side of the main staircase at Castle Grant and this alone could account for the wearing of almost identical tartans — apparently modelled on another Waitt portrait, that of Patrick Grant of Milburn — by both subjects. Waitt could certainly draw tartan when he wished to but there is a strangely unfinished look about that of the Champion and this may be the reason for the small differences that exist between these two.

There is a great lack of evidence to show that the pattern of a tartan had any important significance in the early eighteenth century and stories have been told of itinerant artists travelling round the Highlands with pack horses loaded with canvasses already complete except for painting in the faces. It does not matter if these stories are true, only that their truth is possible and that clients were therefore not unduly fussy about the precise accuracy with which their tartans were depicted. Since in the last resort it was the sitter (or his wife) who decided whether or not the portrait was a good one, perhaps we need not expect a high degree of accuracy, even by intention, in the delineation of tartan, the sketchiest representation being adequate for the purposes of the picture. When the hunt was on for the correct pattern of the Earl of Inverness' tartan, the portrait painted of the Earl (as Duke of Sussex) by Sir William Beechey was consulted but because of bad colour and indifferent draughtsmanship gave no help; however, when a specimen of the tartan made for the Earl came to light, it became clear that Beechey had, according to his lights, painted the same thing.

Allan Ramsay painted many fine portraits of Highland gentlemen in the years immediately before The '45. In *his* portrait, Norman, 22nd Chief of the Clan MacLeod, wears a plaid of the Murray of Tullibardine tartan in which blue, green and black are all shown as black. Since MacLeod had Murray connections this has not been considered inappropriate — artistic license was granted for the changes of colour — but also among Ramsay's clients were the Earl of Loudoun, who wears a plaid of a pattern remarkably like Tullibardine and the Jacobite Duke of Perth and David, Lord Ogilvy who both wear plaids for which it could have served as a model. Dare we suppose that all these had Murray affiliations or is it more likely that Ramsay had a plaid about his studio and draped it over a lay figure so that he could go on painting after his clients had gone home? Incidentally, in the MacLeod portrait and in that of the 7th Earl of Wemyss and his wife, Ramsay painted trews cut *with* the cloth instead of on the bias. Can we really believe it?

David Morier, whose standards of accuracy were high enough for him to be commissioned to execute a whole series of paintings depicting the uniforms of the British Army, also fell into the tartan trap. His painting of a Grenadier of the 42nd Regiment (Frontispiece) shows diced hose in which the red and white squares join side by side, a circumstance that cannot occur; with tartans un-mixed colours can meet only corner to corner.

Morier is best known for his painting of 'An Incident in the Rebellion', which was painted after Culloden on the orders of the Duke of Cumberland. Showing a group of men of Barrell's Regiment repelling a Highland charge (the first time they had ever stood against one and the last time they ever had to) this points a different moral, providing a splendid example of the way in which a blind leap to a conclusion can gradually become an incontrovertible fact. Recently, it has become possible to read that the Highlanders in the painting were modelled by Jacobite prisoners; earlier versions were that they 'are thought to have been', 'may have been' and 'probably were' but the original was by Lord Archibald Campbell[1] who wrote 'The Highland soldiers must have been painted from prisoners, as it is impossible that an English soldier, sitting as a model, could have put on the Highland dress so well.'

If 'Put not your trust in portraits' is a sound maxim, a sounder is to treat reproductions of them, either painted copies or in the form of coloured plates in books, with reserve. I have already pointed out that in colour printing handwork on the blocks or inaccuracies in registration can introduce spurious detail and despite improvements in techniques and materials this risk remains; three reproductions of the Grant 'Champion', two coloured and one black and white, show three very slightly different tartans. As for painted copies, these are subject to both human error and artistic license. In the late 1970s there could be seen in Inverness an excellent modern copy of Morier's 'Incident', excellent, that is, except that some of the 'Rebells' were wearing tartans that were not invented until nearly a hundred years after the battle.

It is not only the artist-copier, painting what he does not understand or what he thinks should be there, who can perpetrate such howlers: so widely have the tartan myths been spread that any script- or guide-book writer will, in complete ignorance, write the most arrant nonsense and never think that it might not be true. When the new Culloden Centre of The National Trust for Scotland opened in 1984 the film show of the battle had some of its Jacobites in tartans from the *Vestiarium Scoticum* and others in 'reproduction' colours that were invented in the late 1940s. Of course, this is 'only for the tourists' but those tourists are gullible and think that they are being given factual information. Once false information has been disseminated by a supposedly authoritative body it is virtually impossible to correct it.

All this being said, it must be recognised that an artist painting from life will probably not make serious mistakes; if he does make a mistake it is likely, like the dicing of the 'Grenadier's' hose, to be so obvious that no-one will be misled. His work is, in any case, the best record we can get of that particular tartan and we must therefore make the best possible use of it. Painstaking reconstruction of a sett by extracting and collating fragments from different parts of a painting of a plaid or shawl will in most cases yield a plausible result for which some corroboration may then be sought. Once in a while, as in the case of the Earl of Inverness' tartan, a reconstructed sett may correspond with one recorded elsewhere, but otherwise some similarity to other tartans known to have originated in the same locality may come to our aid. Failing these, it will be necessary to take a painting at its face value, always keeping it at the back of the mind in readiness for the day when something like it does turn up.

NOTES

1 *Highland Dress, Arms and Ornament*. Constable & Co 1899. Reprinted by Dawsons of Pall Mall 1969.

Military Tartans

In view of the importance which Government departments attach to their files it is somewhat surprising that War Office records reveal so little information about the early military tartans. This may in part be due to the practice of having specimens submitted every two years (which was the interval between the issue of new plaids and jackets) for Royal approval; since the earliest tartans were made more or less locally there would have been no need to keep a central record, the approved patterns being returned to the local military authorities to be handed on to the people who were going to make the tartan. However it may have come about, the fact remains that we have no official records of the earliest military tartans or their origin and so their history, which is essentially the history of the Black Watch tartan, is compounded in large measure of legend, regimental tradition and pure surmise, to which is added a very little ascertainable truth. In a matter so poorly documented as tartan, legend and tradition, containing, as they nearly always do, an element of truth, are valuable sources of information, but it is always necessary to remember that there may be no more than a grain of the essential ingredient and that even this may be distorted out of recognition. The element of surmise in any tartan story is difficult to isolate, for we usually come upon it in its third or fourth generation, when what may originally have been only a blind and illogical guess has been copied and paraphrased from book to book until it has taken on the appearance of a proven fact.

The accepted theories concerning the origin of the Black Watch tartan are well known. It is (a) an old Campbell tartan chosen for the Regiment because the majority of the Independent Companies that formed it were commanded by Campbells, or because the Earl of Crawford, the Regiment's first Colonel, had Campbell connections, or (b) it was specially designed for the new regiment because the Earl, being a Lowlander, had no tartan of his own to give it; it has also been claimed as a Grant pattern[1]. Some of those who support the second theory have suggested that the new design was arrived at by combining the tartans of the six companies and removing distinguishing overchecks but this idea rests upon the assertion by General David Stewart of Garth[2] that before embodiment each Independent Company wore the tartan of its commander which we now know to be untrue, certainly after 1733; some broad similarity between the tartans is also implied and this would be unlikely if they were 'clan' setts. D. C. Stewart[3] made out a tentative case for the tartan to be a dark version of Royal Stuart and this theory was unfortunately accepted as a fact and publicised as such in the 1960 revision of *The Clans, Septs and Regiments of the Scottish Highlands.* A further hypothesis is that it derives from the Fraser tartan (Plate 4 (f)) as a compliment to Simon, Lord Lovat, who is reputed to have proposed the formation of Highland regiments and to have retired to the Jacobite camp in a fit of pique when the suggestion failed to meet with approval. If the red of this tartan is changed to green and the green to black something very close to Black Watch appears but to pay a compliment so well concealed that two hundred and fifty years passed before it was understood seems hardly worth the trouble.

Although it is not part of the story of the origin of the tartan, it is appropriate to refer here to the tradition that when Lord John Murray was Commandant of the 42nd (*c.* 1750) he had two red lines added to the regimental tartan as a mark of distinction for the Grenadier Company. This has caused some puzzlement, for the resulting tartan, supposedly exclusive to the Grenadiers and called the 'Athol Sett' is the same as Murray of Athol. David Morier's painting of a Grenadier of the 42nd (Frontispiece), painted about 1750, is adduced by Lord Archibald Campbell[4] as evidence of the accuracy of this tradition and his word has been relied upon by almost every writer on military tartans since.

Any one of these stories can be made to sound convincing if delivered with a sufficient air of authority but I believe that all are seriously in error and that a much more accurate and logical picture can be drawn with the aid of information that has come to light during the last twenty years or so, though *controlled* guesswork is still necessary.

Let us begin in the tradition of the best detective stories and set down what we can claim to know, beyond reasonable doubt, about the early military tartans:

I In May 1725 General Wade issued an instruction regarding clothing for the Independent Companies saying "... the plaid of each Company to be as near as they can of the same Sort and Colour". This might be taken to mean that each company had its own tartan but any ambiguity in this direction is cleared up by a letter written by the factor of Ballindalloch on 11th July 1733. Covering the despatch of 269 ells of tartan for the use of the Independent Companies, the letter refers to 60 ells of cloth not quite ready, which 'any that wants may have in two dayes if it's called for', and, 'If my Lord Lovat has not enough, he may get that 60 ells:'. Later, the factor, Robert Grant, asks the recipient to see that the bearer of the letter receives payment from 'the Capts. that get the tartan.' This letter is supported by Ballindalloch Estate accounts and makes clear that, even if the Independent Companies did not all wear the same tartan in 1725 they certainly did so in 1733[5].

II In the early 1970s, a researcher working in a library in America came upon a piece of tartan with a note attached saying that it had been 'sent to Lord Loudoun for his Highlanders' in 1747, when they were stationed in the Low Countries. The Earl of Loudoun was a Campbell and a staunch Hanoverian. He was given authority to raise a Highland regiment in April 1745 and his officers' commissions were dated 6th June in that year. After an inauspicious career which included the Rout of Moy and the capture of three of its Companies at Prestonpans, Lord Loudoun's Highlanders, as they were known, were sent to the Low Countries in 1747 and were brought home and disbanded at Perth in June 1748.

As the second Highland regiment it might be supposed that had the present Black Watch tartan then been in existence Loudoun's Regiment would have worn it or a simple variation upon it. However, the specimen is a plain blue, black and green check with a red line guarded with black on the blue and a yellow line on the green (Plates 2 (a) and 4 (b).[6]

III Late in the eighteenth century Wilsons' of Bannockburn were making a tartan designated '42nd Pattern Kilts' which was a simple blue, black and green check having a red line guarded with black on both blue and green (Plates 2 (b) and 4 (c)). Thread counts are given in a manuscript notebook[7] thought to date from before 1800 for three qualities of cloth for officers, sergeants and privates and on 16th September 1795 an order was placed by John Mackintosh & Co., Inverness, for 220 yards of 'Tartan for Privates Kilts of the small pattern of green blue and black with stripes of red.'[8] These threadcounts appeared in company with counts for ordinary Black Watch tartan, which was also termed '42nd Pattern', but are for kilts *only* whereas the ordinary tartan is given as both kilts and plaids; by the time the 1819 Key Pattern Book came to be compiled the pattern with red lines seems to have fallen into a degree of disuse, for it appears in only one quality under the name (42nd) Coarse Kilt with Red.

IV Garth tells us[2] that soldiers of the Grenadier Company of the 42nd had a red line *added* to the green of their tartan and James Logan[9] says that, while the regular colours of the tartan "are blue, black and green" a "red stripe in the middle of the former is often introduced", adding that this was done to distinguish the philabeg from the belted plaid[10]. These two accounts do not necessarily conflict. Garth was a soldier and might be expected to know where the red line was added but Logan, the observer and not always a good one, knew only what he saw; the Black Watch kilts were pleated to show blue and so a red line on the green would be hidden where vertical and would show horizontally only on the crossing of blue and green. Logan saw a red line on the blue and Garth knew there was a red line on the green; Wilsons' 42nd Pattern with red lines conforms to this and we need therefore look no further for the 'Athol Sett'. However, if Wilsons' really did not make plaiding of this pattern — and there is no evidence that they did — Morier's Grenadier cannot be wearing it and we must assume that the 'Athol Sett' came into use at some time after the painting was executed; nor can he be wearing whatever it was that Logan saw, for this was specifically the philabeg and not the belted plaid. Unfortunately, the extraction of any regular pattern from Morier's painting (Frontispiece) calls for a degree of perspicacity bordering upon a vivid imagination and it is impossible to discover what pattern the artist intended if, indeed, he meant to give anything but an impression of tartan. The whole painting measures only 39cm × 49cm and the kilted part of the plaid is about 6½cm × 5cm and so absence of fine detail is not surprising.

V Garth also tells us that the first pipers of the 42nd wore the Royal Stuart tartan and Logan repeats this but illustrates a piper wearing a green tartan, going on to say that "The band (i.e. the military band) continue to wear tartan of the same red pattern which formed the original dress of the pipers and drummers". Wilsons'[11] give explicit instructions for making this tartan: "To make the Band, or Musicians', Plaids you have only to put scarlet in place of the black in the Sergts. plaids. The Band and the Sergeants are of the same quality." (Plates 3 (b) and 4 (h)). A military print of 1842/43[12] shows the military band of the 42nd on the march; the bandsmen wear red kilts and plaids and the drum major green. Royal Stuart is a plaid setting of the Prince Charles Edward tartan which figures among Jacobite relics of the '45 and from which it probably inherited the

> 'Royal' prefix. It does not seem to have been named as such much before the end of the eighteenth century and so, although it is possible that Garth used the name retrospectively, it would appear that he merely confused the two red tartans. He was getting on in years when he wrote his book and relied much on his own recollections and those of his old comrades as a result of which he made several minor errors.

The important facts that emerge from the foregoing are (a) that there were two different tartans, both called 42nd Pattern, being made by the same manufacturer at the same time and (b) that there were two military tartans, both blue, black and green checks with a red line on the blue and that one of these — that to which the red line had been added to the green — was a variation on a third, unrecorded pattern. The first disposes of the belief that the same tartan was always meant when 42nd Pattern was mentioned, the second spurs us on to find the missing link.

Although it is known that when Lord Loudoun was choosing a tartan for his regiment his friends advised a blue, black and green one because it was the cheapest, I find it difficult to believe that, in the climate of the times, the authorities — and especially the King, on his rather unsteady throne — would have looked favourably upon the idea of Highland gentlemen, even staunch anti-Jacobites like Loudoun, raising private armies and kitting them out in their own livery at the ultimate expense of the Government. Rather do I think it almost certain that some degree of uniformity would have been imposed and to have laid down a more or less standard basic tartan pattern, to which small but distinctive variations could be made for different formations, would have been the obvious way of doing this. On the evidence at our disposal 'Anything you like, so long as it is blue, black and green with a red line on the blue' would appear to have been the rule, though it may have been less rigid even than this; Wilsons' 'Grant tartan' (Plate 4 (d)) has its red lines on the green but it is difficult to account for it as anything but a military or quasi-military sett though it may be later than those we are now considering. One thing is clear and that is that the raisers of regiments did not have tartan matters entirely their own way. Lord Loudoun tried hard to get a red tartan for his men almost until the time when the regiment was disbanded but he never succeeded.

All the arguments then are in favour of our mystery tartan following this rule and it only remains to determine the colour of the overcheck, if any, on the green. Garth's remark could be interpreted as meaning that there was none but I consider that the design requires that the green, like the blue, should be divided. Introduction of extra colours into a tartan makes more work for the weaver and increases the cost of the cloth; in any case, red and yellow are ruled out by their subsequent use for other purposes. Black and blue are therefore the most probable colours and of these black, repeating the border colour of the green squares, must be regarded as the more likely. A colour strip of this admittedly hypothetical tartan is shown at Plate 6 (a).

I believe that this was the tartan worn by the Independent Companies, probably from 1725 and certainly from 1733, and that it was carried forward into the new Highland regiment, originally the 43rd and later renumbered as the 42nd, and eventually superseded by what we now call the Black Watch tartan. It may also have been worn by the earlier Independent Companies with distinguishing overchecks according to the individual fancies of the Commanders and thus have given rise to Garth's assertion (page 25). When the new tartan superseded the old we cannot tell, but I suspect that it may have been much later than we have hitherto supposed. The argument that the new tartan was issued when the regiment was formed hinges upon the supposition that each of the Independent Companies wore a different tartan, so making a new uniform tartan necessary, but we now know that this was not so. It is difficult to imagine that the Treasury, famous for parsimony, would have authorized a complete renewal of the Regiment's plaids unless it was strictly necessary and far easier to expect that all the old plaids were worn out and all stocks of material used up before any consideration was given to the new tartan. Then came the Mutiny of 1743, shortly followed by the events of The '45, in which the 43rd's brother regiment, Loudoun's, failed conspicuously to cover itself with glory, to throw doubt on the whole future of the Highland regiments. Taking all this into account, I feel it likely that the issue of the new tartan was considerably delayed, perhaps until the 43rd was renumbered in 1749 or, maybe, even later, until the next batch of Highland regiments, Keith's and Montgomery's, were formed in 1757. When it came, the new design showed very little real difference from the old. There were no *distinguishing* coloured lines to be removed but removal of the red line from our hypothetical design would leave a pair of black lines centred on each blue square and if these pairs are moved from the centre to the edges of each alternate blue square we are left with the Black Watch tartan as we know it to-day (Plates 3 (a) and 4 (g)). Who knows, it may even have been a weaver's mistake, but by doubling the number of checks in each repeat of the pattern it creates much greater scope for regimental variations and removal of the red lines would probably have paid for the additional complication.

The new tartan became the basis of the majority of the tartans worn by Highland regiments, those of some of the Fencible regiments, of which the

Breadalbane Fencibles (Plate 6 (1)) and the Inverness Fencibles tartans are examples, and of countless 'clan' and family setts. A bewildering variety of overchecks has been added to the basic pattern but we are concerned here only with those of known military origin. Gordon (92nd Regiment) and Mackenzie (78th Regiment) are well known and the former is well documented[13]: almost unknown outside the field of tartan research are two tartans set out in the manuscript notebook previously mentioned and named 'Drummers' Plaids 71st Regiment' and 'Drummers' Plaids 92nd Pattern' (Plate 4 (j) and (k)). The descendants of those regiments, the Gordon Highlanders and the Queen's Own Highlanders, have no knowledge of these tartans and are politely sceptical of their existence but Wilsons', though they were not always right about everything, were in the business of making and selling tartan, not of hoaxing posterity. It is recorded that some regiments, in order to circumvent War Office strictures, recruited pipers and put them on the books as drummers; if as Logan says, the pipers of the 42nd wore the red band plaid, might these other drummers have been pipers in reality?

In the 1819 Key Pattern book, Wilsons' tell us that the "Clothing of the 93rd Regiment is the very same in every particular as the 42nd Regiment" but at least one modern authority[14] has it that although the sett of the tartan is the same the colours are lighter. It was Garth who first put about the story that the Black Watch was so called because of its dark tartan and it would appear that it is because of this that the Regiment now has the darkest possible tartan short of black while the 93rd retains colours that are, by intention at any rate, approximately those of the original.

Alone of the original kilted regiments the 79th (Cameron's) did not adopt a variation of the new 42nd Pattern, taking instead the dark Clan Donald tartan and replacing the two fine red lines centred on the blue with a single yellow line. Tradition ascribes the design to Lady Cameron of Erracht, mother of Alan Cameron, the founder of the Regiment. The usual story has been that, as the red of the Cameron tartan did not go well with the red of the soldiers' coats, Lady Erracht, herself a MacDonald, took her own Clan's tartan and added the yellow line from the Cameron. However, Lady Erracht was actually a MacLean and although there was a red tartan abroad in the Cameron country at the time and it did have yellow lines, these did not form a central feature of the pattern as did those of the tartan 'discovered' by the Sobieskis some thirty years later. A much more probable origin would have been for Lady Erracht to have taken a local pattern and varied it according to fancy, as any weaver might do in similar circumstances. In view of my earlier suggestion that restrictions were placed on the choice of military tartans it may be asked how Alan Cameron got away with it. He was a redoubtable gentleman, who did battle with the War Office more than once[15] but there is no record that he did so on this occasion. Perhaps his proposed tartan conformed sufficiently closely to the standard or possibly the 76th Regiment, MacDonald's Highlanders, provided a precedent.

There remains one purely military tartan for consideration and from this the work of D. C. Stewart[16] has mercifully removed all need for major guesswork. This is the so-called 'Childers Universal Tartan'. In the 1880s the then Secretary of State for War, the Rt. Hon. Hugh C. E. Childers, conceived the notion of putting *all* the Scottish regiments into tartan, the tartan chosen being the Black Watch, which now became the 'Universal' tartan. The Lowland regiments liked this idea as little as the Highlanders had liked schemes for taking *their* tartans away and called the tartan 'MacChilders' (and, presumably, other and less repeatable names). The plan did not go through but early in the present century certain of the Gurkha regiments developed affiliations with Highland units and adopted tartan for parts of their pipers' uniforms. In earlier editions of his book *The Clans, Septs and Regiments of The Scottish Highlands* Frank Adam includes comprehensive tables which list all the tartan-using regiments of what was then the British Empire and gives details of the tartans and in what parts of the uniforms they were worn, recording that the 8th Gurkha Rifles were using the 'Universal' tartan for pipe ribbons and bag covers. A footnote says that the tartan "appears to be a variety of the Black Watch or the Sutherland." The 1st Battalion, 1st Gurkha Rifles is recorded as using a tartan called 'Childers' for plaids, ribbons and bag covers and another footnote tells that this was dark green with red stripes; a further footnote in the 1934 edition (partially revised by Thomas Innes of Learney, Carrick Pursuivant of Arms, later Sir Thomas and Lord Lyon King of Arms) discloses that the tartan was designed by H. B. Mackintosh of Elgin and says that "it is really the Mackintosh tartan with the colours transposed". These tables are omitted from the 1960 edition but reference under the heading of Stewart in the section entitled *Notes on the Plates of Clan Tartans* shows that Childers and Universal have become one and that the "Childers Universal tartan, a nineteenth century W. O. invention — a converse of the Mackintosh sett" is ordained for the use of Englishmen and other aliens! Thus is history — or that part of it which is bunk — made. The 'Childers Universal' tartan is neither Childers nor Universal, nor is it a nineteenth century invention; it was designed in 1907 for a distinguished regiment of the Indian Army and should be respected as such. It is impossible to reach any conclusion as to what constitutes a 'converse of the Mackintosh sett' but the tartan is Mackintosh on a black ground with green of a shade described as that of beech leaves and the blue changed to 'ash leaf green'; there is a red line between the 'beech' green stripes in place of the blue line of the original.

From time to time various regiments and units of the Royal Air Force have adopted tartan for particular uses. These tartans are liable to change with the times and to fall in and out of use, so it is not possible to give an up-to-date list. However, many of the established tartan picture books give information on tartans in current use at the time of publication and the enquiring reader must be referred to these; a serious attempt some years ago to discover to what extent tartan had invaded the Royal Air Force foundered on lack of knowledge on the part of the authorities.

NOTES

1 As a recent example, *The Field* for November 1987 reported that Colonel William Grant, "a younger son of the fifth laird of Rothiemurchus, raised one of the independent Highland companies incorporated to form the 42nd Regiment, better known as the black Watch, *and gave it his plaid.*" (Author's italics)
2 *Sketches of the Manners and Customs and Present State of the Highlanders of Scotland.* 1822.
3 *The Setts of the Scottish Tartans.* Shepheard-Walwyn 1974.
4 *Highland Dress, Arms and Ornament.*
5 Regimental and other records quoted by J. Telfer Dunbar: *History of Highland Dress.*
6 Oblique confirmation of this tartan is to be found in J. Telfer Dunbar's *History of Highland Dress* wherein is reproduced an engraving taken from Allan Ramsay's portrait of Lord Loudoun "in the Regimentals of the Highland Regiment", the text stating that the tartan is "green, blue and black with a red overstripe." The tartan in Ramsay's painting is a red one and it is difficult to see how such a mistake could have been made without some knowledge of the regimental tartan.
7 In the Royal Museum of Scotland, Queen Street, Edinburgh.
8 Copy in the author's possession.
9 *The Scottish Gaël.*
10 Strictly speaking, one cannot have 'the former' of three, but R.R. McIan's lithograph entitled "Shaw" in *The Clans of the Scottish Highlands* shows that Logan meant 'the first', i.e., blue.
11 1819 Key Pattern Book.
12 'The Highlanders No. 12.'
13 *History of Highland Dress.*
14 Robert Bain: *The Clans and Tartans of Scotland:* Margaret O. MacDougall edition. Collins 1953.
15 Loraine MacLean of Dochgarroch: *Indomitable Colonel.* Shepheard-Walwyn 1986.
16 Unpublished.

The Tartan Cult

The regular chequered pattern and the twill weave that are the fundamentals of what we now call tartan were known in the third century A.D.[1] and therefore by 1745 there had been nearly one and a half millennia for its development. The fragment of material cited is woven in natural undyed shades of wool, but this is no proof that the people of Pictish times did not know about dyes. Roman commentators are clear that the Celtic peoples wore clothing of bright colours and while it is possible that the inhabitants of North Britain, being further from what was then the hub of civilisation, took longer to acquire the art of dyeing than did their southern neighbours it may be that they were more concerned with warmth than with ornament. In later times the Highland village weavers showed themselves to be fully equal to English weavers and to the Flemings who, in the fourteenth century, were brought in to improve the quality of English cloth, so it is unlikely that they remained in ignorance, if it was ignorance, for very long. There is no obligation to use colour in a tartan pattern and there are several examples of plaids from as late as the seventeenth century made with natural colours.

At the very beginning of the eighteenth century Martin Martin[2] recorded that the pattern of a man's plaid gave some clue as to where he lived and although this claim (see page 12) has a rather sweeping style that suggests some exaggeration, we have already noted the way in which basic patterns prevailed over wide areas and were modified by local weavers for their own ends. It can easily be seen that a local pattern of this kind, made for a captive clientele, might have become identified with the people of that locality who were themselves predominently of one Clan or family group and its adherents and, when the belief grew up that Clan tartans had been worn since the beginning of time, have become, by retrospection, the Clan tartan of that group.

There is no evidence that the Highlanders themselves looked on tartan in that light, however, and when the Dress Act was repealed in 1782 the demand was for 'latest patterns' and 'bright colours'. Lack of brightness of colour was a constant source of complaint by the merchants and Clan tartans, of which few were listed anyway, received scant mention.

That Clan tartans were believed in by this time seems indisputable. The Government, in framing the Dress Act, appears to have recognised in tartan some kind of group significance, and although by 1815, when Stewart of Garth and Robertson of Struan were concerning themselves with the question, the ban had been raised for as long as it had been in force, it is too much to expect that these gentlemen invented Clan tartans as a subject for correspondence and then set about collecting the figments of their imaginations. Whatever we may think about the origin of the Clan Tartan Cult, it cannot have been launched, ready made, upon a gullible public.

We cannot be certain of all that had happened between 1782 and 1815 but there had certainly been an upsurge of feeling in favour of the Highlanders. The Government no longer feared the Jacobites and The '45 had become a Romantic Adventure. The Highlands had attracted their first tourists and the public conscience had been smitten with the plight of the Highlanders in the aftermath of Culloden; Highland Societies had been founded in England and in Scotland to find ways of mitigating those circumstances and what were afterwards called 'do-gooders' were abroad in the land. Lowlanders no longer feared Highlanders and Highland soldiers had proved themselves and earned the respect of their comrades in the Continental and American wars. The Highlander had achieved 'noble savage' status and the way was open for the fictionalising and romanticising of Highland life and history.

Under the Clan system every member of the Clan was *supposed* to be descended from the Clan's founder and, hence, all were members of the same family. Family loyalties were important and social distinctions were based not on class but on the respect of children for parents. If everybody was part of the Chief's family everybody had to behave like a Chief and if this resulted in some arrogance and some bloody quarrels it also produced a standard of good manners, learning and social behaviour above the average for its day. All this looked very peculiar to the outside eye, as did the spectacle of a Highland Chief living in style and in a single storied, dry-stone-built, thatched cottage and going around the house barefoot and in his shirt-tails[3]. Such paradoxes were more than a gift to the romantic fictionalists; they were a challenge!

Sir Walter Scott was first in the field with Rob Roy, whose real character was not quite spotless, as the prototype Highland Gentleman. Scott had travelled extensively in the Highlands on legal business, collecting stories and legends on the way, and had grown to like the Highlanders too much for strict veracity. General David Stewart of Garth treated history in much the same way as Scott had treated fiction, seeing in every Highland frog a spellbound prince. When these two stage-managed the King's visit to Edinburgh in 1822 they fixed the Clan Tartan Idea in the public mind. Tartans that had previously been only numbers in a pattern book suddenly became 'Clan' tartans and one cannot fail to suspect that some Chiefs, in search of their 'genuine and ancient' setts had lines that were not selling well unloaded on them by cunning merchants.

James Logan toured the Highlands in search of lore and traditions in 1825 and his version of Highland history, *The Scottish Gaël*, was published in 1831. Logan took the line that everything Highland was rooted impossibly far in the past and gives an implied justification of this attitude saying that the Highlanders "tenaciously preserved their primitive institutions, their costumes, language, poetry, music etc., and remained for many ages little known to the rest of the kingdom". The Rev. Alexander Stewart, who edited the second edition of *The Gaël*, which was published in 1875, after Logan's death, pokes gentle fun at his approach, quoting a footnote from a *Pall Mall Gazette* of March 1875:

> THE PHILOLOGY OF TARTAN. . . . A recent traveller to Zanskar, struck by the Scottish pronunciation of these Tibetan mountaineers, has ascertained from a Gaelic scholar that the Highlanders of Scotland and the inhabitants of this province belong to the same race. Zanskar is simply Sanquhar. Bonnets, brooches, and plaids are worn and the woollen garments of these Asiatics are checked and striped in brilliant colours, after the manner of Clan tartans. R & N being interchangeable consonants, it is possible that Tartan comes from Tartar, while almost every name in this locality has a Gaelic meaning. The traveller also darkly alludes to another legend not generally known which was related to him by a learned friend, 'who insists that the word tartan obtained its present application when the Assyrian general Tartan (Isaiah XX 1-4) took Ashdad, and carried away the Egyptians captive in an imperfectly clothed condition, which must have made them bear a striking resemblance to Scotch Highlanders in their native dress.'

Such 'history', advanced with a straight face and a sufficient air of authority found a receptive and credulous readership.

By this time, tartan had developed a long, if largely spurious, lineage and while it had been doing so the Continental and American wars had ceased and the Colonies had become to a large extent self-sufficient. The tartan manufactories that had grown up to supply the Army and the export trade found themselves with a large surplus production capacity and competition from other textiles. Most of the loss had to be made good from the home market and the tartan industry, never lacking in initiative, set to with a will. Undoubtedly, tartan has some mysterious aesthetic attraction for most people and they need very little encouragement to buy it. A name linking the pattern with some place, person or happening is enough and such names began to appear in the pattern books with increasing frequency from 1815. 'Waterloo', 'Wellington', 'Regent', 'Sir Walter Scott' and 'Flora MacDonald' were early in the field and there were also 'Meg Merrilees', which soon became the Merrilees tartan and 'Maggie Lauder', to which the Sobieski brothers gave a new lease of life by calling it 'Mak Phersone' and pretending that it belonged to the sixteenth century. Tartan was now beginning to *need* a name in order to *be* a tartan, a process of evolution that soon led to 'tartan' becoming synonymous with 'clan tartan'.

The revelations of the Sobieski brothers[4] must have been a great encouragement to the tartan trade, providing seventy-five hitherto unknown tartans of undisputed (at least, few people disputed it) antiquity and showing, for the first time, the existence of Lowland tartans. The cult was gathering strength and tartan was no longer 'Highland', it had become 'Scottish'.

When the Queen herself became captivated by the Highlands and the Highlanders, who could fail to follow her example? When the great sporting estates were opened up the wealthy came to shoot, fish and stalk and the very wealthy brought their servants with them. After the railway came North the less wealthy came as well, for holidays, and all the time there was a demand for information about Highland tradition and lore. Some of those who provided it were themselves ill-informed and some copied from others with no attempt at verification until, after several transpositions, what they wrote took on the appearance of truth. There was plenty of fiction as well but, whatever it was, the Clans and their tartans sold well and, as is the way with such writings, it all got mixed up in the public mind and the myth of tartan as a kind of heraldry became established, not only in the eyes of the outsiders; even the Clansfolk believed it!

Propaganda begets counter-propaganda and as the belief grew that Clan tartans had always been, and should always be, worn as a means of identification, there were those who made it known that only Scots or those of Scottish descent might wear the kilt and that no-one could sport a Clan tartan unless related in some way to the Clan. This was just what was needed to put the tartan cult on a firm footing. The unattainable is naturally sought after, so people began to want to be of Scottish descent in order to wear tartan, which thereby became a sort of status symbol; even to-day, really nice and respectable people will almost apologise for being unable to claim a tartan when there is no reason at all why they should claim one. To cater for this need the 'What is my Tartan?' lists came into being. Parts of these are true but they owe a great deal to a kind of acrobatic genealogy which places people according to name and not to descent. In the lists, all the sons of Walter, Watt, Watson, MacWattie or whatever are held to be the sons of Sir Walter Buchanan and wear the Buchanan tartan; Williams', Wilsons and MacWilliams are Gunns, because there was a Will Gunn who fought a long feud with the Mackays; all Taylors are Camerons, there having been a tailor Cameron who worked as hard with his Lochaber axe as he did with his needle. Many more examples can be found without difficulty but perhaps the most absurd is the name Quay. If you pronounce this as spelt you are a Mackay, but if you call it 'Key' you are of the Clan Chattan. For those who could not readily fit into a Clan there were 'septs'. A sept is difficult to define but perhaps is best described as a group of people within a Clan all of whom bear the same surname which, however, is different from the Clan name. They may be smiths, weavers, carpenters, bowyers or any others distinguished by having some trade or idiosyncrasy and, of course, they wear the Clan tartan. Since Scots descent was good enough to qualify for a tartan, a grandmother or even a great-grandmother was an adequate claim but there are those who have the required relative whose name does not figure in the lists and for them there are 'District' tartans, setts named after the places where they were found or made or, even, because the maker just fancied the name. For those with neither Clan, Sept nor District, there are the 'general use' tartans, Hunting Stewart, Jacobite and Caledonia. The first two are of respectable age and Hunting Stewart does seem to have been a general tartan early in the nineteenth century. Caledonia is also old but its name is a mistaken one.

It was the Victorian standards of ostentation and etiquette that regimented tartan and gave us hunting tartans, dress tartans and even funeral tartans. Rarely can there have been such a prolific marriage of supply and demand and it continues. Year after year new 'tartans' appear in the shops for the benefit (or otherwise) of the tourist; tartans having no real authenticity and often without even the sanction of good design, but they are given names that sound well and the customer is left to assume that they are genuine. No-one will disillusion him.

NOTES

1 The so-called 'Falkirk tartan'. See Wild, J.P. *Textile Manufacture in the Northern Roman Provinces*. Cambridge University Press 1970.
2 *Description of the Western Isles.*
3 Burt, *Letters from the North of Scotland* (No. 12). 1754, reprinted 1974 by John Donald Publishers Ltd.
4 *Vestiarium Scoticum.*

Women and Tartan

It is probable that the earliest form of outdoor dress worn by Highland women was simply a blanket, caught up in haste and draped over the head and shoulders to give protection from inclement weather. In due course this developed into the arisaid described by Martin Martin[1] and the stripes of the blanket became regularised into arisaid setts. This fashion in dress and tartan clearly persisted for a long time, for it was 'yet wore by the vulgar' in Martin's time and in 1814 Elizabeth Grant of Rothiemurchus wrote[2] of "old, smoke-dried, shrivelled-up witches with pipes in their mouths and blankets on their backs." By that time it was the dress of the lower orders and white plaids were not usually worn by gentlefolk though in Badenoch women reputedly wore white plaids for St Columba's day.

When Lowland ladies took to tartan as an anti-Union or a Jacobite symbol they followed the lead of their Highland sisters who, by this time, were wearing tartan gowns and riding habits or tartan 'screens' — light shawls — or plaids as accessories to dresses made from imported materials. Somewhat later, Sir William Beechey painted a charming portrait of the Marchioness of Queensbury wearing a tartan hat trimmed with feathers.

A fashion that remained in vogue for many years was that of a Highland bride wearing a new plaid as part of her wedding outfit. I have been unable to find out if this plaid was part of the trousseau or the gift of the husband, the evidence being both sparse and inconclusive. In 1775, William Wilson, the 'Son' of William Wilson and Son, the Bannockburn weavers, named 'Janet Wilson sett', a new pattern of plaiding, after his spouse, Janet Paterson, but a lady who showed me her grandmother's wedding plaid could not tell me her grannie's name, either maiden or married. A length of plaiding in 'Crieff sett', worn by the bride of a Grant, *could* have been bought by mistake for the 'New Bruce' tartan but at the time of that wedding, if our other information is correct, 'New Bruce' had not yet become the Grant tartan. On balance, it seems not improbable that a man would make a present to his bride of a plaid in a tartan appropriate to her new status.

Janet Wilson sett and the Crieff sett plaid are both narrow width, hard tartan material typical of the late eighteenth century but the other, in

Forbes tartan, is fine, soft merino material such as Wilsons' began to make during the first quarter of the nineteenth century. To judge by the number of similar plaids that has survived these plaids must have been very popular for general wear as well as for weddings and the style — approximately a yard and a half square and fringed all round — lasted well into the synthetic dye era. They came in a very wide range of patterns apart from recognisable Clan tartans, some with warp and weft different and some apparently made up from assembled elements taken from 'standard' tartans.

Several fine examples of tartan wedding dresses have survived, some in silk, and from these it might be supposed that the wedding plaid was a usage of the less affluent. However, the well-to-do seem also to have had their wedding tartans; the well-known Ogilvie, sometimes known as Drummond of Strathallan, is one of these and a MacInroy/MacDonald wedding is commemorated by a version of the dark MacDonald tartan in which red and green are interchanged.

With the near-demise of the kilt for daily wear, tartan became more usually worn by women than by men, who are not generally able to display anything larger than a tie, so the popularisation of tartan leaned heavily in the female direction. A catalogue of 1908 lists, among other more usual feminine accessories, blouses, petticoats, underskirts and stockings in a wide variety of tartans — ninety-seven in the case of petticoats, though only eight in stockings. Men had to be content with braces, ties, cummerbunds and socks. Of course, these were 'clan' tartans. The old arisaid tartans, of which Wilsons' 'Blanket sett' (Plate 5 (a)) was perhaps the last survivor, had long since been forgotten and, half-remembered, had become 'dress' tartans for men's evening wear, though one of them was named 'Victoria' after the Queen who had done so much to boost the sales of tartan.

There were no notions of 'clannery' about the old arisaid setts and so nothing upon which the romantics could hang a myth. There was therefore no incentive to preserve the patterns, which might have offered an interesting field for study. As it is, we have only a few 'bar blankets' to give some idea of the general appearance of an arisaid sett. With these in mind I have devised a type of sett based on conventional tartans (Plate 5 (b)) which appeals particularly to those women who prefer setting the trend to following fashion and is exclusive into the bargain.

Tartan *can* march with the times and new does not have to be nasty. Where good taste prevails the ties of convention can be loosened and I have seen modern evening dresses in patterns of the tartan type in which 'Lurex' thread is used to good effect, as silk was in former days.

NOTES

1 *Description of the Western Isles.*
2 *Memoirs of a Highland Lady* 1898. Republished in two volumes by Canongate Publishing Ltd, 1988.

The Types of Tartan

In the beginning, the Highlander had his *breacan* and was well content with it. He had good reason to be. It kept him warm day and night and protected him from the weather out of doors. It hid him from prying eyes, human and animal, on the hill and it lasted well. It satisfied his artistic sense and love of colour. The family blankets were of much the same material and his wife was content to take one of these and drape it over her head and shoulders if she had to go outside in inclement weather; perhaps on special occasions she might arrange it more elegantly as an 'arisaid'.[1]

This state of affairs must have persisted for a very long time, but quite suddenly — in the context of centuries — things began to happen to tartan. Highland dress ceased to be barbarian and became to some extent *de rigeur:* the Romantics took it up and spread their strange notions of what Highland life was like in olden times. Synthetic dyes were invented and mechanisation of the textile industry made quantity-production easy: the old thin, hard tartans, so unkind to the soft skin at the back of town-bred knees, were supplanted by soft and hairy ones which were also thick and heavy. Tartan became popular and was taken up by many people whose recent ancestors would have taken shelter behind barred doors and shuttered windows at the first sight of a flurry of tartan at the street corner.

Mass-production does not only make production in large quantities easy, it makes production in small quantities impossible or at least uneconomical. Manufacturers needed to sell as much tartan as possible and the best way of doing so was to convince people that they needed to have several different patterns. The strident colours of the early aniline dyes made 'hunting' tartans an almost natural development, for which the writings of George Buchanan[2] appeared to give some historical justification, and in an age when everybody (or everybody who could afford the necessary finery) 'dressed' for dinner, 'dress' tartans found ready acceptance. Some clans were lucky enough to have two tartans and in such cases a dark one could be called 'hunting' and a bright one 'dress'.

In Victorian times few people had the Highland attitude towards funerals and so the next development was in the direction of black and white tartans, which we were asked to believe were 'funeral' or 'mourning' setts. The Sobieski brothers made no suggestion that their black and white MacFarlane tartan was anything but a Clan tartan, however, though the ready acceptance of the *Vestiarium Scoticum* as a sixteenth century source led to some of their designs being called 'ancient' or 'old'. Much more confusion was to come.

About the end of the Great War 'ancient' or 'old' colours were invented, based on the idea that the colours of old tartans had been lighter than those then in use, which now became called 'modern' colours. It thus became possible to have 'ancient' tartans in 'modern' colours and all possible other arrangements of these, quite meaningless, descriptions. The final development in the way of colours was the 'Reproduction' range invented in the late 1940s. It was claimed that these were derived from a piece of tartan dug up on Culloden Moor and tartans made in these shades certainly have the appearance of having been buried in peat for two hundred years; I do not believe, however, that any Highland Dyer would have regarded them as satisfactory. The name 'Reproduction' was registered as a trade name and so the copies that very quickly appeared were called 'Muted' tartans.

The number of possible combinations of all these is bewildering but it helps sales. If you want one, you can have an 'ancient' tartan that was designed yesterday or one in 'modern' colours that are older than 'old' colours; if you do not like any of these you can have a 'reproduction tartan that is not a reproduction of any tartan.

However hard one tries — and some people have tried very hard — it is not possible to fit everybody with a 'clan' tartan and this is where the 'district' tartan comes into its own. Wilsons' of Bannockburn in their early days made a number of tartans that were given the names of places or of organisations associated with places. Some of them were just names, like *Aberdeen Sett* and *Dundee Sett* but some, on grounds of pattern, look as if they came from the places they were named after; these include *Lochaber Sett, Crieff Sett* and, intriguingly, *Caledonian Sett*, which turns out to be the red Mackintosh tartan. District tartans are supposed to have been worn by people who lived in areas not inhabited primarily by one clan and almost any excuse for wearing one will serve. Nowadays, any tartan with a place name is marketed as a 'district' tartan regardless of its origin. The tartan that originally belonged to the Stirling and Bannockburn Caledonian Society is now the Stirling and Bannockburn District tartan, a coat left on Culloden battlefield is the Culloden District tartan — and has a 'dress' version — and the favourite of a Marchioness of Huntly is the Huntly District tartan. The spread of tourism has produced a great proliferation of tartans that are presented to a gullible public as 'district' setts; though they have, in most cases, no pretence to genuineness they are given names that sound real and the unshakable belief that the customers have in all the tartan myths does the rest.

When even 'district' tartans fail to provide the answer there still remain the so-called 'national' tartans. The best known of these are *Jacobite*, which D. C. Stewart, who knew about such matters, thought probably originated in Barcelona, *Caledonia*, named in error about 1953, and *Hunting Stewart*, which was in existence in 1819, was probably altered by the Sobieski brothers about 1828 and was thought by James Grant[3] to have been in general use as a universal tartan from the early part of the nineteenth century. The Black Watch tartan has been proposed for general use, apparently because the War Office once called it 'Universal', and on the same grounds the '*Childers Universal*' has been offered for the same role; in the 1930s the National Association of Scottish Woollen Manufacturers launched a tartan that they named '*National*', but this has never caught on.

All these types of tartan present a confused and confusing picture in which it is impossible to avoid seeing some advantage to the tartan trade. I doubt if any great effort is made to exploit the advantage; with so many lambs rushing to the slaughter it is hardly necessary, but the story would be less muddled if the people behind the shop counters had a better understanding of their goods and some feeling for the art and history of tartan.

NOTES

1 *Scotland's Clans and Tartans.* 1974.
2 *Rerum Scoticorum Historia.* See Chapter 2.
3 *The Tartans of the Clans of Scotland* (1886).

The Art of Tartan

Tartan is an art form of considerable antiquity which owes much of its beauty and liveliness to the interplay of colour and the action of light and sight along and across the diagonal ribs of the twill weave that is traditionally used in making the cloth.

Martin Martin[1] wrote of "Plads" in "Stripes" and the Sobieski brothers, with their "settiss or stryppes of Tertinnis" and their patterns of "stryppes vpon ane fylde", succeeded in making this appear to be an ancient way of describing the pattern but, although the weaver sees the pattern as stripes of warp and weft, the true basis of tartan is the check in one form or another.

To say that colour is important to tartan may sound like a statement of the obvious but it is a fact that the use of colour in relation to tartan design is little understood. Colours for tartan work require to be clear and unambiguous and bright but soft, to give good contrast of both colour and brightness and to mix well so as to give distinctly new shades where two colours cross without any one swamping another. These conditions were amply fulfilled by the traditional range of tartan colours though the modern versions of these fall far short of the ideal. The very dark greens and blues and the harsh reds and yellows of the so-called 'modern' colours almost obliterate the details of the design and the washed-out, pastel shades of 'ancient' colours do not differentiate sufficiently between blue, light blue and green; 'reproduction' or 'muted' colours are scarcely colours at all in the tartan context (Plates 6 to 9). Although actual shades are known to have varied with location and period, the Highland dyers appear to have experienced no difficulty in obtaining a fairly bright red, a good yellow, a clear, dark blue and a definite green from the sources available to them. Green was usually rather lighter than blue, and being dyed with blue on top of yellow, was very variable as was black, which usually called for similar methods; the root of the white water lily (*Nymphaea alba*) is reputed to give a good black but is somewhat difficult and risky to harvest. Unbleached wool was a good enough white and there are some grounds for suspecting that light blue, initially at any rate, came from the accidental use of a weak or old dyebath. Post-Proscription and pre-aniline tartan manufactories employed largely imported vegetable dyes and numerous examples of the colours obtained from these have come down to us with the Wilson records. Wilsons' made a bright scarlet, a deeper red called 'rose', a dark blue, purple (which was a dark blue with a hint of warmth and nothing like as bright as a present-day purple), a rather light and slightly olive green and a somewhat 'muddy' yellow; light blue was usually a duck-egg shade. Less common colours found in Wilson patterns included 'Bloom' — a pale pink — Bottle green, 'Shade' green — which seems to have borne much the same relationship to green as light blue did to blue — 'Officers' blue — a brighter blue than the standard indigo — and 'Sextian' blue. Sextian blue has not yet been positively identified but may have been mauve. 'Sextian' clearly has something to do with six and at my primary school, which was a bit old-fashioned, I learned *eight* spectral colours of which the sixth was mauve. Of the native dye-plants the Crowberry (Empetrum nigrum) gives, in strong concentration, a good purple and in reducing strength successively mauve, lavender and zinc grey; if it is over-heated it gives a greenish khaki.

Every stripe of the warp crosses every stripe of the weft and, since the colours are woven into the cloth, where a stripe crosses another of the same colour solid plain colour results but where it crosses a stripe of another colour the result is a mixture of the two in equal proportions. The number of mixtures increases in rapid disproportion to the number of colours that we start off with, in accordance with the formula:

$$M = \frac{C^2 - C}{2}$$

where M is the number of mixtures and C the number of colours. Two colours, that is a simple check, give only one mixture (three shades in all) but six colours give fifteen mixtures, twenty-one shades: thus the more colours to begin with the more subdued the final effect. This is not the only paradox to be found in tartan!

In plain weave the mixture of colours is of the 'pepper and salt' variety but in the traditional twill weave the two colours appear alongside each other as alternate diagonal lines of shading and these present a different appearance according to whether one is looking along or across them. Because of this, even a draped piece of tartan shows 'life'; in motion, it has a vitality of its own. A fine, smooth yarn gives a sharper 'picture' and so is preferable to a thick and hairy one. Anyone who doubts this should compare a piece of fine worsted tartan with its Edwardian counterpart.

Deriving directly from the shepherd plaid, the simplest type of tartan pattern is the plain check in natural shades of undyed wool but this gives the designer very little scope even when intermediate natural shades are introduced. In particular, there is a lack of contrast between the elements of the design which limits the use of overchecks and the pattern cannot be enlarged to any considerable extent without becoming unacceptably loud. The introduction of colour alters all that. Not only do we have more than dark brown, medium brown and cream from which to compose the pattern but we also have the power to adjust the contrast, both in degree and kind; we may have contrast of light and dark, as with indigo blue and light green, or of colour, as with red and green or blue and yellow. In a satisfactory design the background checks will show a firm but not harsh contrast and the overchecks will be such as to show clearly on both. It is important that the overcheck lines should not only be of suitable colours to show against the backgrounds but also that they should be wide enough to be seen. In normal circumstances a single line should be of at least four threads.

It would almost certainly be untrue to claim that the possible number of arrangements of overchecks is infinite but there is as yet no sign of an end to them although it is sometimes difficult to arrange an adequate distinction between two similar setts. The simple check may be overchecked, divided to give Sobieski-style 'stryppes vpon ane fylde' or separated by having a narrow edging line around one of the checks. The overchecks may be single or numerous and if the latter they can be separated or grouped. But they are always built into the pattern and it is a mistake to regard them as being merely a 'differencing' in the heraldic sense. A selection of variations upon the simple check is shown at Plate 11.

The Sobieski brothers leaned heavily upon the check pattern and about one third of the setts illustrated in the *Vestiarium* are of this type, but few can be called inspired. The introduction of a third colour into the base pattern makes a big difference. Instead of the simple check the base now becomes the 'superimposed check' in which a square of a third colour is placed centrally upon one of the others, which may be enlarged for the purpose; this has the effect of broadening the pattern and allowing further modification of contrasts as well as widening the scope for meaningful variations. Tartans of this type fall naturally into several well defined groups, such as MacLeod (green on the black of a blue-and-black base), Mackintosh (green on the blue of red-and-blue), Black Watch, and the abbreviated Black Watch type beloved of the Sobieskis and Royal Stuart. A selection of these is shown at Plate 12.

A further development of the check is used in the Ross and MacRae group of tartans and comprises multiple checks, typically red, blue, red, green. There are few variations on this scheme and some of them are shown at Plate 13.

A fourth and very important type of design is not a check at all and comprises overchecks or groups of them nicely disposed on a plain-coloured background. The ancient arisaid setts were of this type which seems to mark the transition from the blanket pattern to the more conventional tartans. This is not to say, however, that such patterns can be regarded as primitive. Some of them are highly developed with numerous miniature setts within the overall pattern. To design one of these must have been a real test of skill and it is impossible to re-construct one from a fragment because apparent pivot lines occur with frequency throughout the sett.

In attempting to emulate the old-time weavers it is important that we should realise that they did not go to any unnecessary trouble. Their designs were usually simple and broad, 'Impressionist' rather than finely detailed, and they did not go out of their way to include a couple of threads of a special colour in the pattern or boggle at the idea of using up some yarn that had gone wrong in the dyeing if they thought they could get away with it. Colours were just colours to them and the modern nonsense of 'blue for the summer skies, white for the winter snows, purple for the heather' and so on had not been invented. In an old tartan you would be unlikely to find both white and yellow or blue and black overchecks but in a two-hundred-year-old piece of Crieff tartan what should be purple is the greenish khaki of overheated crowberry.

The end product of the tartan designer's work is a balanced and harmonious work of abstract art. The drawing board is an aid to the achievement but in the end the pattern must be made on the loom, making the most of the qualities and the limitations of the materials and colours to hand and adjusting the proportions of the pattern accordingly.

NOTES

1 *Description of the Western Islands of Scotland.*

Tartan for Weavers

Tartan is a practical art and its first practitioners were the Highland village weavers. To-day, in order to reach a complete understanding of tartan and to answer some of the questions it poses it is necessary to follow in the footsteps of those village weavers and weave tartan for ourselves. To carry this activity to its logical conclusion it would be necessary to set out to *become* a seventeenth century handloom weaver, a formidable task which would not be in the power of many to accomplish. Most students will find that a simple four-shaft table loom and an adequate instruction book will take them far enough along the road, enabling them to weave any specimens that may be required and to explore the structure of tartan. The student, weaving tartan for its own sake, is in a different case from the practising weaver weaving it for his living and it is to the former that this chapter is directed, for among amateur weavers the admission that one weaves tartan habitually and as a matter of course frequently causes some surprise (which may be tinged with respect) for tartan seems generally to be regarded as exceptionally difficult to weave.

In truth, tartan weaving is simple weaving but it is different weaving. The tartan weaver has to weave lengths of fine, close and even cloth with good selvages as quickly as possible and more or less automatically. Not for him the carefully regulated beating to get the right number of threads to the inch or the laying in of the weft at exactly the right angle to counteract the tendency of the web to narrow as it is woven. All that has to be incorporated in a technique that will fit to a smooth and rhythmic action at the loom and leave the weaver free to concentrate on the pattern and the thread count. In short, the tartan weaver is a production weaver; his art is in the design of the pattern and this is set before the warp goes on the loom.

Most of the 'domestic' types of loom available to-day are too light and will skid around the floor under the influence of the heavy beat needed for weaving close material and anyone thinking of tartan weaving seriously would do well to consider a really heavy machine of the 'English' or 'Kentish' type, either of which can have a seat for the weaver incorporated in the frame. Extra weight can also be built in by the use of the 'weight box' method of tensioning the warp which, although old-fashioned, offers several advantages over the conventional pawl and ratchet brake. It gives slightly when the shed is opened instead of stretching the yarn between two fixed points, it gives sensibly even tension throughout a moderate length of cloth, the cloth can be wound on without the need for frequent trips to the back of the loom to release the warp — it can easily be arranged so that release of warp is entirely automatic — and it is easy to contrive. (See Appendix A)

Close weaving is greatly aided by setting the eyes of the heddles about three-quarters of an inch above or below (it does not matter a great deal which) the straight line joining the breast beam and the back beam of the loom. By this 'differential shedding' when the shed is opened one half of the warp threads carries the weight of the box and the other half is left slightly slack. Work as closely as possible to the reed, using a deep shed so that the warp threads open wide to receive the weft and beat on the open shed so that the weft is beaten into the slack pocket caused by the differential shedding: change the shed on the beat so as to lock the weft into place. By these means a 2/16s worsted yarn can be set at 34 – 36 ends per inch on the loom and will pull in to about 40 during the weaving; when the finished web is immersed in hot lather the threads will absorb water and swell, 'nudging' each other into a completely even pitch.

A firm worsted yarn set to such closeness will not tolerate the usual doubling of the selvage threads in the reed. Such additional packing will not leave room for the weft to be beaten close and this will cause the body of the cloth to be loose; it will also cause the selvage threads to stretch with consequent uneven selvages. A better arrangement is to have selvage strips of twenty threads and to thread five of these in the space of four in the main body of the cloth. These strips are then tensioned separately from the rest of the width and pulled up rather tighter; this will cause the fell of the cloth to curl away from the reed at the edges and allow the body of the cloth to take the full weight of the beat.

In fine, close weaving some pull-in is inevitable and a temple is an essential piece of equipment when weaving full single-width cloth for holding the web to its full width and preventing obstruction of the beat by the selvages.

Suitable shuttles are an aid to good selvages and a heavy 'skid' type is infinitely preferable to the lightweight roller sort. Shuttles of the type used on the 'Hattersley' looms upon which Harris tweed is woven are excellent; they run smoothly through the web and the yarn unwinds very smoothly from the fixed 'pirn' which can hold up to half an ounce of yarn. The tension of the yarn can be adjusted so that the weft pulls right up to the selvage and no more at every throw and although the metal ends are a bit rough on the fingers to begin with, one soon gets used to that. The big drawback to this kind of shuttle is its cost and it is usually worth looking around the suppliers of professional weaving equipment before taking a trip to the local craft suppliers.

It is rare for a thread count to be suitable for the loom as it stands and some adjustment will almost always be needed to fit it to the size of sett required and the gauge of yarn to be used. Since in most cases the weaver has to put up with whatever yarn is available in suitable colours, the choice is narrowed to the use to which the material is to be put and a size of sett that is both suitable and fits exactly into the width of the web as complete setts or half-setts. There is a relationship between the use of the material and the size of the sett in that it appears to be necessary for the eye to take in the pattern in a single sweep, so that an article normally seen in close-up must have a smaller sett than something viewed from a distance. A tie sett is therefore small, a plaid sett large and kilts, skirts and scarves somewhere between. Since for all except scarves the pattern has to be fitted into the width of a single-width web, nominally twenty-seven inches, convenient sizes of sett are for ties, three inches, for kilts and skirts, six inches or so and for plaids and shawls nine or thirteen-and-a-half inches, the equivalents of 9, 4 or 4½ and 2 or 3 setts to the width. Scarves allow greater latitude and are best arranged symmetrically about the centre line with a broad band of colour at the edges.

When the number of setts or half-setts to the width has been decided the number of warp ends to each follows automatically but even at this early stage in our calculations it may be found that some adjustments have to be made to the number of warp ends in the web in order to fit in an exact number of pattern sections.

When the number of ends to each repeat has been determined the final stage of the process, that of enlarging or reducing the given count to the same number, can begin. Basically, this is a matter of simple arithmetic but it is not *quite* so simple as that because straightforward multiplication or division will, unless we are very lucky, call for odd numbers and fractions of threads and these have somehow to be disposed of. A simple rule of thumb for this is, in the case of an enlarged sett, to 'round down' the numbers of threads in the finer lines and to distribute the surplus progressively over the wider stripes. For a sett that is to be reduced the reverse applies and the finest lines should be kept substantial and the wider stripes robbed for this purpose (See Appendix B). In general and if possible, except in the case of 'guard lines' to overchecks no line should be less than four threads — the smallest number that will give a 'solid' appearance — wide. Tie settings have to be exempted from this rule and it will be noted that many of the small fancy patterns that I have quoted at the end of the book have two threads of a colour. This can cause problems since these patterns were set on the loom at about 52 ends per inch, a fineness that the modern hand weaver will find hard to match if only because of the difficulty of obtaining suitably fine yarn in casual quantities. No-one wants to take on a large stock of special yarn for the purpose of occasionally making something different but a satisfactory answer to the problem is to use two threads of fine yarn where calculations call for one of the normal thickness — two of 2/32s instead of one of 2/16s for example. A pound of thin white yarn will go a long way and can be dyed quite easily as required with any domestic dye.

In former times it was common for the light-coloured overchecks — mostly white and yellow but sometimes red — to be woven in silk which not only gave brighter and clearer colours but also, being a glossy fibre, gave some 'sparkle' to the cloth. The present-day amateur can use sewing silk for this purpose but it will have to be used double, two threads of 100/3s silk in place of one of 2/16s or 2/18s worsted. The shuttles will also have to be wound with a double thread and a watchful eye must be kept on the web for loops caused by uneven unwinding of the two threads. There is some difference in the shrinkage of worsted and silk but if the cloth is woven really closely this should cause no trouble.

Silk is a delightful material to work with and no weaver should miss an opportunity to make a piece of silk tartan, however small. But beware of string heddles; unless they are suitably fine they will be bunched close together and threads that are being raised by the eyes will catch in the knots of the next row and be pulled down, causing several breakages at every shed. Heddles for silk weaving can be knitted in blocks but the thread pitch is then fixed and all the heddles have to be changed if yarn of a different count is used.

Another method of embellishment used by the old-time weavers for plaiding was to incorporate an ornamental edge pattern or 'selvage mark'. Plaiding was made in narrow widths — commonly 19 inches — with one 'fair' selvage, the unused weft threads being carried along the other in the usual way. The selvage mark was put into the fair selvage and two lengths of material were joined along the other to make a plaid two yards long and 38 inches wide. There was no set arrangement for the selvage mark. In the case of dark tartans it was frequently just a band of black about an inch-and-a-half wide but in bright setts something more elaborate would be used. Some examples of these will be given later but a typical arrangement would be, starting at the outside, a narrow line of the ground colour followed by a broad band of the darkest colour in the tartan

— blue or purple — another line of the ground colour and one of the same width in the colour of the main band. The selvage mark was usually threaded in herringbone or chevron pattern and this can sometimes leave a single thread at the edge that is not picked up by the weft. If this should occur the loose thread is put in the same heddle as the previous one. The selvage mark is not applicable to straight yardage of cloth but makes an attractive and distinctive finish to a kilt or shawl and the herringbone weave seems to help the selvage.

With few exceptions the Wilson pattern books quote complete weaving data for each pattern. The thread count for either the whole or the half sett is given, from *centre to centre* of the pivot strips in the case of reversing patterns, and is totalled, providing an instant check on the accuracy with which the count has been written down or copied. The number of setts or half setts to a given width is also stated or the number of 'gangs' to the width is given. A gang is the same as a portee but the term is applied to multiple-thread warping: a pattern described as '14 gangs of 30' would have 2 × 14 × 30 — 840 — warp ends to the width. Reeds were described by a number, either in the hundreds, denoting the number of 'splits' or dents to the Scotch ell of 37 inches, or in the tens, which is the number of 'porters' of twenty splits in the same length. There seems to be some affinity between the Gaelic word for twenty — *fichead* — and that for a weaver — *figheadair* — but the precise connection is not clear, unless it is that weavers frequently counted in twenties, and may be imaginary. Unless otherwise stated, Wilsons' put four threads to the split. Non-reversing patterns were called 'cheek' or 'cheeck' patterns and this has commonly been mis-read as 'check'. Finally, Wilsons' counted their yarn in 'hesps' to the pound. A figure of 1800 yards has been suggested for one hesp but calculation suggests that 1200 yards would be more accurate.

Tartan Research

Tartan research is a fascinating business. Much ground remains untrodden and the possibility of an important discovery lurks round every corner. It is a science in which one feels one's way without the constrictions of rigid guidelines but one which can absorb a wide range of skills. The most useful assets that can be brought to it are an inquisitive mind, the ability to make logical deductions and a willingness to keep them continually under review. There is a great deal of work to be done in the comparatively narrow fields of individual Clan and Family tartans and the development of the early tartan trade as well as in the wider area of the origin and development of tartan as a textile and although the ability to weave tartan is an essential aid to the full understanding of it much can be achieved by the simple process of sitting and thinking and wondering 'Why?'

It is best, of course, that students should be able to weave specimens for themselves, but failing this capability or having no benevolent tartan merchant in the family, an 'instant' tartan collection can be purchased in the form of one of the 'tartan picture books' that are put out primarily for the tourist market. These come in three kinds, good, bad and indifferent and, since none is likely to have a great deal to say about tartan — and that often ill-informed or misleading — the choice is governed by the quality of the tartan pictures. Sharpness, accurate registration and clarity of colour are all important and, of course, every picture, like any woven specimen, should show enough of the pattern to cover a complete half-sett of the tartan.

What used to be called a reading glass is the best kind of magnifier for examining tartan as it has a wide field of view with sufficient, though comparatively low, magnification; if it is mounted on a stand so that you can get both hands to the specimen, so much the better. A jeweller's eye-glass is a useful accessory but will seldom be needed. On the other hand, a nearly essential aid is a set of colour filters, red, green and blue. Coloured cellulose film can be used but photographic 'tri-colour' filters are best. These can be bought — with some difficulty — in the form of two-inch squares of gelatine which must be bound between two glass cover slides for protection. Seen through a filter of its own colour any colour appears lighter; its complementaries are darkened and neutrals are unchanged. The blue filter is the most important, it often being impossible to distinguish between blue and black without one.

Because of the structure of the twill weave taking a thread count is much less difficult than most people think. In twill, each thread crosses alternately over two and under two of every other thread to form the diagonal ridges in the cloth. Each ridge is therefore counted as four threads; if the stripe being counted begins with a ridge and ends with a valley, or vice-versa, the number of threads will be a straight multiple of four, but if it starts *and* finishes with either two extra threads have to be added. Counting is most easily done at a contrasting edge, where the colour being counted and that crossing it will appear as alternate dashes. A pointer with which to mark off the dashes is a great help and a cocktail stick is highly suitable. Do not use the tip of a ball-point pen, the nib of a fountain pen or the point of a pencil; any of these may mark the fabric.

In old tartans the true count appears only in the warp; the weft count is typically about two-thirds that of the warp and may also be irregular since the yarn of the weft was often of uneven thickness and the weaver simply put in enough to make a square pattern. Another way of telling which is the warp way, in the absence of a selvage, is by the marks that were often left by the reed. It is a wise precaution to take counts *and* measurements in both directions of the specimen.

The more information that can be collected on any specimen the better but the most comprehensive notes lose a great deal of their value if they are not properly filed. By far the best filing system for tartan studies is 'Sindex' which D.C. Stewart invented to help in compiling *The Setts*. A measure of its efficiency is that although it was originally intended to deal with no more than a couple of hundred tartans it has coped quite successfully with the entire collection of The Scottish Tartans Society. The information for each tartan is recorded on a single 8″ × 5″ record card which carries the colour strip along the top edge; below this on the left is written the name or other identification of the tartan and on the right the filing code for the particular card. This occupies the top margin of the card and below this are the thread count, cross indexing, notes on sources and any other information; this last can overflow on to the back of the card but this a rare circumstance. The inventor's own instructions for operating 'Sindex' are given in Appendix C.

Since the death of its inventor some users have made changes to 'Sindex' which include the introduction of additional colour letters the meanings of which are not immediately apparent. The reasoning behind these changes is difficult to follow since they are an unnecessary complication and affect adversely the system's value as a means of rapidly identifying a specimen. Nor do they do anything to overcome the only weakness of 'Sindex', the occasional difficulty of deciding if a colour is A, LtG, N or dirty W; R or T. The important features of 'Sindex' are its straightforwardness and simplicity. It has not and was never intended to have any role in comparing patterns. For this the human brain with a long experience of tartan is, at present the only apparatus available though a system of classification by pattern is under development. (See Appendix D.)

Colour strips should be drawn so as to include a little more than one whole repeat of the pattern and although the job can be done with felt-tipped pens or even coloured pencils an altogether better result can be obtained by the use of the water-soluble paints known as 'designer' colours. These are both opaque and free flowing and the blocks of colour can be outlined with a ruling pen and then filled in with a brush. Where the situation demands, a finished strip can be outlined in white to give it sharp edges. For exhibition purposes and especially for reproduction, when evenness of colour is important, a strip can be built up from coloured adhesive film which is marketed in a wide range of colours under various names of which 'Letrafilm' is probably the best known. The technique for this is to work from one end of the strip to the other, section by section, laying down a strip of film, trimming the end, butting the next to it and so on. When the strip is complete, trim all round the outside and rub down firmly. The best background surface is an artist's fashion board and guide lines must be drawn *outside* the area of the strip as pencil marks will show through the film.

Even with long practice it is not always easy to interpret a colour strip and it is sometimes necessary to make a pattern in two dimensions. For this two methods are available which are much quicker and less laborious than weaving. For those with some skill at the drawing board it is not difficult to imitate the 'machine painting' process (page 20) by drawing fine, closely spaced and parallel lines in 'designer' colour. The knack of getting the lines fairly evenly spaced comes quickly with practice but there can be some difficulty in getting the colour to run smoothly *and* give a dense line and the paper wears away the edge of the pen quite quickly, necessitating frequent re-sharpening. Those less well placed in the matter of drawing board skills can make a tolerable representation of a tartan pattern by laying strips of 'Letrafilm' on to a background material. The method is similar to 'machine painting'; the strips are laid down one colour at a time first one way and then the other but this time the backing is white and the darkest colour is laid down first. Darkness, however, is a relative term; all the colours should be of low density so as to avoid blocking the colours behind them. A grey of 20% strength will return to the eye about 30% of the light falling upon it and this will appear sufficiently black; even this may be strong enough to show through a light colour placed over it.

The camera is an indispensable aid to tartan research, allowing the collection of all kinds of information for leisured study, and it is possible to collect large cases full of expensive apparatus in an effort to cope satisfactorily with all aspects of such collection. However, in what older photographers regard as defiance of reason, the better kinds of modern 'compact' camera are entirely adequate. Since conditions will rarely be conducive to the production of perfect results readable results are all that need be aimed for; copies of documents must be legible, photographs of cloth must be 'thread-countable' and those of portraits must show sufficient detail for the sett to be extracted. These demands call for a camera which will focus at a short distance and, preferably, one to which a long-focus lens can be fitted, since the most interesting pictures are always hung high up. A large lens (or slow shutter speeds and a tripod) are desirable features which enable the best use to be made of available light; flash is useful in this respect but even with the greatest care is inclined to reflect from the subject matter. For document photography an extra-fine grain black and white film is best (my favourite is Ilford Pan F but other manufacturers have similar films by which their devotees swear) but if colour film is in the camera by all means have a go with that; modern colour films are very good indeed in sharpness and contrast, so the chances of getting a usable result are reasonably good. For colour records I prefer prints, though I supplement these with transparencies where possible; remember that artificial light will affect the accuracy of the colour, so take copious notes.

To everyone, the camera and film he or she knows best are the best for any work but there is one golden rule to be followed, to seek permission before photographing, whether in museum, art gallery or private collection.

Part Two

THE TARTANS

Introduction

With something like two thousand tartans on record and more coming almost daily it will be obvious that any choice limited to five hundred or so patterns must be to a large extent arbitrary; however, it has not been haphazard.

The Setts of the Scottish Tartans is long out of print and, so far as an author and his publisher can foretell the demands and the possibilities of the future, is likely to remain so. I have therefore included all the thread counts contained therein with the accompanying commentaries which I have revised, brought up to date and added to where necessary. In order to distinguish between the original notes and new material the former are in sans serif type-face though the reference numbers of the tartans have, of course, been altered.

I have taken relatively few counts from *The Tartan Weaver's Guide* but have included a fair sprinkling of Canadian Provincial tartans and a number of the officially recorded patterns issued by the Office of the Lord Lyon.

I have drawn heavily upon the pattern books of William Wilson & Son, the Bannockburn weavers, in the way of named tartans, tartan-style patterns known to them only by numbers and the small check patterns that they made in tartan cloth; all these show the kind of cloth and patterns that were in demand in the first quarter of the nineteenth century.

The remaining counts have found their way into my collection from various sources and are included because of some special interest or lesson to be learned; in this category come one or two of my own recent designs which show how I think a practical handloom weaver would have tackled tartan design.

Tartan is no longer purely Highland nor even necessarily Scottish-related and I have also borne this in mind when making my choice.

I have deliberately refrained, except in special cases, from providing colour strips of the patterns. Colour strips are very pretty but they are also very expensive to reproduce and their interpretation calls for considerable experience of the woven cloth; they are useful for comparing patterns but their usefulness is curtailed if they are fixed to the printed page and cannot be placed cheek-by-jowl when required. I recommend most strongly that those who have a use for colour strips should draw them for themselves, choosing a method to suit their needs from those outlined on page 56 where I have also dealt with some ways in which two-dimensional representations of tartan can be made on paper. There are many occasions when these can be useful and they take far less time to produce than does a woven specimen.

Thread counts taken from the Lyon Court registers, the majority of those from *The Tartan Weaver's guide* and nearly all of those from *The Setts* are in reality tables of proportions reduced to the smallest number of threads required for each stripe in order to reproduce the pattern accurately: those taken from the Wilson pattern books or from woven specimens give the actual numbers used in weaving the particular piece of material. The practical weaver will almost always find it necessary to adjust the given count to suit a particular size of sett or gauge of yarn, or both. This is seldom a matter of straightforward arithmetic and too-slavish adherence to the exact proportions of the count can, especially in small and simple patterns, have a very adverse effect on the appearance of the tartan. (See Appendix B.)

The thread counts give the stripes of the warp in sequence and the number of threads in each stripe. Except in the case of asymmetrical tartans, the first and last colour in the table is in bold type, and these constitute the pivotal stripes about which the design is symmetrical. Take for example the BARCLAY (16). The notation for this is:

R	G	B	G
2	32	32	2.

R 2 and G 2

are the pivots on which the design reverses. In setting up the loom preparatory to weaving, a start would normally be made at one of the pivotal stripes, preferably the less important. From here the threads are counted in one direction until the other pivot is reached; this is counted once only and the counting continued in the reverse direction. Thus the BARCLAY would run:

G	B	G	R	G	B	G	B
2	32	32	2	32	32	2	32

and so on.

In the case of an asymmetrical pattern, such as the BUCHANAN (40), a full repeat is given; the end stripes are not in bold type, and the count, on reaching the end, must be taken up again from the beginning, not carried back in reverse. There are a few exceptions to this general rule. In these the departure from symmetry is not readily noticed. The CAMPBELL OF ARGYLL (57) is an example of this type, the difference lying in the alternation of two colours, in this case yellow and white, at the same point in an otherwise reversible sequence. In such cases the notation is given as for a reversible design, except that the two colours are both indicated in the one position, separated by an oblique stroke, thus — Y/W. The intention is that one colour should be read in the forward order, the other on the return.

In the majority of the tables the following letters are used to indicate the colours:

A	=	Light blue (Azure)	Mn	=	Maroon
B	=	Blue	N	=	Grey (Neutral)
C	=	Rose (Crimson)	P	=	Purple
D	=	Dark (+ Colour)	R	=	Scarlet (Red)
G	=	Green	T	=	Brown (Tan)
K	=	Black	W	=	White
L	=	Light (+ Colour)	Y	=	Yellow

Other colours are named in full.

(This table evolved with 'Sindex'. *The Setts* used Az for Light Blue, Cr for Crimson, Bk for Black, Gy for Grey and wrote Brown in full; Dk was for Dark and Lt for Light.)

Some of the counts issued by the Lyon Office employ different symbols:

Az	=	Azure/Sky blue	Purp	=	Purpure/ Purple
Gu	=	Gules/Scarlet	Bu	=	a duller blue
Vt	=	Vert/Grass green	Red	=	a duller red
Br	=	Brown	C	=	Crimson
Bk	=	Black	Gr	=	a duller green
Wh	=	White	Y	=	Yellow

It is important to understand the fundamental difference between these two sets of symbols. The first defines the colours loosely, so that the artist-weaver can use his skill and the colours at his disposal to get the best results, while the second attempts to define setts put up for approval and registration. It might have been better to have defined the colours by reference to standard shades and to have chosen symbols less liable to mis-reading, confusion and typographical error than 'Br', 'Bk' and 'Bu' or 'Gu' and 'Gr'. I can do no more than warn of the pitfalls.

The Setts of the Tartans

1 ABERCROMBIE

G	W	G	Bk	B	Bk	B	Bk	**B**
28	2	14	14	4	4	4	4	14

The only published record of this family tartan is that given by Logan in 1831; the design does not appear in any of the illustrated works. A strict rendering of Logan's count is given here. It shows an unduly clumsy sett, and in view of the many aberrations that occur in other of his tables, the liberty might be taken of modifying this one to give a more satisfactory result, by enlarging the main blue stripe and by contracting the narrower blue and black stripes. Also, it may be that in the above count the 28 should be read as 14.

The Wilson of Bannockburn records show that a rather different ABERCROMBIE tartan was popular during the first thirty years of the nineteenth century. This is the tartan now known as GRAHAM OF MONTROSE. (141) Wilson's also produced what they called 'Abercromby with yellow', which is identical with the CAMPBELL OF BREADALBANE (61). Another variant, MACCALLUM (201), has the light line in red. The MACNEIL OF COLONSAY (286) also resembles their ABERCROMBY, with one black stripe changed to blue.

Logan claimed that he had 'not inserted any fancy tartan' in his pattern tables but Wilsons' thought otherwise and wrote saying "we are sorry that you have allowed several Fictitious and Fancy patterns to get amongst the Genuine Clan Tartans — we allude particularly to Douglas, Abercrombie, Graham and some others." They also complained that "the greater part of the scales given for the different Tartans are incorrect at the extremeties" (*sic*) and several patterns were declared to be 'defective' or 'never seen before'.

Wilsons' record of the tartans they supplied to Logan and a list of their comments on the pattern tables as published have been preserved and if they are not greatly enlightening they at least give some food for thought. In this case they supplied an unspecified quantity of their No. 64 or Abercrombie Pattern (which, they say, was named after Sir Ralph Abercrombie in the late 18th or early 19th century) but Logan's table relates to another fancy pattern, No. 158 — also known as GRAHAM TARTAN — which has somehow acquired a pair of black lines, Black Watch fashion, around the edge of the blue square instead of a single central overcheck (Plate 16 (a) and (b). No. 158 is the same as GRAHAM OF MENTEITH (140), with white in place of light blue, and comparison of this with Logan's Abercrombie shows quite clearly that the central panels of the latter, both blue and green, should be doubled in size.

2 ABERDEEN SETT

W	C	R	W	K	LG	W	R	C	W	C	R	W	A	W	P	R	C	W
4	6	46	4	32	8	2	12	6	2	6	12	2	20	4	6	16	6	4
C	R	P	W	K	LG	K	W	P	R	C	W	C	R	P	W	P	A	W
6	16	6	4	24	8	24	4	6	16	6	4	6	16	6	4	12	8	4
A	P	W	K	LG	**W**													
8	12	4	32	8	4													

A late eighteenth century plaid pattern from the Wilson records. It is sold as a 'District' tartan but it is unlikely that it was ever intended as such. Wilsons' named many of their patterns in honour of people or places and it is possible that some of the latter were named after the places where specimens were found. These, however, are all simple patterns with some territorial characteristics and quite unlike this type of pattern.

3 ALBERTA

G	K	Pink	K	LB	K	**Y**
24	2	2	2	4	2	8

The official tartan of the Province of Alberta, approved by provincial legislature in 1961.

4 AMERICAN SAINT ANDREWS

DB	B	Mid B	A	W	A	Mid B	B	DB	K	R	W	R	W	R	W	**R**
28	2	2	2	2	2	2	2	40	40	34	8	6	6	6	6	10

J. C. Thompson inspired the design of this tartan in celebration of the Bicentenary of the United States of America. The allusion to the 'Stars and Stripes' is evident though the full range of blues needed to show the stars clearly is rarely, if ever, used. I feel that many of my American friends still think that I introduced the black bars in recognition of the Southern States or as some obscure British joke but the fact is that 'flag' red and 'flag' blue are such strong colours that an equally strong neutral stripe is essential to separate them.

5, 6 ANDERSON

(5)

R	Az	R	Bk	R	Az	Bk	W	Bk	Y	Bk	Y	Bk	R	B	R	G	R
6	12	2	4	2	36	6	6	6	2	2	2	8	2	8	6	12	4

G	**R**
12	8

(6)

R	B	K	R	K	B	P	W	K	Y	K	Y	K	R	P	G	K	R
8	12	2	4	2	32	6	6	6	4	4	4	10	4	10	14	2	4

K	G	**R**
2	14	6

Recently become popular for feminine wear, this elaborate pattern gives the impression of being made up of elements from older designs not very successfully blended. The ground is variously rendered in grey, turquoise, or pale blue. Slight variations on the present sett are to be found.

Among six or eight versions of the basic tartan differences are minimal but the count (6) is for a somewhat more masculine design.

7 ARBUTHNOT

B	K	B	K	G	W	G	B	G	W	G	K	B	K	B	K	**B**
8	8	38	38	14	4	16	16	16	4	14	38	8	8	8	8	36

A family tartan of Black Watch parentage registered at the Lyon Court 11.10.1962.

8 ARMSTRONG

G	Bk	G	Bk	B	Bk	B	Bk	B	**R**
4	2	60	24	4	2	2	2	24	6

In earlier times the name of Armstrong was not only respected but feared in Liddesdale and throughout the Borders, but has no Highland associations. The tartan first appears in the *Vestiarium Scoticum*.

9 AUSTIN

See "No. 75 or Austin" among the reversing patterns, page 178.

10 BAILLIE SETT

B	K	B	K	B	K	G	K	Y	K	G	K	B	K	**R**
56	8	8	8	8	56	54	6	10	6	54	56	54	6	10

The tartan of the Inverness-shire (or Baillie) Fencibles 1794-1802. The pattern is taken from Wilsons' 1819 Key Pattern Book and is for the 28 reed.

11, 12 BAILLIE OF POLKEMETT

(11)	**G**	R	K	B	**W**												
	4	40	24	24	6												
(12)	**B**	K	B	K	G	W	G	W	G	W	G	K	B	K	B	K	**B**
	2	2	16	18	18	2	2	2	2	2	18	18	2	2	2	2	22

Both these tartans are said to have been designed by A. W. Geddes (of Andersons', Edinburgh) in 1937.

13 BAIRD

P	G	P	G	Bk	B	Bk	**B**
6	2	2	16	16	16	4	6

The family tartan of the Bairds, who are first heard of in Lanarkshire, but were long associated with the counties of Banff and Aberdeen.

14, 15 BALMORAL

(14)	**Gy**	R	Gy	Lavender	Bk	Gy	Lv	Gy	Lv	Gy	Bk	Gy	**R**
	4	2	16	4	4	2	2	2	8	4	2	2	2
(15)	**R**	LN	K	LN	DN	LN	DN	LN	K	DN	LN	R	**LN**
	5	5	5	11	23	5	5	5	12	12	55	15	9

The design derives from the ROYAL STUART (406), but has been formed without regard for the basic structure of the latter. It was first illustrated by D.W. Stewart in *Old and Rare Scottish Tartans* with the following note:

> The object of including this beautiful modern yet rare design in a collection of Old and Rare Tartans is that collectors may possess a pattern greatly desired by them. Hitherto, on account of the conditions imposed on Messrs Romanes & Paterson, Edinburgh, the manufacturers of tartans to the Royal Family, it has been impossible, even for the connoisseur, to procure an example of it. For the purposes of the present work, however, Her Majesty the Queen has not only granted permission for its publication here, but has also graciously afforded information concerning its inception in the early years of the reign, when the sett was designed by the Prince Consort. It has continued to occupy a conspicuous position in the dress and appointments of the Royal Family and its retainers, when these partake of a Highland character. On the occasion of a Royal marriage, Her Majesty's gifts to the bride include articles of costume of this tartan.

This represents only one use of the tartan, extending from about 1860 onwards. In its original form it was produced in much heavier material, having the present red and black stripes, but two shades of grey, the darker of which became the lavender of the material intended for feminine wear. The earliest material was made in two weights, a heavy one for the Balmoral male staff and a lighter one for the royal wearers. These woollen tartans were not in the normal twill weave, but something much more complex, and the grey yarn was not self-coloured but spun three-ply in two proportions of black and white. The effect of these peculiarities was a texture remarkably similar in appearance and feel to rough-hewn granite.

It should be remarked that the BALMORAL tartan is not produced as an article of commerce.

I find it difficult to accept the suggestion that the lighter-weight cloth for ladies wear would have used lavender instead of grey and think it more likely that the lavender shade was 'D.W.'s' attempt to match the mixed grey of the worsted yarn by a single colour of silk. Several of the examples shown in *Old and Rare Scottish Tartans* cast doubt on 'D.W.'s' accuracy in matters of colour.

In the count (15) the dark grey yarn is three-ply with two plies of black to one of white; the light grey areas are made by weaving alternate picks of this and white up to the stated total.

16, 17 BARCLAY

(16)	**R**	G	B	**G**		(17)	**W**	Y	Bk	**Y**
	2	32	32	2			2	12	12	2

The design of the Barclay family tartan is presented in two colour schemes. In one the ground is yellow; the other, the Hunting version, has a green ground. This latter form derives from the *Vestiarium Scoticum,* where the blue is rendered much darker than the green. The Dress tartan, of later date, is often given the more robust proportions here shown.

18 BHUTAN

C*	Y	G	Y	Cr*	W	B*	W	**C**
4	4	12	4	16	4	12	4	6

The conditions which led to the development of tartan in the Highlands applied also to other isolated and self-sufficient communities and often had much the same result although the extravagent propaganda that goes with the Scottish product was absent.

Bhutan, a small mountain kingdom whose National dress is not dissimilar to Highland dress, is a case in point; the specimen from which this pattern was taken is modern but there is no reason to suppose that the design is not traditional.

In the count given the stripes marked with an asterisk are green in the weft.

19 BIRRAL SETT

R	W	P	A	W	A	P	W	G	W	R	C	P	C	R	W	**P**
130	4	16	8	4	8	16	4	64	4	16	8	4	8	16	4	32

A late eighteenth century plaid pattern from the Wilson 1819 Key Pattern Book. With four threads to the split in a 600 reed three half setts go to the width of 19″.

20-26 BLACK WATCH

	B	Bk	B	Bk	B	Bk	G	Bk	G	Bk	B	Bk	**B**
(20)	22	2	2	2	2	16	16	2	16	16	16	2	2
(21)	24	4	4	4	4	20	24	6	24	20	22	4	4
(22a)	60	10	10	10	10	64	64	10	64	64	62	10	10
(22b)	56	8	8	8	8	58	54	8	54	58	56	8	8
(22c)	48	6	6	6	6	48	46	6	46	48	46	6	6

	R	K	B	K	G	K	**R**
(23a)	10	6	88	94	90	6	10
(23b)	10	6	72	78	74	6	10
(23c)	8	6	62	66	62	6	8

(24)	**R**	K	B	K	G	**K**
	6	6	46	48	46	6

(25)	**B**	R	B	R	B	R	G	R	G	R	B	R	**B**
	56	8	8	8	8	58	54	8	54	58	56	8	8

(26)	**B**	K	B	K	B	K	G	K	G	K	B	K	**B**
	32	6	6	6	6	32	30	6	30	32	30	6	6

All the accounts of the inception of the Black Watch tartan speak of it as a design new at the time when the regiment was formed. In that it is not identical with any then existing pattern, this is true enough. There remains the possibility that it was an abstraction from patterns already in use. Many of the tartans of to-day are founded on the scheme of the BLACK WATCH, and some of them we know to have been admittedly built on it, such as the FORBES (120) and the GORDON (134). But there are others that may be earlier than the BLACK WATCH. Unfortunately, it is difficult to fix the age of these. Yet, in addition to the merely traditional designs, there are several actual fragments, of great age, in which the characteristic feature of the BLACK WATCH is to be seen. D.W. Stewart shows the design of a fragment, named the MACRAE HUNTING (309), and dating from before 1715, which is clearly of the BLACK WATCH type; and the fragment (434) he describes as having been worn by Prince Charles Edward while in the Mackintosh country contains the same germ-idea. A similar specimen, with much the same history, but described as ROBERTSON, also shows this motif, in an attenuated form. A remarkably similar sett is shown in the McIan-Logan work as MACDONALD OF KEPPOCH (214), and has there attached to it the same tradition as D.W. Stewart gives in connection with a somewhat different design (213) — that it was from a plaid given by Keppoch to the Prince and later cut up for distribution among Jacobite enthusiasts. Whatever the actual sources of these fragments may have been, they seem to rule out the idea that the Black Watch tartan was entirely original, and at the same time rule out the necessity for supposing that such tartans as the ATHOL MURRAY (348) derive from the BLACK WATCH. A plaid found at Culloden also deserves consideration in this connection (435). Two counts are given here: one (20) based on Logan's Sutherland tartan, and a more robust version (21) taken from later examples. Specimens from before Logan's time show considerable uniformity in the sizes, with all the broad stripes about one inch wide and the narrow about one sixth of an inch, making the repeat about thirteen inches, though similar tartans were sometimes smaller.

Thus wrote D. C. Stewart, but that was over forty years ago. My own later thinking is dealt with in detail under the heading 'Military Tartans' and all that remains to be done here is to consider the patterns quoted.

It seems that the belted plaid continued in military use for some long time after it had been superseded for civilian wear by the kilt and it must indeed have been an excellent campaign dress in the hard-soldiering days of the Napoleonic Wars. The threadcounts (22) are taken from the 1819 Key Pattern Book and are for Officers', Sergeants' and Privates' plaids for the 27, 24 and 18 reeds respectively. The Silvage (*sic*) Marks are 106, 100 and 80 threads and the breadth is given as 26 inches in all cases, two lengths being joined edge to edge to make the plaid 52 inches wide. "To make the full width put on three full half setts and so much of the fourth until all the green in it is put on after which conclude with the Black Silvage Mark." There is nothing in the pattern to indicate that the selvage was woven in herringbone but this was usual.

The counts (23) are for OFFICERS', SERGEANTS' and PRIVATES' KILTS, 42nd

PATTERN and come from a manuscript notebook of about 1790 in the Wilson records; the reeds used were 28, 22 and 400 respectively. In this case some detective work is called for to complete the weaving data given for we are given a selvage mark of 104 threads but not the width of the web for the Officers' kilts and the widths (20 gangs run with 30 threads and 23½ gangs run with 30 threads) but not the selvage marks. Following the principle set out above but using five half setts and the green of the sixth we arrive at 95 threads for the selvage mark of the sergeants' kilts and 78 for that of the privates' kilts while the officers' kilts are shown to have been warped with 28 gangs of 30 threads.

I have stated my belief in the possibility that the new 42nd Pattern tartan derived from that of the Independent Companies and my reconstruction (24) of the latter is taken directly from the counts for Privates' plaids (22).

"To make the Band, or Musicians', Plaids (25), you have only to put scarlet in place of the black in the Sergts. plaids. The band and the Sergeants are of the same quality."

Finally, I give '42ND COARSE KILT' (26) for the 17 reed, 19 inches wide with a selvage mark of 48 threads. Once again this is taken from the 1819 Key Pattern book which contains numerous settings of this, one of the most popular tartans of the day. See Plates 2 (b), 3, 4 (a), (c), (g) and (h).

27 BLAIR

B	R	B	K	G	R	G
12	4	40	32	40	4	12

A modern family tartan of simple but effective design.

28 BLAIRLOGIE

K	R	B	G	B	G	K	G	W*	G	K	G	B	G	B	R	**B***
80	6	20	6	10	50	2	2	6	2	2	50	10	6	20	2	8

This pattern comes from a pattern book shown to me by the late Dick Dalgliesh, originator of Reproduction tartans. In itself it is not of great interest but the pattern between the asterisks above — W6 to B8 — is identical with that given in the *Vestiarium Scoticum* as MACNEILL (287).

29, 30 BLANKET SETT and BORDER SETT

(29)	W	K	R	W	G	R	W	R
	90	4	38	4	38	44	4	4

(30)	W	R	W	G	W	K	R	K	W	G	W	R	W
	90	38	40	40	40	4	44	4	40	40	40	38	40

This is another of Wilsons' "Old Superfine Tartan Setts" from the 1819 Key Pattern Book. The count (29) is from centre to centre of the pivotal stripes. Four half setts were put on and followed by the border (30) to make a total of 1386 warp ends which, woven in the 28 reed, gave a width of 19 inches (Plate 5 (a)).

31 BLUE

R	MidB	R	MB	A	DB	W
4	22	6	22	24	20	4

I designed the Blue tartan in 1985 for a family of that name, a sept-name of MacMillan. Naturally enough, a predominantly blue tartan was asked for and the three shades arranged as a superimposed check fulfilled this requirement. The red lines are taken from the hunting MacMillan tartan (277) and balance at the opposite pivot is provided by the white line on dark blue.

32 BOYD

Y	Gr	Bk	Bu	Bk	Bu	Bk	Gu	Gr	Gu	Bk	**Wh**
10	44	4	4	4	4	20	76	10	8	8	10

This is a modern family tartan registered at the Lyon Court in 1956. It has a close resemblance to the *Vestiarium Scoticum*'s Stuart of Bute (404), the Boyds having come from that part of Scotland. Note that the colours are given in the symbols used by the Lyon Office.

33 B.C. PROVINCIAL

G	K	G	A	Y	A	R	K	R	A	R	**W**
8	2	16	16	2	16	16	2	16	4	16	2

The tartan of British Columbia, circa 1966-67.

34-36 BRODIE

(34)	**Bk**	R	Bk	Y	Bk	**R**
	4	32	16	2	16	4

(35)	**R**	B	G	Bk	Y	Bk	**R**
	4	16	16	16	2	16	4

D.W. Stewart traces this to the beginning of the nineteenth century, adding that, about the same period, the HUNTLY (156) was also known as BRODIE.

The Dress version appears in the *Vestiarium Scoticum*, where the yellow line is about half the width shown here; the HUNTING BRODIE is of later date.

A quite different Brodie sett was in use about the middle of last century. The count is as follows:

(36)	**R**	W	B	Bk	R	B	R	**Y**
	96	8	8	8	24	8	2	8

The count (36) is taken from the manuscript of William and Andrew Smith's 'Authenticated Tartans'. It dates to the mid-1800s at the latest and its authenticity is challenged only by the *Vestiarium Scoticum*. See Plates 8 and 9.

37, 38 BRUCE

(37)	**W/Y**	R	G	R	G	**R**
	2	16	4	4	12	2

(38)	**R**	G	K	W	K	Y	K	A	Cr	**W**
	48	44	4	12	4	4	30	12	12	4

The Bruce tartan has alternate yellow and white lines. The design comes from the *Vestiarium Scoticum*; no other authority can be given.

BRUCE OF KINNAIRD (38) can be taken as yet another variation upon the well-worn Royal Stuart theme. However, there is another possible source in a non-reversing pattern, Wilsons' No. 17 which, if woven as a reversing sett, is almost identical with this.

(No. 17)	A	K	Y	K	W	R	G	K	W	K	Y	K	A	R
	24	32	6	4	12	88	50	4	12	4	6	32	24	12

39 BRUCE COUNTY, ONTARIO

W	B	R	G	R	G	R	G	R	G	R	**Y**
2	2	14	4	4	12	2	12	4	4	16	2

The official tartan of the County, registered at the Lyon Court in 1965.

40-43 BUCHANAN

(40)	**Bk**	Y	Bk	B	Bk	G	B	G	Bk	B	Bk	R	W	R	Bk	B	Bk	**Y**
	2	12	2	8	2	12	8	12	2	8	2	16	2	16	2	8	2	12

(41)	**Az**	G	Bk	Az	Bk	Y	Bk	Y	Bk	Az	Bk	R	**W**
	4	32	2	4	2	8	2	8	2	4	2	32	4

(42) **Bk** W Cr W Cr **W**
2 18 8 4 8 4

(43) **B/R** T G T B T
6 28 28 4 28 4

The Buchanan tartan (40) is one of the most popular, and quite the most irregular, of the tartans seen in common use. Is this irregularity due to anything more than an unfortunate slip? The first illustration showing the modern design appears in the McIan-Logan work; the next is the Smiths'. Logan's own threadcount of 1831 indicates a design containing the same elements, but perfectly regular, and of markedly superior quality. Smibert, in 1850, showed a version which, while coarser in its proportions, is substantially the same as the specimen from which Logan made his count. Smibert obtained most of his specimens from Messrs. William Wilson & Son, of Bannockburn, who are known to have been among the original subscribers to Logan's *The Scottish Gaël.* We may presume that the symmetrical version was the one being produced at Bannockburn early in the nineteenth century, but we cannot be certain who had it first — Logan or Messrs Wilson. It would seem as if many of Logan's designs were transmitted through the Wilsons to Smibert, whereas the Smiths depended more on Edinburgh firms for their information, and we must suppose it was from one of these that they obtained the irregular version of the BUCHANAN. Subsequent manufacturers have in general used the Smith work as their source rather than Logan or Smibert, and in this way the irregular sett has been perpetuated. It is possible that several versions of Buchanan tartans were in use before 1850, and McIan may have used for his drawing one of these in preference to that tabulated by Logan. It is significant that in this instance the only comment on the tartan was made by McIan himself, not by Logan. Yet we find in McIan's drawing showing a Robertson tartan irregularities similar to those found in the BUCHANAN, though we do not have to suppose that his version of the ROBERTSON was ever in production by the makers. McIan's was the first illustration of this Buchanan tartan, and there was time for it to be used as a model by Edinburgh weavers before the Smiths made their book, for McIan's BUCHANAN plate was issued in 1843. The Smiths say of it that it 'seems to be universally considered the genuine Buchanan Tartan'. This suggests the existence not only of doubt but of controversy on the matter. Whether or not McIan was actually responsible for the irregular sett, he certainly may have been. There is in use at the present day a 'MacMillan Ancient' (278) tartan, and this undoubtedly derives from McIan's drawing of his MacMillan figure. Logan says in the accompanying text that the MACMILLAN is identical with the BUCHANAN, yet the difference in the drawings is sufficient to justify the supposition that they were distinct tartans. If the weavers of to-day can take McIan as their authority for the MACMILLAN, those of a century ago may similarly have taken his authority for the BUCHANAN. A study of the McIan plates will show that while the outline drawing is done with cor·· iderable care, the colouring is often slapdash and highly misleading. It is un،ortunate that although Mclan's drawings have their use as a check on some of the patterns, they are for the most part worthless as accurate records.

It might be thought that between the publication of *The Scottish Gaël* and the Mclan collaboration Logan had changed his mind about the correct sett. Yet the table he later supplied to M'Intyre North, except for an irrelevant omission, is the same as his original symmetrical sett, and does not countenance the Mclan version. Of all Logan's early tables, that given for BUCHANAN is one of the eight or nine that do not lay themselves open to misunderstanding.

We feel justified in suggesting that Logan's BUCHANAN (41) should replace that now in common use (but see Appendix F).

The design (42) in the *Vestiarium Scoticum* is entirely different from these, and is rarely seen.

The hunting tartan (43) is taken from a specimen presented to the Highland Society of London by Sir Charles Buchanan in 1955. It derives from the *Vestiarium* sett and therefore bears a marked resemblance to HUNTING FRASER. (See Appendix F and Plate 9 (f).

44 BURNET OF LEYS

R	**B**	**R**	**W**	**R**	**G**	**R**	**Y**
120	10	10	4	10	4	10	4

A modern family tartan, one of the first to be registered at the Lyon Court — in 1938.

45, 46 CALEDONIA

(45)	**DP**	R	A	DP	Y	G	R	A	**R**
	4	26	18	18	4	24	26	6	26

(46)	**R**	W	R	K	R	G	Y	K	A	K	A	K	A	**R**
	26	4	26	6	26	42	6	36	18	4	4	4	18	42

In view of its widespread use as a foundation for other tartans it is perhaps not surprising that Wilsons' named the Mackintosh tartan (260) 'Caledonian Sett'. However, this seems to have been something of an aberration, for they also called it 'Lovat or Fraser tartan', as well as by its proper name and they already had a suitable Caledonian tartan in 'No. 43 or Kidd Sett or Caledonia Pattern', which lasted until it was appropriated as the Macpherson tartan (295) in 1817. Concurrently with this, however, they ran a fine Merino 'No. 3 or Caledonia pattern' (45), seven half setts making a twenty-seven inch web.

The 1953 edition of Robert Bain's *Clans and Tartans of Scotland* gave the name 'Caledonia' to another Wilson design, No. 155 (46), a close relative of No. 43, the editor Miss Margaret MacDougall asserting that this was the correct Caledonia tartan and that the Macpherson tartan had, in the previous century, been incorrectly worn as Caledonia. She had, of course, got it wrong. No. 43 was quite correctly worn as Caledonia until the Macphersons took it over and No. 155 had never been named.

47-51 CALEDONIAN SOCIETY TARTANS

(47)	**W**	K	R	A	K	G	K	B	K	B	R	B	R	B	R	B	**R**
	8	2	4	8	4	40	30	8	8	28	4	4	8	4	4	8	28

(48)	**R**	G	R	A	R	K	R	B	G	**Y**
	6	36	8	6	8	26	6	36	4	6

(49)	**R**	G	Y	K	A	W	B	**W**
	80	32	4	16	8	2	10	4

(50)	**R**	B	R	A	R	B	R	G	R	G	R	B	**R**
	18	4	42	4	4	16	4	4	4	34	4	4	16

(51)	**K**	B	G	R	G	K	G	K	G	K	G	B	T	B	T	B	T	**B**
	12	6	8	16	26	6	6	6	6	6	8	8	6	6	6	6	6	6

In 1835 James Logan, at the request of a friend there, designed a tartan (47) for the use of a Caledonian Society in Prince Edward Island and other Societies have at various times had the same idea. Wilsons' produced a tartan (48) for the Stirling and Bannockburn Caledonian Society about 1847 and a coat seen in Banff museum is in a tartan (49) described as 'Ancient Caledonian Society'. A modern and somewhat less satisfactory design (50) — too like Grant (143) for comfort — was made in 1953 for the London Caledonian Games Association.

Some other Societies were less enterprising and were content to wear 'stock' tartans. In 1813 the Glasgow Highland Society wore jackets of 'Abercromby pattern' and in 1821 the Caithness and Sutherland Society sported Mackay kilts and Prince Charles Edward jackets; the Highland Society of London outfitted itself in Royal Stuart. Correspondence with Wilsons' fails to reveal what tartan was worn by the Strathbogie Ploughmans' Society but there is some compensation gained from learning that in 1808 the Highland Society of Scotland ordered a quantity of the Kidd/Caledonia tartan 'for persons rather stout'.

The Glasgow Celtic Society also had its own tartan (51).

52-56 CAMERON

(52)	**R**	G	R	B	W	B	R	B	**R**		
	12	6	12	2	2	2	4	16	8		
(53)	**G**	R	G	R	G	Bk	R	B	R	B	**Y**
	16	2	2	6	32	32	2	32	6	16	4
(54)	**Y**	R	G	R	G	**R**					
	2	32	12	4	12	4					
(55)	**B**	A	B	R	K	A	R	G	R	K	**R**
	16	6	80	6	88	6	6	80	4	8	14

Cameron tartans are in general use. The Erracht Cameron (53) (Plate 4 (m)) worn by the Cameron Highlanders, is the only one recorded by Logan. This is commonly described as a blend of the MacDonald and the Cameron tartans, made when the regiment was raised in 1793. It closely resembles the dark Clan MacDonald (209), the only foreign element being the single yellow line, so that it is difficult to see what of Cameron there is about it, unless the story relates to a Cameron design now lost to us. The Lochiel contains no yellow, and the *Vestiarium Scoticum* was then unknown.

The Cameron of Lochiel design (52) was first illustrated by the Smiths. Sometimes the lines enclosing the white are rendered in black, but the Smiths show these lines as blue. They quote as their authority for the sett both the then Chief and an ancient fragment of tartan. In general the Smith illustrations contain few slips, and it may be that these lines were formerly blue, and were changed to black in conformity with the practice now common of reinforcing a light line by means of black edges. In early specimens of tartan it is not always easy to distinguish blue from black.

The third Cameron tartan (54), in green on red, with a yellow line, first appeared in the *Vestiarium* but did not come into wide use till late in the nineteenth century.

The Erracht Cameron was for long treated as a Hunting tartan; but at a Clan Gathering in 1956 the following, based on the *Vestiarium* sett (54), was adopted as Cameron: Hunting, so releasing the Erracht for purely regimental use. The count is as follows:

(56)	**R**	G	R	G	B	G	**Y**
	6	20	6	28	32	6	4

Lochaber Cameron (55) is the name given to a Wilson pattern of about 1800 known to them as "New pattern for T. Logan". Nothing has emerged from the Wilson papers concerning the identity of T. Logan but he appears to have been an important early customer. The tartan is related to "LOCHABER SETT" (179).

57-65 CAMPBELL

(57)	**B**	Bk	B	Bk	G	Bk	W/Y	BK	G	BK	B	BK	B	Bk	**B**
	2	2	16	16	16	2	4	2	16	16	2	2	2	2	16
(58)	**B**	Bk	B	Bk	Y	G	Y	Bk	B	Bk	B	Bk	**B**		
	2	2	16	16	2	28	2	16	2	2	2	2	16		
(59)	**B**	Bk	B	Bk	G	Bk	**Y/W**								
	4	2	24	24	24	2	4								
(60)	**Az**	Bk	G	Bk	B	Bk	**R**								
	4	2	16	16	16	2	4								
(61)	**Bk**	B	Bk	G	Y	G	**Bk**								
	6	18	18	18	4	18	18								
(62)	**P**	K	P	K	G	**W**									
	4	2	12	10	10	2									
(63)	**K**	B	K	G	**K**										
	4	22	52	22	4										
(64)	**B**	K	B	K	**G**										
	4	2	14	12	14										
(65)	**R**	K	R	K	**R**										
	8	2	48	44	4										

Five designs are here shown. The most widely used is that known as CAMPBELL OF ARGYLL or CAMPBELL OF LOCHAWE (57), and consists of the BLACK WATCH as a foundation, with alternatively a white and a yellow line centred on the green band. This design is of a type that is not strictly symmetrical, but it does not offend against the principle of symmetry in the way that some tartans, notably the BUCHANAN (40), are seen to do. The Smiths write of it as the oldest of the Campbell designs, and members of the Clan have adduced it to support their claim that the BLACK WATCH is essentially a Campbell tartan. It is one of the two given by Logan under the name of Campbell. The other is the BREADALBANE (58) as illustrated by McIan and by Smibert, and later by D.W. Stewart, Plate 61. Of this and other Campbell tartans D.W. Stewart writes:

> The specimen here presented is a careful reproduction of the tartan of Campbell of Breadalbane, as worn by the Fencibles of that district from their embodiment in 1793 to their disbandment in 1802. The authority is a portion of the regimental uniform of Major Campbell, one of the officers, whose descendants now treasure it as a precious

relic. Wherever the tartan occurs in early collections, dating from before 1790 down to 1840, the pattern agrees with the accompanying illustration. The later date, however, witnessed the inception of a delusion that has prevailed even to the present day; for a tartan similar in some respects, which appears in certain early collections under the simple designation of 'fancy', began about that time to usurp the title of Breadalbane Campbell, and is now received as the correct design. But the existence of this regimental dress now a century [and a half] old, the uninterrupted record of the pattern to 1840, and the proved genesis of the spurious variety, afford the amplest justification for including the earlier pattern in the present work. It is the only Campbell tartan included in the collection made by the Highland Society of London in 1816–17. It is doubtful if any of the so-called Campbell tartans as worn at the present time were in use earlier than the middle of [the eighteenth] century, while several are of more recent introduction. The early Campbell portraits at Langton and Loudoun show designs entirely unlike any Campbell tartans now in use, being chiefly red."

In point of fact, this later 'fancy' tartan appears in a collection made before 1820, where it is styled simply 'Braedalbane'.

The 'fancy' BREADALBANE (61) was first illustrated by the Smiths, who obtained their specimen from the Marquis of Breadalbane. The scheme of this tartan is found again in several others, such as the GRAHAM OF MONTROSE (138), probably belonging to the same period. The design known as CAMPBELL OF LOUDOUN (59), was first shown by James Grant in 1886, though the Smiths give as CAMPBELL OF ARGYLL a very similar scheme, the light lines being white only. The CAMPBELL OF CAWDOR (60), (Plate 4 (e)), on the same foundation, also appears in the Smith work.

The Clan Campbell is spread wide and it is difficult to see how the many branches could have evolved such closely related patterns had they done so entirely spontaneously. The inference is either that all the designs are comparatively late or that at least some of them may have a common origin in an earlier Independent Company uniform. There is some evidence of re-arrangement of attributions among the Campbell tartans: in the Key Pattern Book, Campbell of Cawdor (60) is listed as "No 230 or Argylle pattern" and at that time was probably worn by pupils of the Duchess of Argyll's School. It can usually be taken that a numbered pattern, even if it later acquired a name, began life as a 'fancy' pattern.

Of the additional setts given here (62) is taken from the Provost MacBean Collection at Inverness Museum, where it is named as CAMPBELL OF ARGYLL. CAMPBELL OF LOCHEWE (63) and CAMPBELL OF GLEN LYON (64) are from an unknown source by way of specimens made by the late John MacGregor Hastie who also collected the red tartan (65).

A tartan marketed by Wilsons' as 'NEW LOUDEN' (183) is considered by some to be a Campbell tartan but I regard this attribution as unsound.

66 CANADIAN CALEDONIAN

B	G	Y	R	W	R	G	R	G	W
6	32	2	2	2	12	6	2	6	2

Another 'Caledonia', designed in 1939 by Hastie Cochrane and George MacBeth of Vancouver.

67 CANADIAN CENTENNIAL

R	W	R	G	B	K	B	Y
6	12	4	64	72	4	8	4

A celebratory tartan devised by Peter MacArthur & Co., Glasgow. It demonstrates well how a strong motif, in this case the RWRWR overcheck on the green, can confer distinction upon a simple design.

68 CARMICHAEL

K	G	B	R	B	Y
6	72	56	4	4	6

A family tartan of attractive simplicity.

69 CARNEGIE

Y	G	R	G	R	G	Bk	R	B	R	B	R	B
2	4	2	2	4	12	12	2	12	4	2	2	6

This is a variant of the MacDonell of Glengarry (210), said to have been adopted as such by Lord Southesk, who was active in 'the '15'. The white of the Glengarry here becomes yellow. Though the Carnegie is widely accepted as a separate design, it is more probable that Lord Southesk adopted the MacDonell tartan as it stood, and that the change from white to yellow occurred in the passing of time. Such change would be almost inevitable in a portrait, and this may account for the differentiation.

70 CAROLINA

R	A	K	Y	K	W	K	R	G	R	K	R	W
64	28	32	6	8	8	8	2	6	26	8	8	4

Designed by Dr Micheil MacDonald for the State of North Carolina. Appropriately, it relates closely to Prince Charles Edward (408).

71 CHILDERS

K	AshG	K	BeechG	K	**R**
176	34	16	56	16	12

The history of this tartan has been dealt with on page 32. The count given is that used by James Johnstone & Co., Newmills, Elgin, in 1907, when it was first woven. The yarn was 24cut Cheviot.

72-73 CHISHOLM

(72)	**R**	B	W	B	R	G	R	**B**		
	24	4	2	4	6	16	6	2		
(73)	**R**	W	R	B	G	Bk	G	Bk	G	**R**
	12	2	48	12	4	2	4	2	24	2

The design more often seen is that of the *Vestiarium Scoticum* (73) (Plate 12 (d)), similar in scheme to the Athol Stewart (403), but Logan gives as Chisholm a variant (72) on the Mackintosh (260), having a white line centred on the outer blue stripes. This early tartan is given also by Smibert and by the Smiths, but James Grant shows only the *Vestiarium* design, as do most later editors, who perpetuate an error made in the *Vestiarium* plate. The fine lines usually shown in blue are given in the text as black.

In the hunting tartan the red ground of No. 73 is rendered in brown.

CLAN CHATTAN and CLAN CHATTAN, CHIEF — see Mackintosh

74-75 CLARK, CLERKE

(74)	**A**	K	G	K	**R**						
	24	8	8	8	24						
(75)	**A**	G	K	G	K	G	K	B	C	B	**C**
	6	6	8	28	8	6	28	36	2	8	4

Parsons have, or had, their clerks and Wilsons' "No. 6 or Clark" (74) reflects this, taking the framework of Hunting Macpherson (298) and changing the colours to more secular shades. An aberrant version overshoots the red pivot, placing a black overcheck in the centre of a red ground of twice the correct width. Colour strips of both are shown at Plate 15 (j) and (k). Clerke of Ulva (75) is unrelated.

76, 77 CLERGY

(76)	**W**	Bk	W	Gy	W	Bk	W	Bk	Gy	Bk	Gy	Bk	W	Gy	W	Bk	**W**
	2	10	2	8	2	52	2	20	10	4	10	20	2	8	2	10	2

(77)	**Az**	Bk	Az	Lavender	Az	Bk	Az	Bk	Lv	Az	**Bk**
	4	16	4	8	4	32	4	32	28	4	4

The Clergy tartan has suffered more than most from the vagaries of the illustrators of the tartan books. Sett No. 76 is from Logan's count, and there are no grounds for questioning it, as he names the colour of each measured stripe; but soon after, if not already, an abbreviated version of this, with a partly identical arrangement of stripes, was in use. Wilson's of Bannockburn produced this shorter sett under the name of 'Priest', and the parts of it corresponding to what Logan had described as grey and white had been changed to lavender and light blue. It was this that the Smiths attempted to reproduce in 1850. They used a colour that could pass for lavender, but they mistakenly used it for sometimes two, sometimes three, of the stripes that should have been black; and the light blue lines in some copies of the book came out a greenish grey. These aberrations vary according to the copy one examines.

When James Grant came to illustrate the 'Clergy' sett in 1886 he rendered the light blue lines of the 'Priest' correctly, but the lavender had become a clear blue, and, following the Smith plate, he used it for two of the stripes that should have been black. Yet in his description he says of the 'Clergy' that it was '. . . a mixture of white, black and grey stripes . . .'. This suggests that he intended Logan's sett to appear, but that his publisher substituted a misrendering of the already defective sett published by the Smiths. A later illustrator of the shorter sett described the correct colours as dark blue, light blue and black, but shows the light blue as green, and carries over the Smith error by making some of the black stripes blue.

In the first edition of the present work [*The Setts*] the Author attempted a compromise between these conflicting authorities, adopting the colours named by Logan and by Grant, but arranging them in accordance with one of the defective plates issued by the Smiths. He regrets that this compromise served only to add to the confusion, which he hopes has now been resolved, thanks largely to the more recent discovery of the Wilson specification for their 'Priest' tartan, which belongs to the period before 1850. A comparison of the two colour strips will show how the two setts are related. The count given here (77) is the one Wilsons' used; they wove it with five repeats on a 25 inch web.

Much of the history of tartan is the result of putting two and two together and making the answer twenty-two. It is recorded that the clergy went armed and wore Highland dress and there are well-known and oft-quoted instructions that they were to eschew bright colours. However, we have yet to discover any early clerical outfitter who might have supplied a clerical tartan and there is really no room to doubt that priests and ministers did the same as their flocks and, for the most part, patronised the local weavers. On the face of it, it would appear that Wilsons' thought 'Priest' a good name for a tartan in subdued colours and that Logan got hold of it and muddled the colours and one pivot but there is no definite evidence to that effect (Plate 1).

78, 79 COCHRANE

(78)	**G**	R	G	R	G	R	G	R	G	K	R	B	R	B	**Y**
	32	4	4	2	6	2	4	4	24	24	2	32	4	16	4

(79)	**Gr**	Red	Gr	Red	Gr	Red	Gr	Bk	Red	Bu	Red	Bu	**Y**
	44	8	4	4	4	8	24	24	4	20	8	8	6

The first design is taken from a portrait and was for long sold as the Cochrane tartan. The pattern is that of the 79th Regiment, the Cameron Highlanders, but with two groups of four red lines on the green. In 1974 the 14th Earl of Dundonald exercised his prorogative as Chief to remove one of the fine lines from each of these groups. The new tartan is registered at the Lyon Court but any historical associations are lost.

80, 81 COLQUHOUN

(80)	**B**	Bk	B	Bk	W	G	**R**
	2	2	16	16	2	16	4

(81)	**B**	Bk	B	W	Bk	G	**R**
	8	4	32	2	16	48	8

With slight variation in the proportions, subsequent illustrators give the design as recorded by Logan (80), except that in the *Vestiarium Scoticum* the white lines occur next to the blue band, not the green (81). This difference may merely represent a slip, but it is considered worth noting in view of its source.

In the use of the white lines the Colquhoun (80) resembles the Leslie (174), with which it may easily be confused. Both were in use near the beginning of the nineteenth century.

82 COMMON KILT

B	R	K	G	K	B	K	**R**
4	2	4	50	56	50	4	6

A Wilson pattern from the early 1790s. It was woven in the 17 reed with 810 warp ends to the width. It is likely that there were four complete half setts to the width, the fifth ending with the broad black stripe enlarged to 68 threads as a selvage mark.

83-87 COMYN, or CUMMING

(83)	**Az**	Bk	Az	Bk	Orange	G	R	W	**R**				
	8	4	8	20	2	20	8	2	8				
(84)	**Bk**	R	G	R	G	R	G	W	G	**R**			
	4	48	8	4	8	8	16	2	16	8			
(85)	**Bk**	R	G	R	G	W	G	**R**					
	4	36	12	6	18	2	18	6					
(86)	**Bk**	R	G	R	Bk	B	R	G	R	Bk	R	**B-Bk**	
	2	2	16	2	12	2	12	12	2	16	2	2	2
(87)	**R**	W	R	K	R	G	Y	K	B	G	K	**G**	
	26	4	26	6	26	42	6	36	36	72	4	24	

There is some confusion regarding the tartans bearing the name of this family. Logan records as CUMMIN a tartan (83) having some resemblance to the usual CLAN MACPHERSON (295). Yet Sir Thomas Dick Lauder, writing to Sir Walter Scott in 1829 about the forthcoming *Vestiarium Scoticum*, says: 'Comyn, who was quite ignorant of his tartan, has now worn more than ever at the Caledonian balls in London his 'twa wyd strypes of greine upon ain scarlett field', etc; and so of many more whom the Messrs Hay have enlightened as being their particular friends'. (Here, incidentally, may be the explanation of the presence also of a Lauder tartan in the *Vestiarium*.) It is curious that Comyn should have been thus ignorant, unless he regarded the Cummins as a distinct family.

In the Smith work of 1850 they show a design which they say had the sanction of the head of the family of Cumming. This design (85) closely resembles that of the *Vestiarium* (84), but is in fact the one given by Logan as MACAULAY (192), and illustrated as such by McIan. Commencing with James Grant's book in 1886, a shortened version (193) of the design is given as MACAULAY, and the Logan MACAULAY (85, 192) retains the Smith attribution as COMYN. This shortened MACAULAY can be traced to M'Intyre North's rendering in 1881 (probably erroneous) of Logan's tables of thread-counts. The shortened MACAULAY has the virtue of obviating the confusion of having one tartan attributed to two distinct families; but as the confusion arises from a mistake made about 1850, it is unfortunate that it should have to be got over by perpetuating yet another mistake made about 1880. The modern HUNTING MACAULAY (194) follows Logan's early version. All this trouble was caused by

PLATE 1

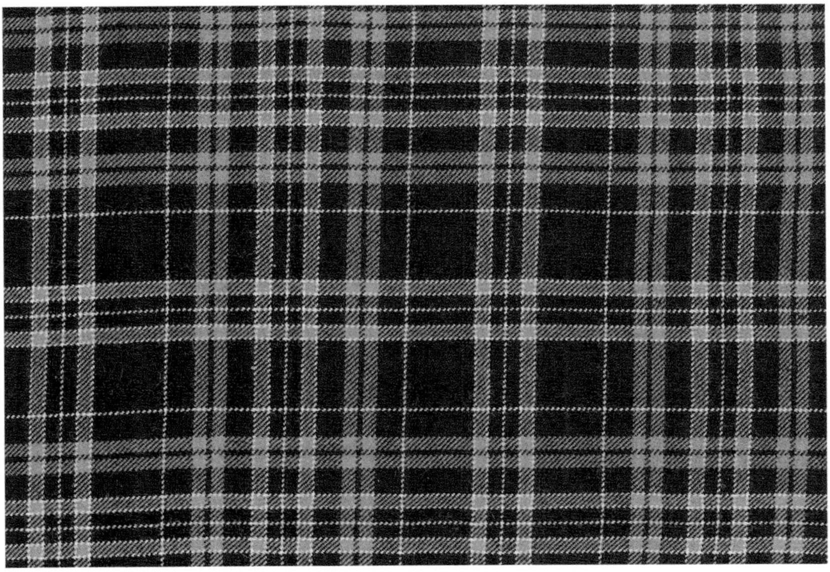

(a) Clergy Tartan (Logan)

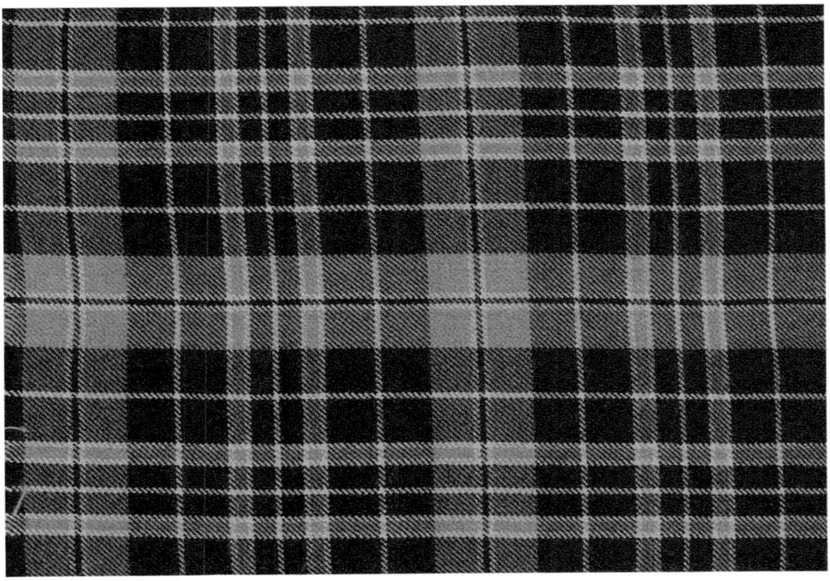

(b) 'Priest' Pattern(Wilson)

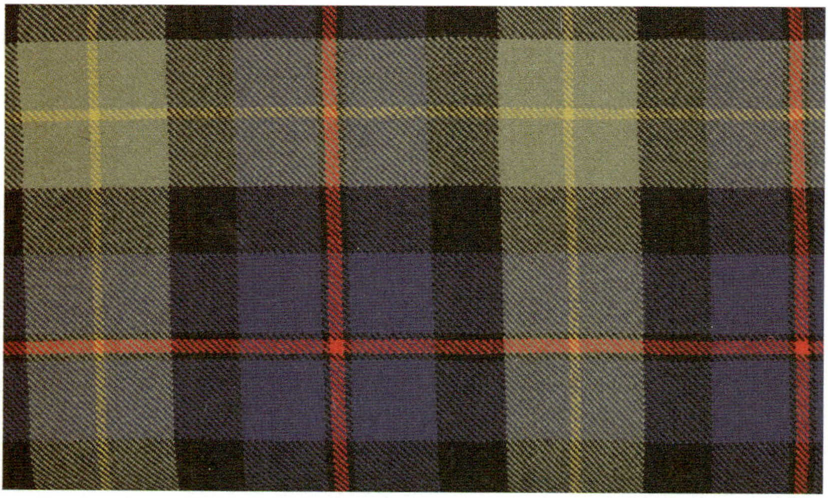

(a) Plaids, Lord Loudoun's Highlanders

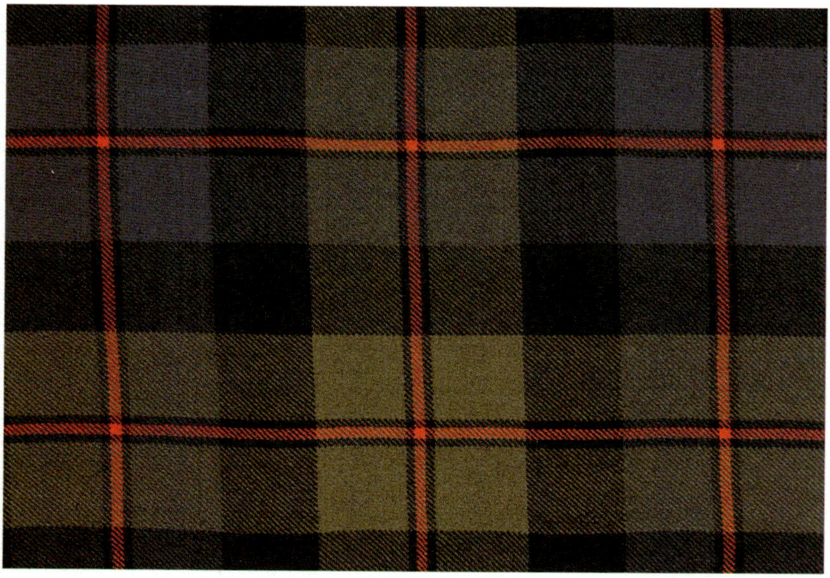

(b) Kilts, 42nd Pattern

PLATE 3

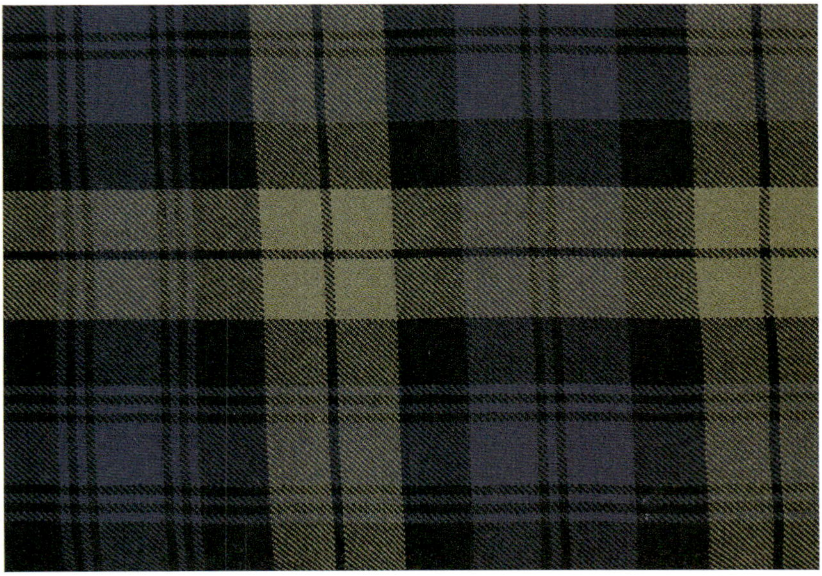

(a) 42nd Pattern, Black Watch

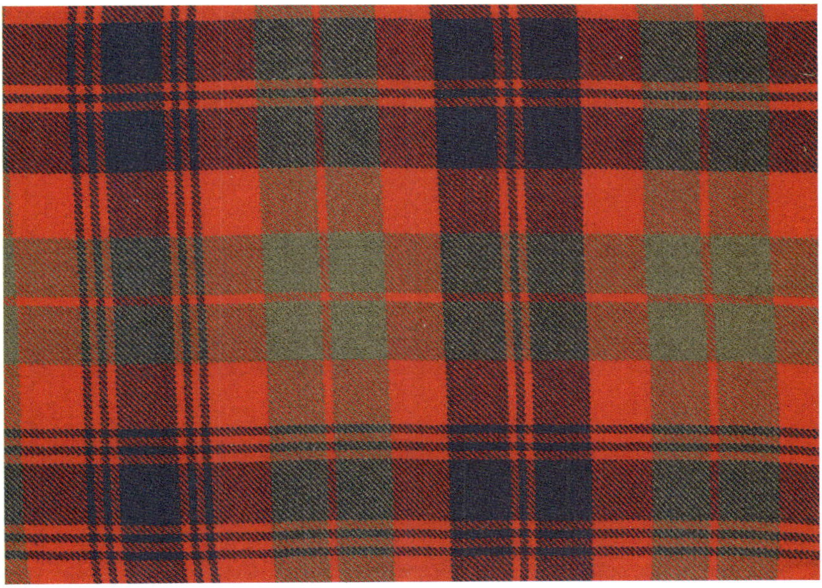

(b) 42nd Pattern, bandsmen's plaids

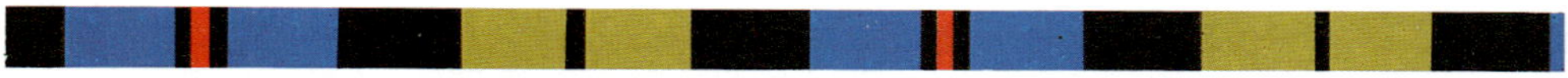

(a) Hypothetical tartan of the Independent Companies

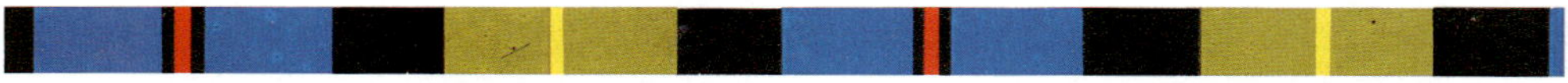

(b) Lord Loudoun's Highlanders

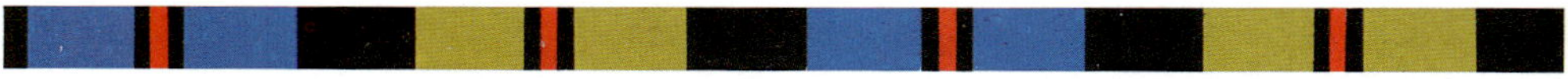

(c) 42nd Pattern, kilts

(d) 'Grant Tartan'

(e) 'No. 230 or Argyle Pattern' (Campbell of Cawdor)

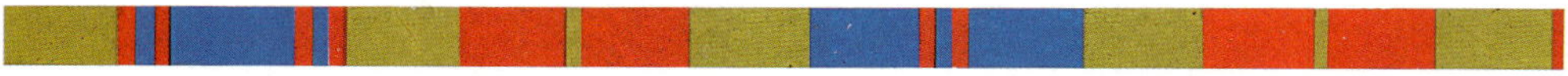

(f) Fraser

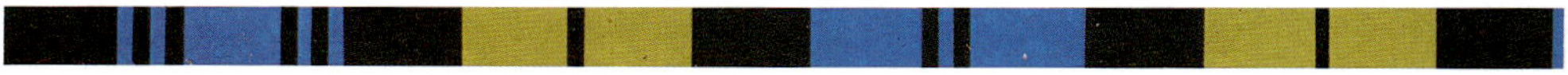

(g) 42nd Pattern, Black Watch

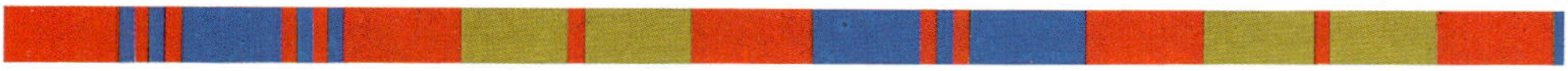

(h) 42nd Pattern, bandsmen's plaids

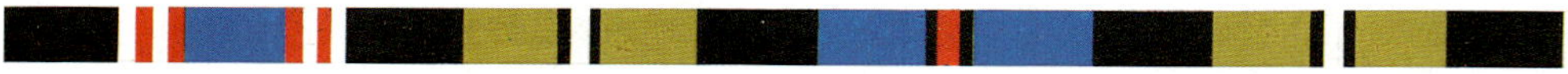

(j) 71st Regiment, drummers' plaids

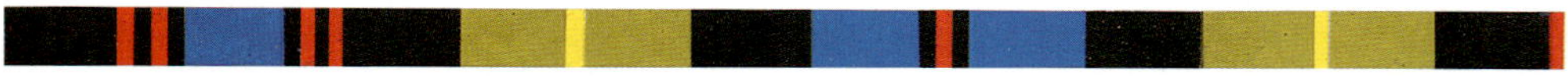

(k) 92nd Regiment, drummers' plaids

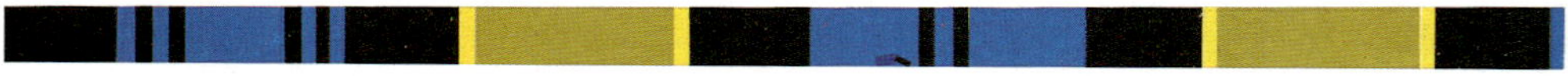

(l) Breadalbane Fencibles

(m) 79th (Cameron's) Regiment

Colour strips of military tartans

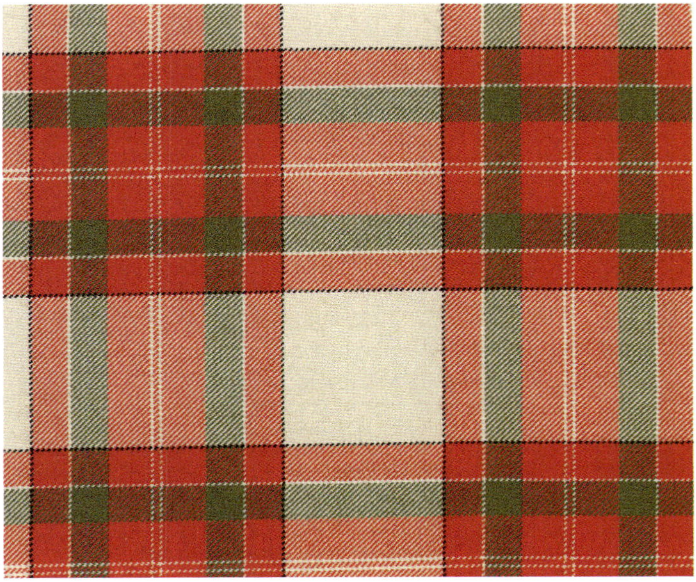

(a) 'Blanket Sett' (Wilson)

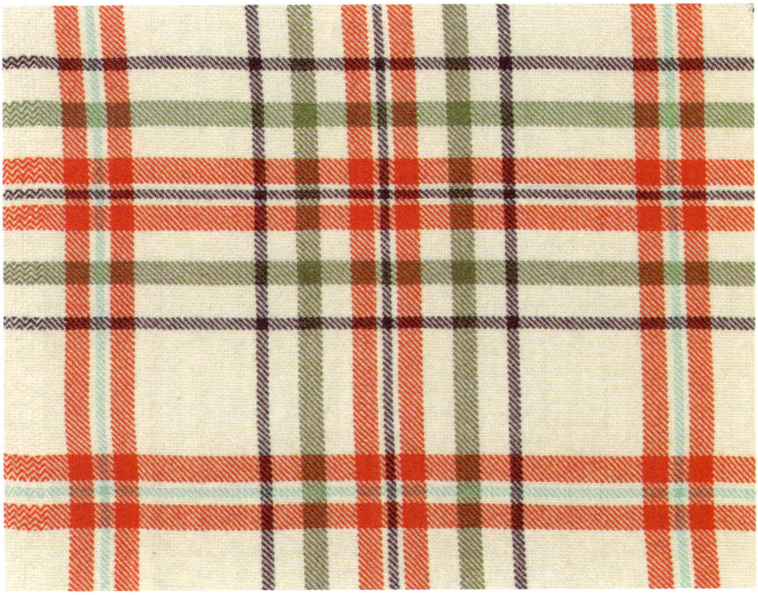

(b) A modern arisaid sett. Note the herringbone weave to the selvage band.

PLATE 6

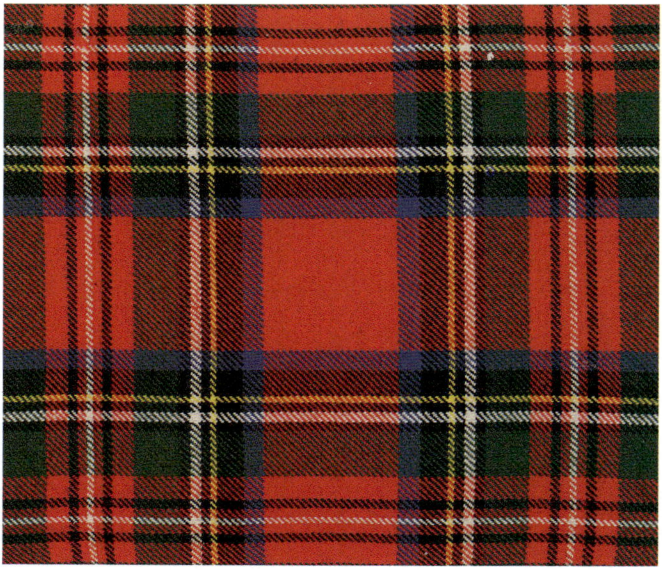

(a) Royal Stuart, 'modern' colours

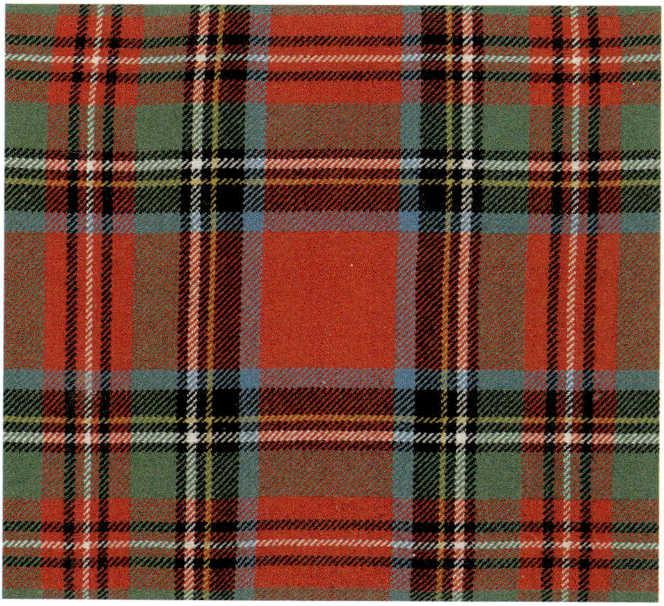

(b) Royal Stuart, 'ancient' or 'old' colours

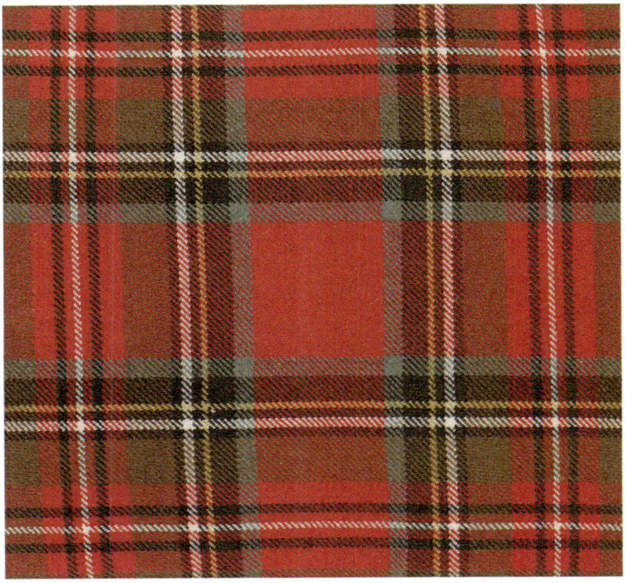

(a) Royal Stuart, 'reproduction' or 'muted' colours

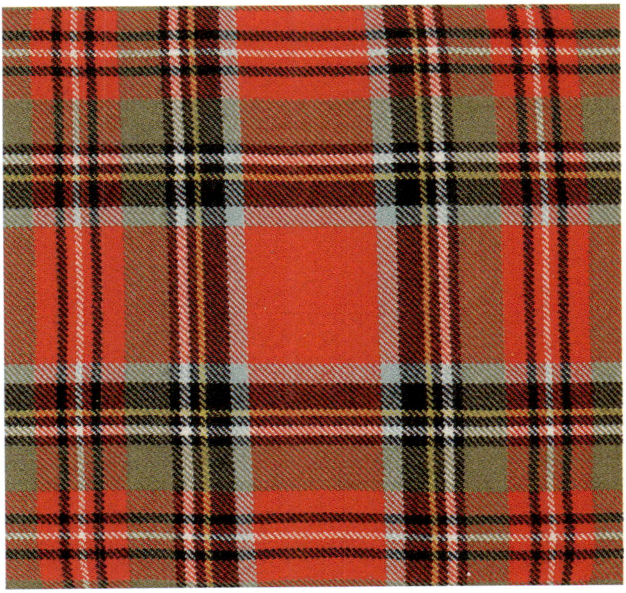

(b) Royal Stuart colours of *c.* 1825-30

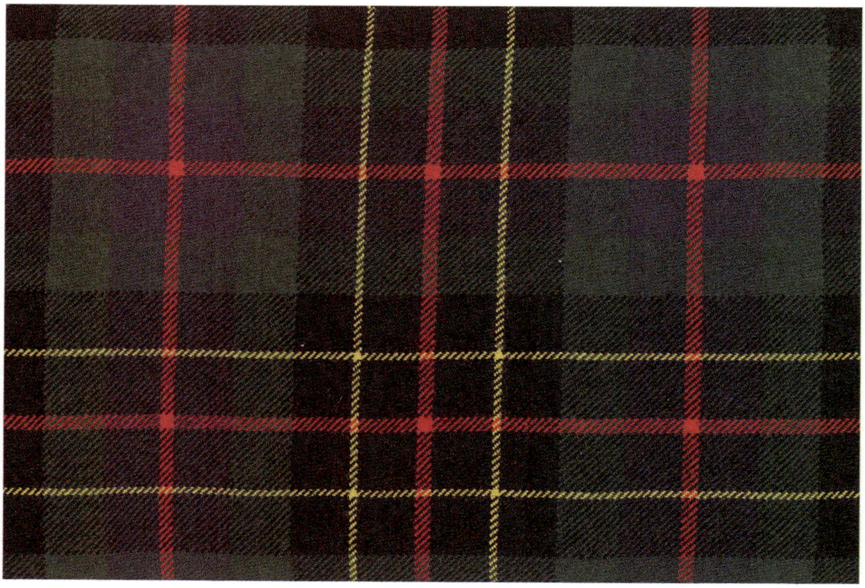

(a) Hunting Brodie, 'modern' colours

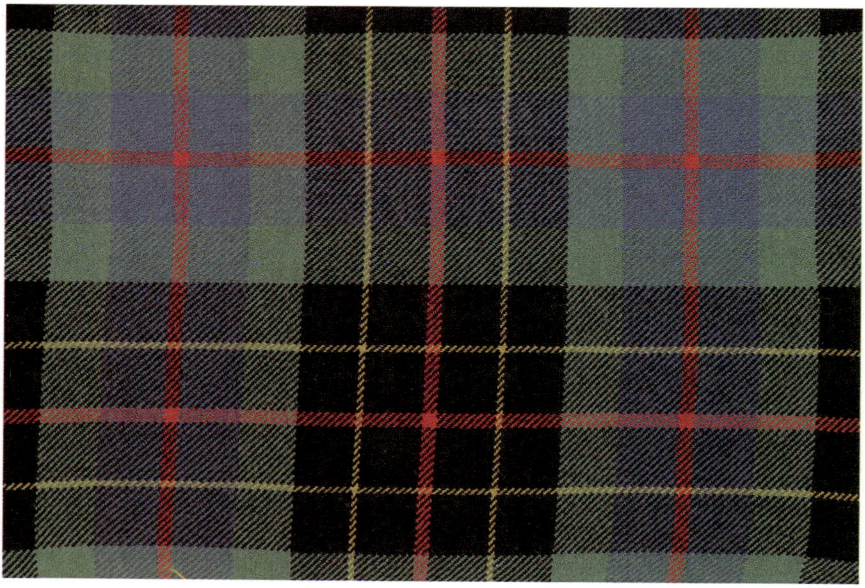

(b) Hunting Brodie, 'ancient' or 'old' colours

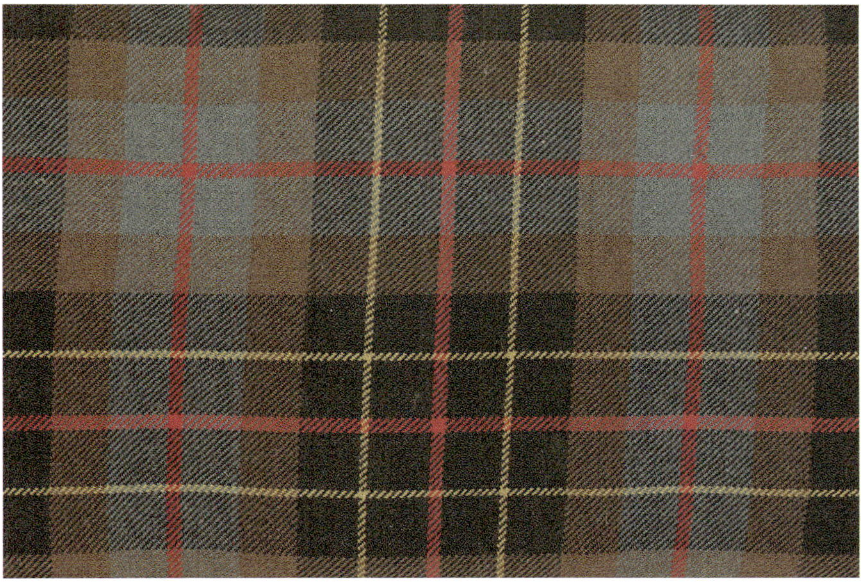

(a) Hunting Brodie, 'reproduction' or 'muted' colours

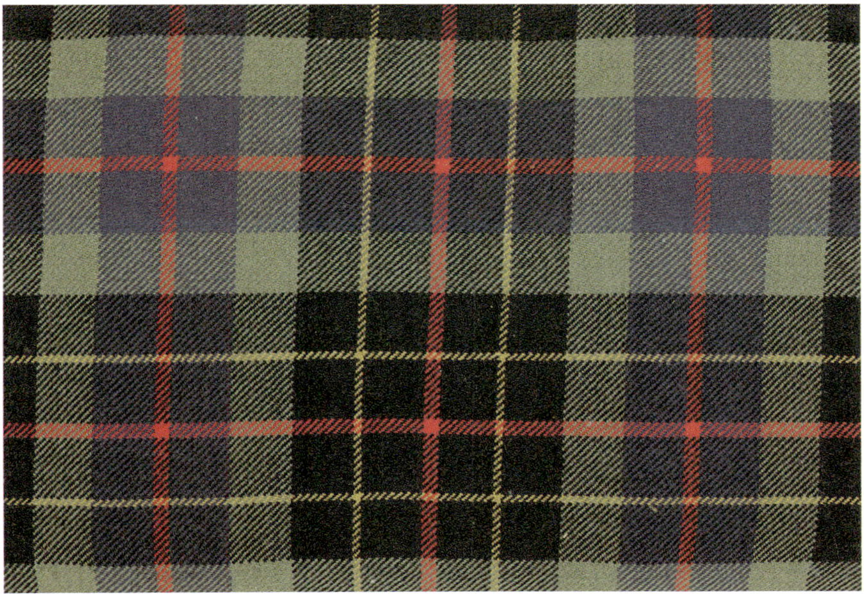

(b) Hunting Brodie, colours of *c.*1825-30

PLATE 10

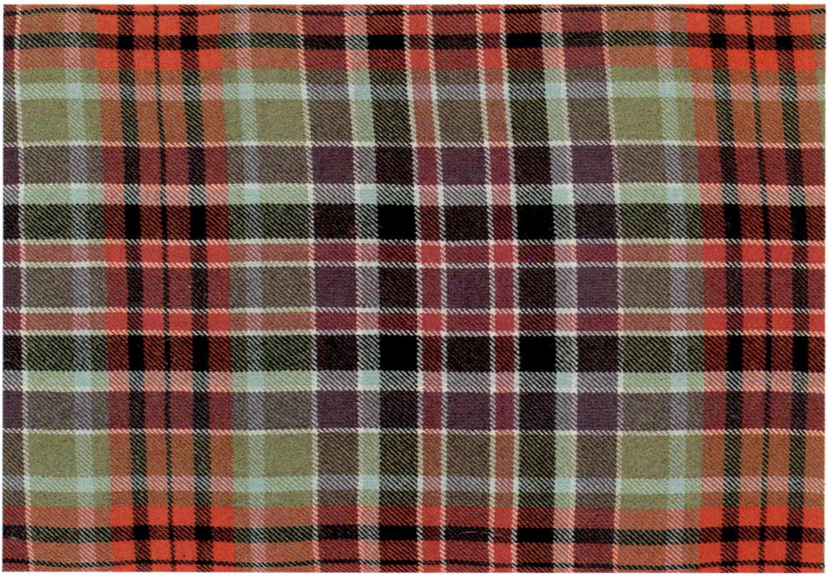

(a) 'Old Huntly' (Wilson)

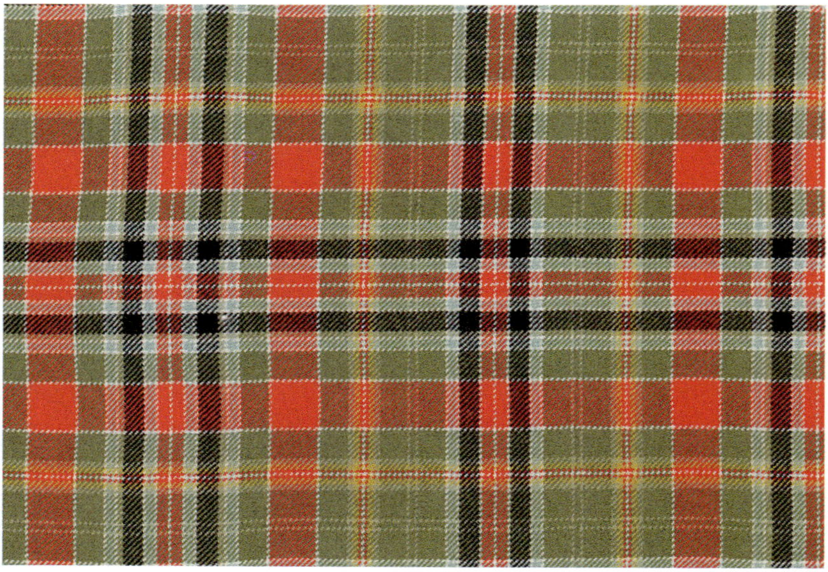

(b) 'Hunter Sett' (Wilson)

Late eighteenth-century plaid patterns

The Check Pattern

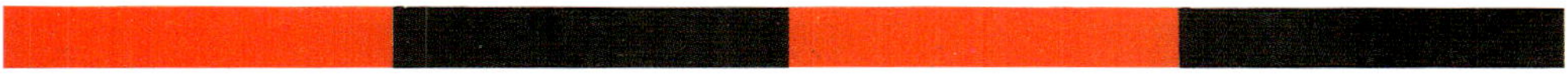

(a) Rob Roy

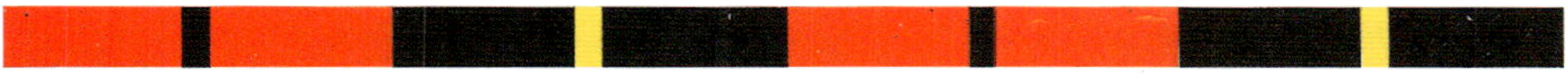

(b) Wallace

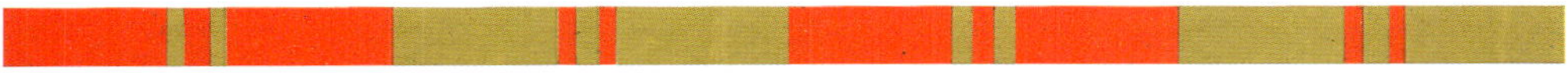

(c) Erskine

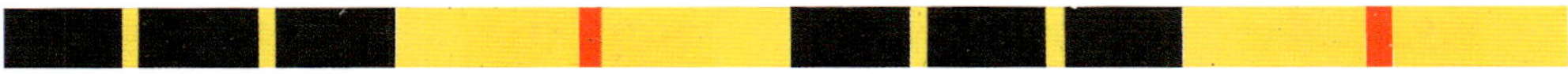

(d) MacLeod

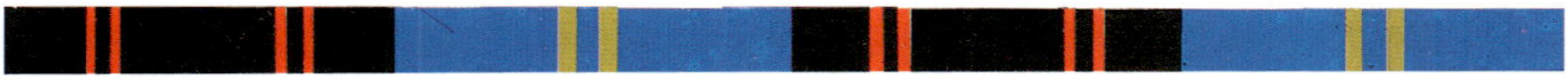

(e) Home

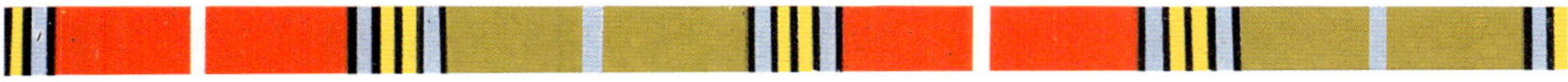

(f) Buchanan

Check patterns

The Superimposed Check Pattern

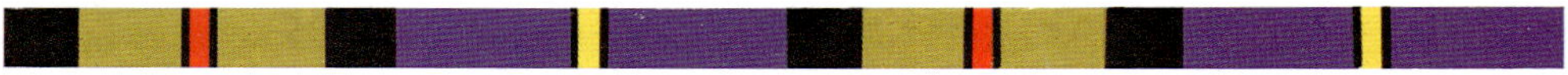

(a) MacLeod

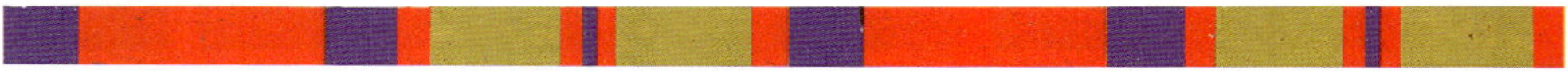

(b) Mackintosh

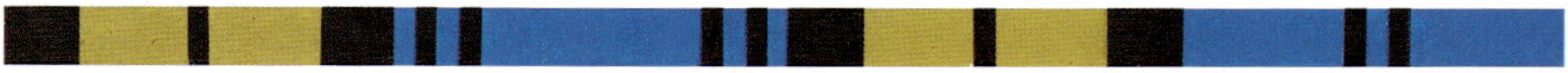

(c) Black Watch

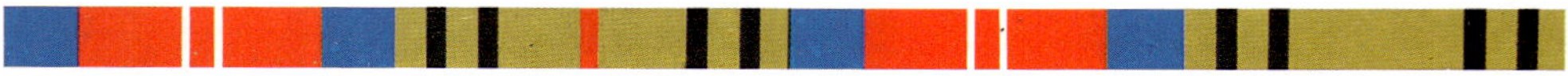

(d) Chisholm

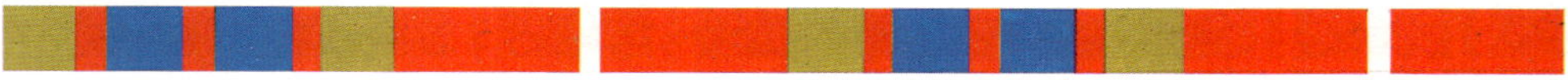

(e) Fraser

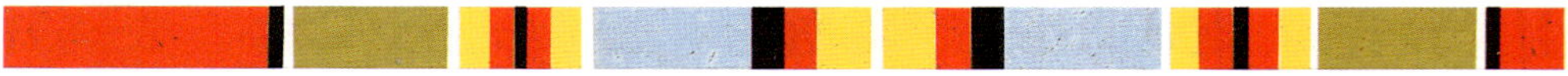

(f) Clan Chattan (Mackintosh)

Superimposed check patterns

The Multiple Check Pattern

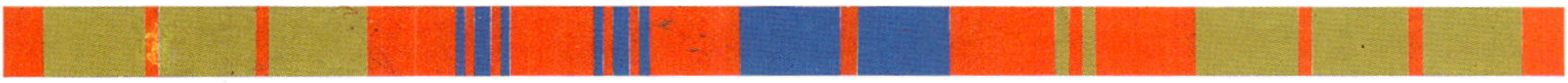

(a) Ross

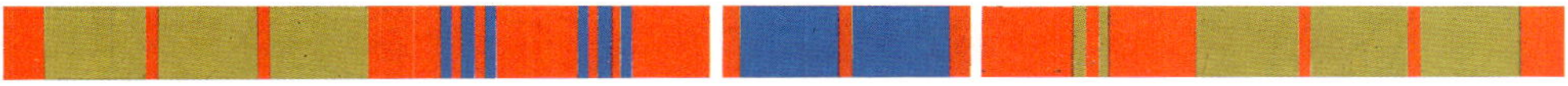

(b) MacRae

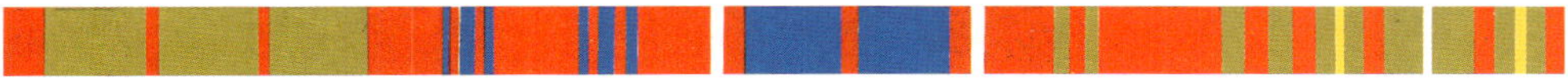

(c) MacRae, 'The Prince's Own'

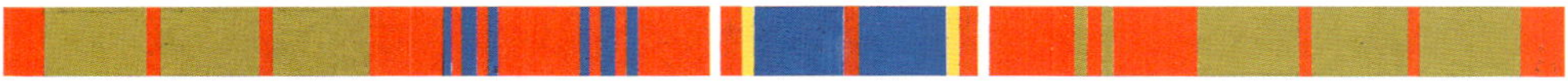

(d) Huntly ('The Marchioness of Huntly's Tartan')

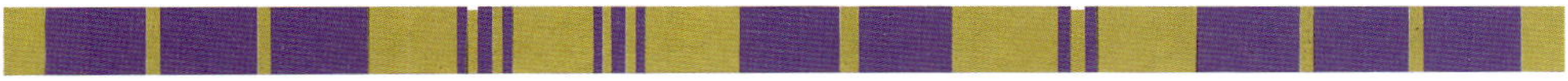

(e) 'Rae Tartan' (Wilson)

Multiple check patterns

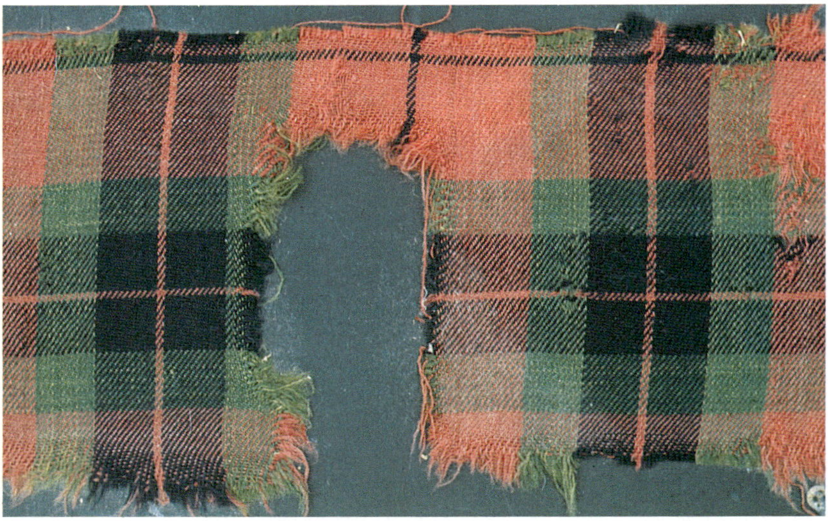

(a) Hugh Fraser of Boblainy's Plaid

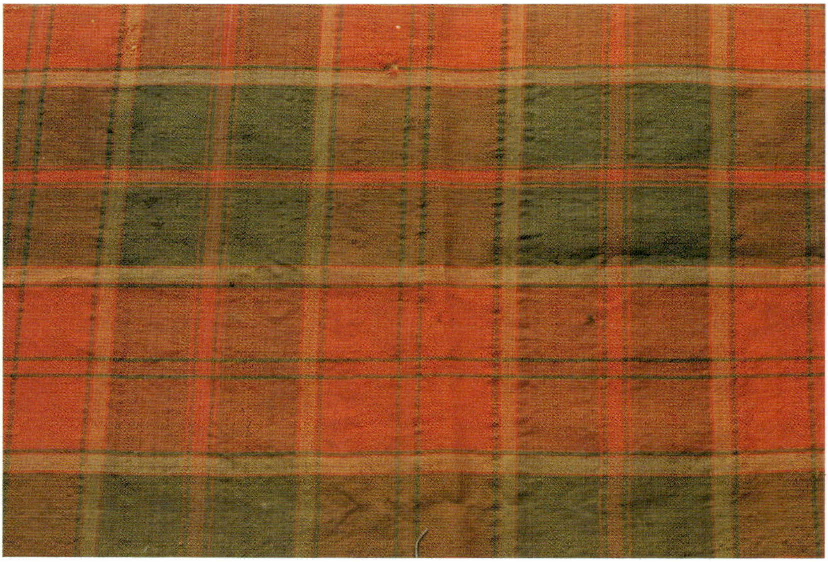

(b) Plaiding in Crieff sett with spoiled purple

Early nineteenth-century plaids

PLATE 15

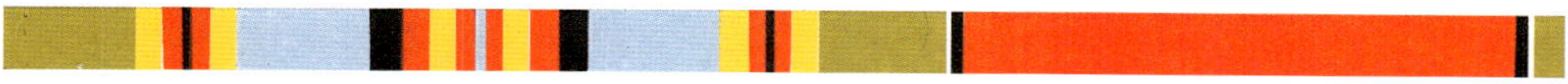

(a) The Crubin Plaid

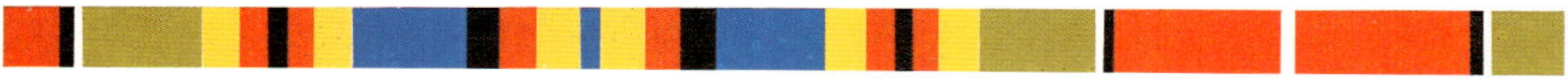

(b) Macpherson (Smith)

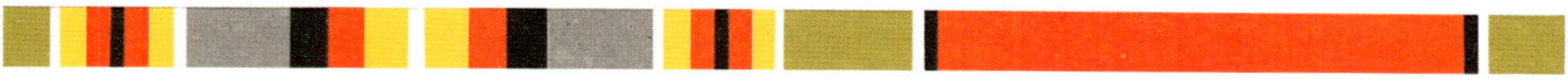

(c) 'Mackintosh Tartan' (Wilson)

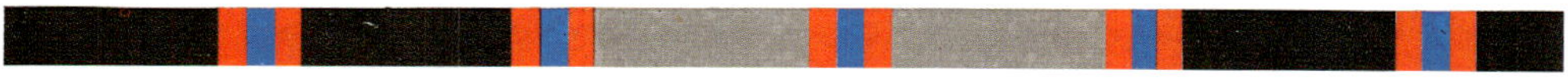

(d) Macpherson, hunting

(e) Macpherson, reputed Clan, with blue and red reversed

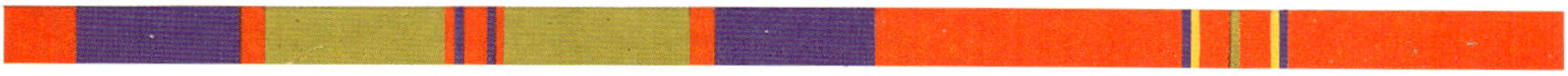

(f) 'Macpherson of Cluny's Tartan' (Wilson)

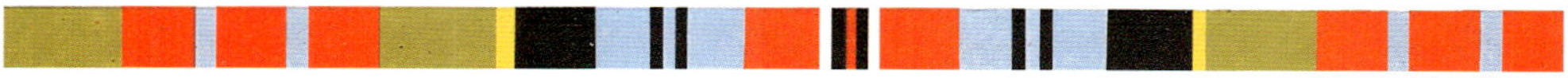

(g) Macpherson (Wilsons' No. 43)

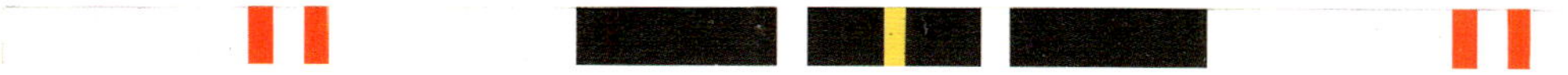

(h) Macpherson, dress ('Maggie Lauder')

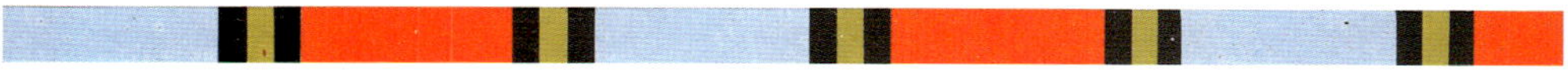

(j) Clark (Wilsons' No. 6)

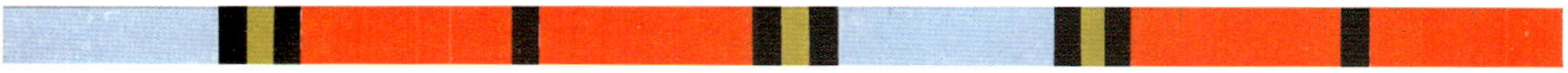

(k) Clark. A count taken with false pivot

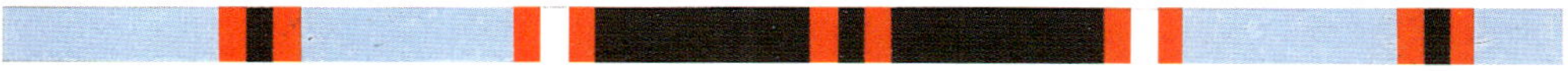

(l) 'Gipsy'

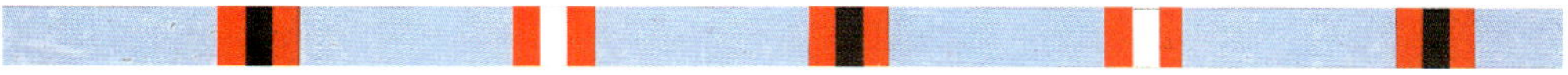

(m) 'Gipsy'. A count taken with false pivot

Colour strips of Macpherson and related tartans

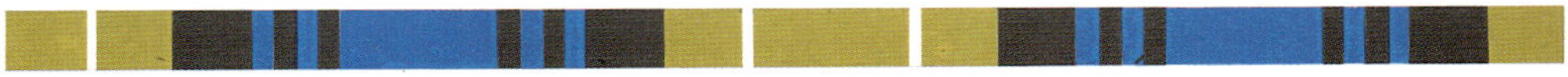

(a) Abercrombie (Logan)

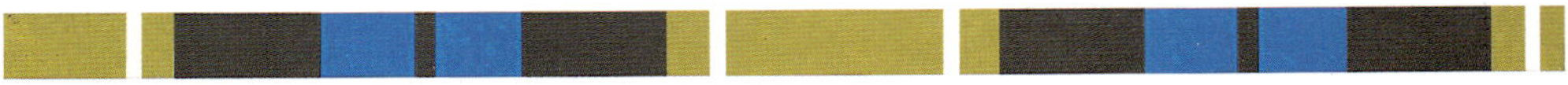

(b) Wilsons' No. 158

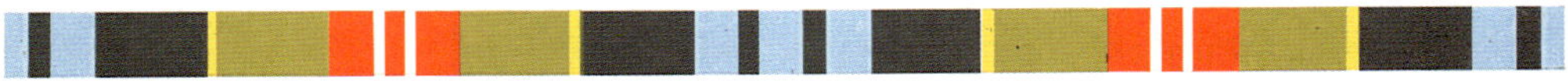

(c) 'Cummin' (Logan)

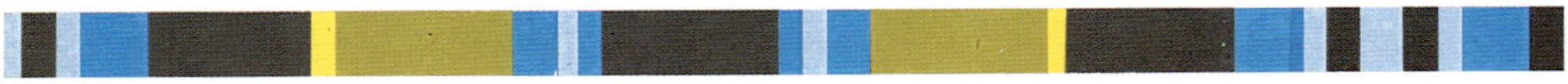

(d) Wilsons' No. 30

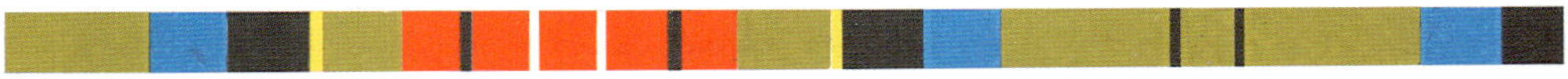

(e) 'Cumin' (McIan/Wilson)

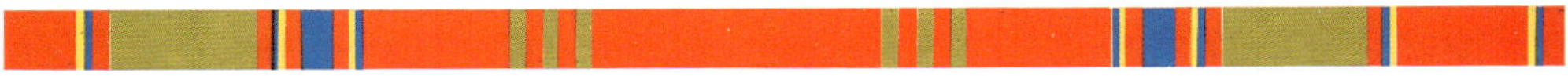

(f) Munro (Logan)

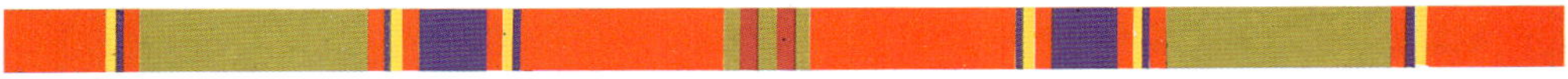

(g) 'Lochiel Tartan' (Wilson)

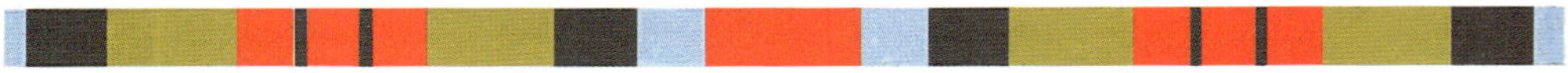

(h) MacDuff

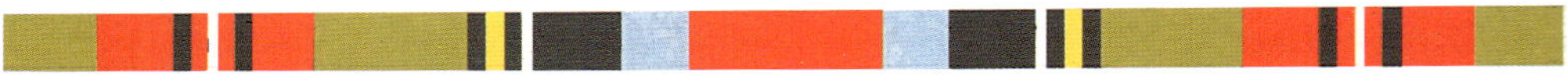

(j) Prince Charles Edward

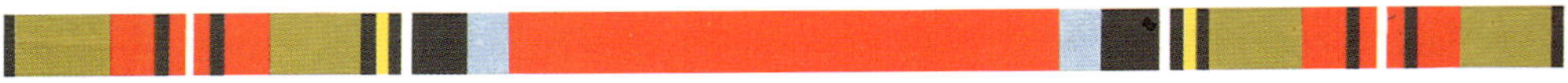

(k) Royal Stuart

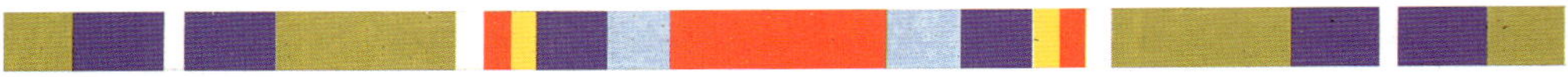

(l) Wilsons' No. 227

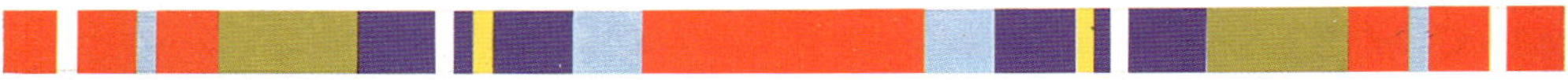

(m) Wilsons' No. 4

Colour strips illustrating some commentaries

the *Vestiarium* design, and the failure to distinguish between it and the pre-existing MacAulay (192).

Still further confusion has arisen from Smibert's illustration of a design (86) under the name of Cumming. Smibert's plate, though somewhat defective, is clearly intended to represent the tartan now known as the MacIntyre or Glenorchy (245, 246). In the Notes on the latter will be found a count for a more extended sett, taken from a specimen in a collection made before 1820, and there entitled 'Cumming and Glenorchy'.

In Wilsons' own list of the tartans sent to James Logan in connection with his work on *The Scottish Gäel* there is the entry "Cummin — an imitation of this pattern made out of No. 155" and it is this that McIan illustrated in *The Clans of the Scottish Highlands.* In their comments on the published work, Wilsons' have this to say: "Have never seen this Tartan but have every reason to believe it to be Fancy Pattern. We have several of this description and it is quite unlike a Clan Tartan. We have no authentic Cummin Tartan — this we have sent is very generally . . ." (the sentence is incomplete). (See Appendix F.)

All this seems to imply that Wilsons' knew of a Cummin tartan and, though they did not make it, were sufficiently familiar with it to make a fair imitation. D. C. Stewart remarks that the tartan (83) given by Logan bears a resemblance to Macpherson (295) and so it should, for No. 155 is almost identical with Macpherson (Plate 15 (g)), so it would appear that Logan's *intention* was to tabulate the details of the imitation that Wilsons' provided and for which a reconstructed count (87) is given. (See Plate 16 (c), (d) and (e).)

88 CRANSTOUN

R	**LG**	**B**	**G**	**B**	**G**	**B**	**G**
4	24	12	6	2	2	2	28

This tartan is rarely seen. The only early illustration of it is in the *Vestiarium Scoticum*. In the text of that work the green adjacent to the red line is described as being the colour of the leaf of a tender ash tree, the remainder being grass-green.

89 CRAWFORD

Cr	**W**	**Cr**	**G**	**Cr**	**G**	**Cr**
12	4	60	24	6	24	6

From the story of the formation of the Black Watch, in 1739, we know that there was at that time no Crawford tartan. This design first appears in the *Vestiarium Scoticum*, where the ground colour is given as crimson.

90 CRIEFF SETT

C	R	G	R	G	R	P	R	G	R	G	R	C
4	12	8	4	170	4	42	4	8	140	8	12	4

Another late eighteenth century plaid pattern from the Key Pattern Book. It is for the 600 reed and 1332 threads make up the width of 19 inches.

"In the first place, put on two full half setts, then, go into the third half sett till the large scarlet mark of 140 threads is finished after putting on which close with the following silvage mark: P8 R4 P76 R16."

A four-yard plaid length which has somehow survived for nearly two hundred years without being made into a plaid has G180 (126 in weft), P32 (24 in weft) and R146 (116 in weft). R12 in the warp becomes 10 in the weft and the selvage mark is P6 R6 P58 R4, the last two stripes being woven in five bands of herringbone; the extra threads are taken into the outermost band. The 'purple' in this piece is actually a light drab, which may indicate that it was dyed with crowberry as this gives a good purple with alum but various drab shades result if it is overheated. (Plate 14 (b).)

91 CUNNINGHAM

W	R	B	R	Bk	R	Bk
6	2	2	56	60	2	6

Cunningham was one of the names used by the broken and scattered MacGregors. Based on the old black and red MacGregor tartan, this design, like so many others attributed to Lowland families, derives from the *Vestiarium Scoticum.* Its similarity to the Erskine (112) and the Ramsay (364), from the same source, is worth noting.

92 DALZELL

G	Cr	G	R	B	W	R	B	R	W	B	R	G	R	B	W	R
12	6	4	64	4	2	8	12	8	2	4	8	64	8	4	2	48

This tartan, which occurs in Logan's 1831 list, but not in the M'Intyre North reprint, is a variant on the Munro (343), though there is no clear reason for the association. The Dalzell differs in having white lines in place of the yellow in the Munro, and in the changing of two scarlet lines to crimson. The MacColl (197) resembles both these, but lacks the light lines. [See Note 1 at end of Appendix F.]

93-95 DAVIDSON

(93)

W	G	Bk	B	R
2	12	6	12	2

(94)	**R**	B	G	B	G	Bk	G	Bk	G	Bk	**R**
	2	12	2	2	12	2	12	2	2	12	2

(95)	**B**	R	B	K	G	K	W	**K**
	6	4	16	16	16	6	4	6

D.W. Stewart writes:

The evidence of the early date of this design rests entirely upon specimens in collections of old hard tartans. Diligent research reveals no portrait in Highland costume of a member of the clan, whose leading representatives, moreover, are without any account of the origin either of this pattern or of another bearing the same name and differing from it mainly in the omission of the white stripe. From the collation of many authorities and the inspection of many samples, however, the conclusion has been reached that of the two the design here represented [93] is the earlier. It is preserved in a collection of examples of tartans made by the Highland Society of London in 1822; in that of Messrs Ogilvie & Co., Edinburgh, dealers in Tartan about the same period; in that of the Mackintosh at Moy Hall, and in many others.

Smibert presents this design, with narrower bands of blue and green. Mclan also illustrates it, but with the red and white lines transposed. The more recent Davidson (94) differs from this in much more than the omission of the white stripe. The bands of pattern are alternately in blue and in black. The same pattern and alternation form the basis of the Henderson tartan (152).

About 1847, Wilsons' produced a version (95) of the earlier tartan with the red and white lines doubled, naming it 'Double Davidson'.

96 DEAS

G	K	R	K	R	K	B	K	B	K	Y	K	G	K
42	4	16	12	16	4	42	4	4	24	6	24	4	4

In his remarks on the Robertson tartans (*q.v.*), D.C. Stewart stresses the need for the careful balancing of tone values in tartan weaving. The Deas tartan, originally from a pattern book of Garry & Deas, Perth, is a prime example of this need. If it is woven in 'modern' colours, with almost black blue and a discernably lighter green, it appears strongly asymmetrical, but if 'ancient' colours, in which blue and green are of almost equal weight, are used, the result appears quite symmetrical.

97, 98 DOUGLAS

(97)	**Bk**	Az	G	B	**W**
	4	4	16	16	2

(98)	Gy	Bk	Gy	Bk	Gy	Bk	Gy	**Bk**
	4	2	32	16	2	2	2	32

Though Logan says he lists no family tartans, he gives the DOUGLAS (97) evidently considering that family to rank as a Border clan. From Smibert onwards the azure lines become narrower.

Wilson's of Bannockburn were weaving this design long before Logan's named sett was published, but only as 'No. 148'. Their 'No. 176' was the same with yellow for white. The name may have been given later, from the increased demand in the 1820s for named tartans.

The black and grey DOUGLAS (98) first appears in the *Vestiarium Scoticum*, where the scheme is used again for the HOME (153).

In the list of tartans sent to Logan *c.*1830, Wilsons' record that No. 148 had been sold as Douglas for a 'considerable' time.

99 DRUMLITHIE ROCK AND WHEEL

R	C	P	R	P	G	P	R	C	P	**R**
4	4	6	30	40	40	4	30	4	6	4

Rock and wheel was an early type of soft tartan made with a 'rock-' (spindle-) spun warp and a wheel spun weft. The count given here is taken from the manuscript pattern book previously referred to. It has been suggested that both pivots should be the same but there is no evidence to support this, nor, if we accept the suggestion, is there any indication as to which is the correct arrangement.

100-103 DRUMMOND

(100)	**R**	W	B	Y	G	R	B	Az	**W**						
	72	2	6	2	32	16	6	4	2						
(101)	**R**	B	R	B	R	Az	R	B	R	G	R	G	R	B	**R**
	12	2	4	4	64	2	4	16	4	4	4	48	4	4	12
(102)	**R**	B	Y	G	R	B	Az	**W**							
	96	6	2	28	16	6	8	2							
(103)	G	R	G	R	G	Bk	G	Bk	G	R	G	**R**			
	8	2	2	56	16	2	2	2	36	2	2	8			

The uncertainty attending the attribution of tartans to clans is well exemplified when we come to the tartans of Drummond, Fraser and Grant. Logan gives a distinctive pattern for each. These are respectively the DRUMMOND OF PERTH (100), a FRASER (124) almost identical with the LOVAT and found in collections dating back to 1790, and the GRANT (143) which is often called DRUMMOND (101). This last design is used by McIan to illustrate his Drummond figure, but in the accompanying text Logan complains that it had come to be worn by the Drummonds although it was a Grant tartan. It certainly seems to have been worn by the Drummond contingent attending the visit of George IV in 1822, but then so also was the ROBERTSON (369). The sett employed on that occasion had the narrow red, blue, and green stripes (but not the azure) of about half the relative width shown here. It is shown by Smibert and by the Smiths in almost the same form both for DRUMMOND and for GRANT, and it appears in the *Vestiarium Scoticum*, minus the azure line, as GRANT (144). The DRUMMOND (103) of the *Vestiarium* is quite different, and resembles the HAY (151). D. W. Stewart contends that, whether as DRUMMOND or as GRANT, this debated tartan is of much later date than the DRUMMOND OF PERTH, and seeks to replace it, as the earliest Grant sett, by that appearing in the *Vestiarium*, and now generally accepted, as FRASER (126). This so-called FRASER he traced to a portrait of Robert Grant of Lurg (1678–1777), in the collection at Troup House, and writes: 'It was accepted by some only of the Fraser families in 1842, because it was illustrated under their name in the *Vestiarium Scoticum*'.

The re-attribution of this (126) as a Grant tartan is a disturbing one. The evidence rests on the portrait of Robert Grant, and it can hardly have been usual for a notable member of one clan to sit for his portrait in the tartan of an unrelated clan. This evidence may not seem conclusive; but the evidence for the tartan being a FRASER consists only in its appearance as such in the *Vestiarium*.

Fortunately, there is no confusion as between the DRUMMOND and the Fraser designs, but it was thought best to deal with the disputed FRASER in connection with the Drummond-Grant question.

A variant (102) on the Drummond of Perth tartan was reproduced by D.W. Stewart, and its source is a cloak said to have been worn by Prince Charles Edward, and left by him at Fingask Castle. The omission of the outer light line will be noted. The count given here is that of the original cloak.

See Appendix F.

DRUMMOND OF STRATHALLAN — see OGILVIE

104, 105 DUNBAR

(104)	**R**	Bk	R	Bk	G	**R**
	8	2	56	16	42	12

(105)	**K**	W	K	**R**
	26	4	8	56

The tartan of a once-powerful Lowland family. Its source is the *Vestiarium Scoticum.*

The pattern (105) is said to have been woven by Wilsons' but no other record has been found.

106 DUNBLANE

W	B	R	W	G	W	G	W	G	W	Y	**G**
2	4	30	2	4	2	10	2	4	2	10	12

This tartan was first illustrated in the Smiths' work, where it is described as taken from a portrait of the 2nd Viscount Dunblane, who died in 1729. It seems to have been revived in 1822, doubtless on the occasion of the visit of George IV to Scotland, in anticipation of which event there had been much hunting round for old tartans to wear.

107 DUNCAN

Bk	G	W	G	B	**R**
8	42	6	42	42	8

No early record can be given for this design. One might seek to relate it to a ROBERTSON, but, though the colours are the same as in one of the Robertson tartans, the resemblance ends there.

108 DUNDAS

Bk	G	R	G	Bk	B	**Bk**
4	4	2	48	24	32	8

The authority for this family tartan is the *Vestiarium Scoticum.*

109 DUNDEE SETT

W	P	W	A	Y	W	P	W	Y	G	C	K	C	**R**
12	12	4	14	8	4	4	4	8	44	4	30	4	84

110 DUNDEE WALLACE SETT

R	Pink	C	K	R	A	W	P	W	P	W	A	K	Y	W	K	W
8	4	4	6	20	16	4	16	16	16	4	16	36	8	4	4	4

Y	G	W	**R**
8	86	4	104

Two more late eighteenth-century plaid setts from the Key Pattern Book which seem vaguely related. Both are for the 600 reed and are nineteen inches wide. The former has four half setts and the latter seven to the width.

111 ELLIOT

R	B	Maroon	**B**
2	6	8	32

Prominent in Border history, this name has no Highland associations, nor is there any very early record of the tartan.

ELPHINSTONE — see MONTGOMERIE

112 ERSKINE

R	G	R	G	R	**G**
8	2	56	48	2	12

One of the Lowland family tartans of which we first have any account in the *Vestiarium Scoticum*. (See Plate 11 (c).)

113 THE FALKIRK TARTAN

This is a fragment of cloth, now in the Royal Museum of Scotland, Queen Street, Edinburgh, found at Falkirk stuffed into the neck of a jar containing Roman coins and thought by archaeologists to have been buried in about 250 A.D. The pattern is an equal check about 1.5 cm square in natural undyed light yellowish brown and dark chocolate brown; the warp threads are spaced at about 13 to the inch and the weft at about 15. The twill rib reverses at each change of colour. It appears that it has not been launched as the 'Ancient Falkirk District Tartan'; its importance to us is that it shows the use of a regular check pattern and ornamental twill weave in the third century.

114, 115 FARQUHARSON

(114)	**R**	B	Bk	B	Bk	B	Bk	G	Y	G	Bk	B	Bk	**R**
	4	8	2	2	2	2	16	16	4	16	16	16	2	4

(115)	**B**	Bk	B	Bk	B	Bk	G	R/Y	G	Bk	B	Bk	**B**
	56	2	2	2	2	20	44	4	44	20	32	2	4

There are two forms of the Farquharson tartan, both based on the Black Watch. The *Vestiarium Scoticum* gives a design (115) in which the red line and the yellow line are each centred on alternate bands of the green ground.

In Logan the yellow line is centred on each band of green, and the red on each band of blue; in this conforming with early specimens.

116, 117 FERGUSON

(116)	**G**	B	R	Bk	G	**Bk**		
	4	24	2	24	24	4		
(117)	**B**	Bk	G	R	G	Bk	**W**	
	48	16	16	4	16	2	4	

The design given by Logan (116) is known as the FERGUSON OF BALQUHIDDER. Smibert was the first to illustrate the FERGUSON OF ATHOL (117), as also the MACLAREN (266), which it closely resembles. Though for the most part the MacLarens were followers of the Stewarts of Appin, many followed the Murrays of Athol, as did the Athol Fergusons, and it is to this association that we must look to account for the similarity in the tartans.

In one of the early collections there is a design bearing the name Ferguson, but it hardly amounts to a tartan as we undertand the term. It is asymmetrical, and the tabulation for it is

LG	B	R
10	12	2

this occupying only one inch.

118 FIDDES ROCK AND WHEEL

P	G	P	R	Little marks	P	R	**G**
16	16	16	64	6	24	22	24

Fiddes is listed in association with two other Rock and Wheel patterns — DRUMLITHIE (99) AND GLASGOW (133) — in the Wilson manuscript notebook. Analysis of the three counts shows that Glasgow and Drumlithie are for the half sett while Fiddes is an incomplete rendering of the whole sett and it is the corrected count that is given here. The expression 'little marks' is commonly used in early Wilson counts, especially in counts of the Black Watch type, where it is used to indicate the *sum* of the four lines of the 'double tracking' and one interpretation of the extended count gives K2, P2, K2 for these six threads in Fiddes. However, it is known that Wilsons' employed outworkers who specialised in particular types of cloth and the close association of the three suggest that they may have been the product of one of these. Such a specialist would not wish to carry an extra colour just for one minor feature and so I suggest that a colour used in one of the other patterns, probably Rose or Madder, would have been used for the little marks. It is also probable that the marks would have been single lines of six threads each, since Wilsons' rarely used fewer than four threads in such a position; black and purple in a 2, 2, 2 sequence would, in any case be almost indistinguishable.

119 FLETCHER

B	Bk	B	Bk	R	G	**R**
12	2	12	16	2	16	4

This sett is known as the Fletcher of Dunans. The more usual sett has the central line in black, not red.

It is unlikely that there was a distinctive Fletcher tartan at any early date, and it is only in recent years that this design has been illustrated. It bears some relation to Logan's CUMMIN (83).

120-122 FORBES

(120)

B	Bk	B	Bk	B	Bk	G	Bk	W	Bk	G	Bk	B	Bk	**B**
16	2	4	2	4	12	16	2	4	2	16	12	16	2	4

(121)

B	Bk	B	Bk	G	Bk	**W**
2	2	12	12	12	2	2

(122)

R	G	Bk	G	Bk	**Y**
2	32	16	6	8	2

One of the small number of tartans concerning the origin of which we seem to have precise information. It was designed, we are told, in 1822, for the family of Forbes of Pitsligo, by a Miss Forbes, who changed the yellow line of the regimental GORDON to white. That, at least, is what Miss Forbes appears to have done, judging by the scheme of the Forbes tartan (120) first published by the Smiths and consistently used since. Yet the almost complete identity of this design with that known as the LAMONT (170), differing only in that the white line in the latter is not now edged with black, invites scrutiny. Logan gives counts for both FORBES and LAMONT; and while his LAMONT is that reproduced later both in the Smiths' work and in the *Vestiarium Scoticum*, his FORBES (121), though similar at first glance, is not based on the BLACK WATCH but on a simpler foundation. Smibert, in presenting the FORBES and the LAMONT, observes the distinction of the white line being edged or not with black, but over-elaborates his foundation. The *Vestiarium* gives an altogether different design for FORBES (122), one that might be taken for a Hunting sett of the CLUNY MACPHERSON (299).

It seems curious that, since the LAMONT was already in use in its present form, anyone should introduce a design so closely resembling it as does the usual FORBES (120). Logan's counts are both of them unambiguous, and that for the FORBES (121) may have been made within four, and certainly not more than eight or nine, years of 1822. This seems a short time for confusion to arise whereas the Smith version had from 1822 till 1850 in which to appear. If Miss Forbes of Pitsligo was unaware of the Lamont tartan, it would not be unnatural for her to propose a design so like the GORDO (134) yet so easily distinguishable from it; yet the Logan counts lead one to suspect that the Forbes design may at first have been more unlike the Lamont than it now is, and that our second count may be the correct one.

In a collection made some years before 1822, two specimens appear under the name of Lamont, and they conform to the two setts we distinguish as Lamont and as Forbes. We now [1974] know that both forms, our present Forbes (120) and the Lamont (170), were in commercial production years before 1822 under the name of Forbes. This, then, invalidates the story of one of them having been designed by Miss Forbes of Pitsligo, and shows that the slight distinction now made between the two originally had no significance.

123 FORT WILLIAM SETT

K	A	K	G	K	A	K	A	Shade green	A	**G**
8	4	4	60	6	4	42	4	4	4	34

A plaid sett for the 28 reed, a nineteen inch width containing eight half setts. It comes from the Key Pattern Book. It could be expected that a pattern originating in the neighbourhood of Fort William would have at least some of the characteristics of other local patterns, and since this does not it must be regarded as being merely a named fancy pattern.

124-128 FRASER

(124)	**B**	R	B	R	G	R	G	R	G	B	R	**B**
	32	2	2	2	24	32	4	32	24	24	2	2
(125)	**B**	R	B	R	G	R	W	R	G	B	R	**B**
	32	2	2	2	24	32	4	32	24	24	2	2
(126)	**W**	R	G	R	B	**R**						
	2	24	12	2	12	2						
(127)	**P**	R	P	R	P	R	G	R	**P**			
	2	14	44	46	2	46	44	14	2			
(128)	**R**	B	G	R	**B**							
	4	28	28	56	4							

The most popular Fraser tartan is that of the *Vestiarium Scoticum* (126) and Plate 10 (e), and the question whether it is properly a FRASER at all has been discussed in connection with the various Drummond and Grant setts (100-103). Two other, and indisputably genuine, Fraser tartans have also come into favour, the Clan Fraser as given by Logan (124) (Plate 4 (f)) and the very similar one known as Fraser of Lovat (125). These are distinguishable by the respectively green and white lines centred on the red ground. Other variants are known to have been worn, but have passed out of general use. A modern Hunting Fraser is sometimes seen; this is the *Vestiarium* sett, but with brown in place of red, and alternately a white and a red line centred on the ground.

The pattern (127) is reputed to have been woven by Wilsons' *c.*1820.

The count (128) is taken from part of a plaid that belonged to Hugh Fraser of Boblainy who inherited the estate from a cousin in 1805. While there is nothing to say that he did not also inherit the plaid the balance of probability is that it was his own and this would date it to the late-eighteenth or early-nineteenth century. Its present significance is that, apart from the blue overcheck, it could have served for the prototype of the *Vestiarium* sett — "... fovr stryppis vpon ane scarlat feyld, quharoff ye vtterwarde be of grein, and ye ynnerward of blewe ..." See Plate 14 (a).

129, 130 GALLOWATER SETTS

(129)	Y	G	P	A	**K**		
	20	80	38	20	38		
(130)	**R**	K	A	P	W	G	**Y**
	22	66	28	64	4	84	20

The Key Pattern Book has no more to say of these than that they are "very ancient". Both were made in the 600 reed, nineteen inches wide, 'Old Gallowater' (129) having eight half setts to the width and 'New Gallowater' five.

Later on, the pattern of Old Gallowater was used for 'No. 122 or Wellington' for which the count runs as follows:

Yellow silk	G	P	A	**K**
4	28	22	6	8

131 GAYRE

B	G	K	W	G	B	G	W	K	R	G	W	G	R	**K**
36	8	8	8	32	8	32	8	8	10	8	8	6	10	8

The five Gayre tartans are all based upon the same design. Related to the Clan tartan shown, the tartan of the Chief's bodyguard has the first pivot (B36) in red and the hunting tartan has the large bands of green, with their contiguous white lines, in grey, the independent white lines also being in grey. The Dress tartan has light blue in place of dark, with the RKR pivot

AKA. The Arisaidh sett differs more radically than any of the others having first the large bands of green rendered in white and then the single black pivot and the black lines on either side of it each replaced by a KYK sequence of equal fine lines.

132 GIPSY

K	R	B	R	W	R	K	R	K
4	4	20	4	4	4	20	4	4

Like CLARKE (74) this is a derivative of the HUNTING MACPHERSON tartan. The inspiration for both design and name probably lay in the fact that James Macpherson, the well-known freebooter and reputed composer of "Macpherson's Rant" was the natural son of a Macpherson of Invereshie by a gipsy woman. (Plate 15 (l) and (m).

133 GLASGOW ROCK AND WHEEL

G	Madder	P	Mad	G	Mad	P
56	8	50	44	54	8	4

Several counts, of which the one given is typical, appear in the Key Pattern Book; in this case there are four half setts to a width of 19 inches. Scarlet was sometimes substituted for the duller shade of Madder. It must be regarded as unlikely that this is an ancient Glasgow 'district' tartan. There is an alternative version which appears to be a mis-interpretation of this count.

GLENORCHY — see COMYN, and MACINTYRE

134-138 GORDON

(134)	B	Bk	B	Bk	B	Bk	G	Y	G	Bk	B	Bk	B			
	24	4	4	4	4	24	24	4	24	24	22	4	4			
(135)	B	Bk	B	Bk	B	Bk	G	Y	G	Y	G	Y	G	Bk	B	Bk	B
	56	2	2	2	6	24	48	2	2	4	2	2	48	24	36	2	8
(136)	B	K	R	K	R	K	G	Y	G	K	B	K	R			
	36	6	6	6	6	40	36	6	36	40	36	6	6			
(137)	K	R	K	R	G	A	G	W	P	W	A	K	W	C	W	P
	4	16	12	16	12	12	34	4	30	4	12	28	4	14	4	32
(138)	R	W	K	Mauve	Y	G										
	48	2	2	12	2	40										

On the raising of the Gordon Highlanders in 1794 a yellow line was added to the Black Watch to make a new regimental tartan (134); this was subsequently adopted by Clan Gordon, the Huntly (156) being then used only as a dress tartan. A black edge is sometimes given to the yellow line, following the example of the MacKenzie and others, but this was a later addition. The sett shown in the *Vestiarium* (135) is similar, but the yellow is triplicated. The attempt in the *Vestiarium* to pass off this latter as an ancient tartan is particularly clumsy.

It would seem that other regiments followed the lead of the 42nd in having special tartans for the makers of military music; the count (136), which is shown in colour strip form at Plate 4 (k) is for Drummers' plaids for the 92nd regiment and comes from the manuscript pattern book which is the source of so many early Wilson patterns. No information is given as to reed or width but a selvage mark of 82 black threads appears to follow the red pivot.

A tartan that became very popular in the nineteen fifties is that known as Red Gordon or, more correctly, Old Huntly (137) (Plate 10 (a)). Coming from the eastern fringes of the Highlands proper the design differs from the Highland type in being built up from contiguous bands of colour with no discernable area of 'ground'. The pattern given in the Key Pattern Book is for the 600 reed, making six half setts to a width of 19 inches. Newspaper reports have confused the Old Huntly tartan with another red Gordon tartan (138) taken from a portrait of Rachel Gordon of Abergeldie.

139 GOW

R	G	R	B	**R**
8	8	2	8	8

Next to the Rob Roy (242), this is the most primitive tartan we have. Though the Gows, or MacGowans, have been particularly associated with Clan Donald and Clan Chattan, the name was used as a sept name in other clans. The tartan may well be an early design from which the Robertson and other tartans derived, without having been anciently peculiar to the Gows.

140-142 GRAHAM

(140)	**Bk**	Smalt	Bk	G	Az	**G**
	2	24	24	2	4	32

(141)	**Bk**	B	Bk	G	W	G	**Bk**
	2	8	8	8	2	8	8

(142)	G	Bk	G	**Bk**
	24	8	2	8

The first two of these tartans have been mentioned in association with the CAMPBELL OF BREADALBANE. It is curious that just as the GRAHAM OF MONTROSE (141) resembles the second MACCALLUM (201), so there is a resemblance between the GRAHAM OF MENTEITH (140) and the older MACCALLUM (200). Whether there was any borrowing in regard to the later designs — and, if so, by whom from which — it is no longer possible to say. The MENTEITH is found in Logan, and is shown by Smibert; but later Logan, in the McIan work, admits that its antiquity had been questioned. Smalt is the colour named by Logan, but other blues also are employed. Possibly the MONTROSE, shown by the Smiths, had by then become the more popular. It is described by them as supplied by a manufacturer who had been making it for nearly thirty years — which takes us back to 1822, when designs were in short supply and in great demand; but we have seen a specimen reputed some years older. The third design (142) comes from the *Vestiarium Scoticum*, but was never generally used.

143-147 GRANT

(143)	R	B	R	B	R	Az	R	B	R	G	R	G	R	B	**R**
	12	2	4	4	64	2	4	16	4	4	4	48	4	4	12
(144)	R	B	R	B	R	B	R	G	R	G	R	G	**R**		
	8	4	4	4	112	32	8	2	8	72	6	2	8		
(145)	R	G	R	B	R	G	R	G	R	G	R	G	**R**		
	2	2	64	64	16	2	2	2	16	64	64	2	2		
(146)	B	K	B	K	B	K	G	R	G	K	Y				
	44	8	8	8	8	44	44	10	12	4	6				
(147)	R	G	R	B	R	B	R	G	R	G	R	G	**R**		
	24	6	24	16	10	16	8	28	8	28	8	28	24		

The usual design (143) is the one sometimes, probably mistakenly, regarded as a Drummond tartan. It is recorded by Logan, Smibert and the Smiths. McIan shows two figures wearing Grant tartan, but the colouring of his plates was so roughly done in both cases that we can only say they appear to be intended to represent the same design. The *Vestiarium Scoticum* gives a sett (144) differing mainly by the omission of the azure lines. The count here given for it approximates to that of the plate, but according to the text the first and last red stripes should be of twenty and thirty threads respectively, thus conforming to the more usual proportions.

There is an old tartan known as GRANT OF MONYMUSK (147) that is worth recording. It is made up of elements from the Huntly group of tartans, but these elements are closely spaced, leaving no considerable expanse of ground; consequently the design is quite different in character from the usual Grant tartan, being very diffuse. Though the colours are the same, the amount of green has been increased at the expense of the red. [See Note 2 at end of Appendix F.]

For undress the Grants wear the BLACK WATCH, from their early association with the regiment.

The question whether one of the accepted Fraser tartans should be considered as a Grant design is discussed in the notes on DRUMMOND.

The count (145) is a translation of the Logan-style pattern by the late John MacGregor Hastie from an early 18th century wedding plaid in the collection of the late Margaret MacDougal; it has been styled "GRANT OF ROTHIEMURCHUS.

What may have been a Fencibles' tartan (146) is named in the Key Pattern Book simply 'GRANT TARTAN'. The colour strip is shown at Plate 4 (d).

148 GUNN

R	G	Bk	G	B	**G**
4	24	24	2	24	4

The Gunns, the MacKays and the Morrisons belong to Caithness, Sutherland and Lewis, and this regional grouping is reflected in the design of their tartans. The GUNN is sometimes, as in the *Vestiarium Scoticum*, represented as having four black bands on a green ground, with a red line centred on the open ground; but the inner two bands are recorded by Logan, and now usually rendered, as blue. In a specimen dated about 1815 the green was seen to be of a remarkably light shade, though the blue was quite dark.

149 HAMILTON

W	R	B	R	**B**
2	18	12	2	12

The designers of the tartans found in the *Vestiarium Scoticum* seem to have had a partiality for groups of three or four equal bands of a single colour. Several examples in quadruple bands have already been shown, and we have had the GRAHAM (142) with its triple scheme. The use of so much unrelieved blue on a red ground, as in this design, cannot be regarded as satisfactory, though in the *Vestiarium* illustration the blue is very dark.

150, 151 HAY

(150)	**Bk**	R	Y	Bk	R	G	R	Y	R	G	W	Bk	R	P	R	Y	R	P
	6	2	2	4	32	4	2	2	4	30	2	30	2	30	4	2	2	4
	R	Bk	Y	R	**Bk**													
	32	4	2	2	6													
(151)	**W**	R	Bk	R	G	R	G	R	G	R	G	Y	G	**R**				
	12	4	2	4	8	96	24	4	4	4	72	4	8	12				

The design more often illustrated recently is that first shown in the *Vestiarium Scoticum* (151) and resembling the Drummond (103); but Logan gives quite different design (150), illustrated only in the Smith work, where the colours are defective, the narrower of the green and purple stripes being rendered as black. Logan gives the name as HAY AND LEITH, from its use also by the family of Leith.

Hay is the family name of the Earls of Errol, one of whom, as Lord High Constable of Scotland, entertained George IV on the occasion of his visit in 1822. The more elaborate of these two tartans is to be found in a collection made a few years earlier; the specimen therein has blue where Logan specifies purple. A repeat occupies thirteen inches.

152 HENDERSON

Y	Bk	G	Bk	G	B	G	B	**W**
2	12	8	2	32	2	8	12	2

The peculiarity of having the main band of pattern alternately in black and in blue, on a green ground, is shared with one of the Davidson tartans. The Davidsons were of Clan Chattan, whereas the Hendersons were variously associated with the MacDonalds and the Gunns, and there is nothing in their histories to explain the similarity of the tartans. The Clan Davidson tartan which this resembles is not known to be very old, and the same is true of the HENDERSON.

153 HOME

B	G	B	Bk	R	Bk	R	**Bk**
6	4	48	16	2	4	2	56

The tartan of the ancient and notable Lowland family of Home, though differing in colour, has the same scheme as the GRAY DOUGLAS (98). Both first appear in the *Vestiarium Scoticum*. (Plate 11 (e)).

154, 155 HUNTER

(154)

W	R	W	K	W	A	W	G	LG	G	LG	G	LG	Y	R	W	R	Y
4	16	4	30	4	10	4	40	4	8	4	40	6	6	4	4	4	6

LG	G	W	R	W	G	W	A	W	LG	K	W	A	W	R	**W**
6	40	4	64	4	40	4	10	4	8	30	4	10	4	16	4

(155)

K	G	K	R	B	**W**
6	16	16	4	16	4

Named 'Hunter Sett' in the Key Pattern Book, the pattern (154) dates from the end of the eighteenth century and gives three half setts to a web 19 inches wide with a warp set at four ends to the split in a 600 reed. (See Plate 10 (b).)

The tartan (155) sold as 'Hunter' is also named Russell, under which name it appears in a mid-nineteenth-century list, Galbraith (in the Highland Society of London Collection) and Mitchell, a name given in honour of General Billy Mitchell when it was adopted as the tartan of the United States Air Force pipe band.

(156) HUNTLY

G	R	G	R	G	R	G	R	W	R	Y	B	R	B	Y	R	W	R
16	4	16	24	4	6	4	24	2	6	2	24	6	24	2	6	2	24

B	R	B	R	B	R	B	R	B	R	B	R	G	R	G
2	2	4	2	2	24	2	2	4	2	2	24	16	4	16

The striking similarity between the Huntly, the MacRae (308), 'The Prince's Own' (307) and the Ross (374), may at first be puzzling, but the little that is known of their history points to an interesting explanation.

It is unfortunate that the large counts needed to render the designs have latterly led to confusion and error in the illustrations, some of which show incredible versions. Logan gives a count for Ross (375), but he seems to have left off counting too soon, with the result that the pairs of blue bands occur twice as often as the groups of three green bands.

Some of D.W. Stewart's notes bear on our problem. Of The Prince's Own he writes:

> Various circumstances tend to enhance the interest of this design, which is especially associated by Jacobite enthusiasts with the memory of Prince Charles Edward, and which was named during the campaign of 1745–46 from his personal use of it. Authenticated by specimens of contemporary and immediately subsequent dates — invariably bearing the legend of royal adoption — the tartan may be ranked amongst the earliest clan patterns extant in fabric. It is undoubtedly an old pattern of the MacRaes, and it was certainly worn by the Prince in their territory. But whether it was

previously used by members of the clan, or whether it was adopted by them as a compliment to the wearer, cannot be determined. Tradition indicates, however, that the Prince was wont to don the local colours of the various clans in his sojournments in their respective districts. It is now generally known as MacRae; but in all representations hitherto published the omission of the yellow lines has produced confusion as to the true sett.

It is not merely the yellow lines, but all that portion containing the yellow lines, that came to be omitted. The next quotation opens with a reference to the Hunting MacRae, with which we are not at the moment concerned, but it is given in full for later reference:

> The present illustration reproduces the pattern of a piece of old hard tartan from a kilt believed to have been worn by a member of Clan MacRae at the battle of Sheriffmuir in 1715. The fragment ... bears internal evidence of great age, the style of manufacture attesting its connection with the period to which it has been assigned. A tartan somewhat akin to this, and having the same name, is supposed to have been founded on an imperfect acquaintance with the pattern here given. The design is poorly represented in the *Clans of Scotland*, by MacIan and Logan. It has been styled Hunting to distinguish it from a red MacRae, which agrees exactly with The Prince's Own. The Editor was unable to account for the connection between the two latter till he discovered a plaid preserved in a carefully authenticated collection in Inverness-shire, with the description: 'MacRae tartan plaid worn by Prince Charles Edward in 1745'. The plaid being a complicated sett, a large specimen is required to show the complete design, and, either through inadequate patterns or insistent copying, the portion containing the yellow lines has been omitted from all representations of the tartan hitherto published ...

And in reference to the Huntly (156):

> The present example is designated Huntly and Brodie in certain early collections and, like those of Dunblane, Strathearn, and Atholl, it appears to belong to a district rather than to a family. Tradition shows it to have been in use during a considerable portion of [the eighteenth] century by such families as Gordon, Brodie, and Forbes, or at least by members of these touched with Jacobitism, who appear to have assumed this tartan in common, just as many families of different name adopted a uniform wear in various localities.

In one form or another what is fundamentally the same tartan has been worn by the Gordons, the Forbeses, the Brodies, the Rosses, and the MacRaes; the feature of twin groups of three fine lines appears also in the Monro sett as given by Logan. This may be due to an error on Logan's part; yet the Munroes belonged to the Huntly district. Whatever the source of the pattern, it became popular over a wide area about the year 1745. It is reasonable to suppose that the Prince acquired and wore a specimen of The Prince's Own (307) while in the MacRae country, but that it was not then a clan tartan, though used by a leading MacRae; that the Jacobites further east adopted either this or some simplified version of it to mark their sympathies; and that it then became familiar in its new home, and later came to be regarded as a regional tartan. It is hardly likely that so distinctive a pattern would otherwise be in use over so scattered an area as that occupied by the clans with whose names it became associated, or that they would have adopted for its personal associations what had hitherto been a recognised Clan MacRae tartan.

The question may be asked — Who, then, is to wear which? Tentatively, we suggest the following solution. The HUNTLY (156) must continue to be used as in the past, as a district tartan; the MacRaes should use THE PRINCE'S OWN (307), since the more usual MACRAE is hardly distinguishable from the HUNTLY; and the Rosses might well retain the simplified version (374), which is the least likely to be confused with either of the other two. It amounts to the HUNTLY minus the white and yellow lines. What tartan any of these clans wore before 1745 it would be hard to say; yet few clans can trace their tartans even thus far with so much assurance.

In one collection made about 1815 THE PRINCE'S OWN is the only tartan bearing the name of MacRae.

The Key Pattern Book calls No. 156 'THE MARCHIONESS OF HUNTLY'S TARTAN', pointing to its being the choice of some particular Marchioness. Which Marchioness we do not know but it clearly did not take long to become a 'district' tartan. (Plate 13 (d).)

157-160 INNES, MACINNES

(157)	**Az**	Bk	R	Bk	R	Bk	R	Y	R	B	R	Bk	G	Bk	R	**W**
	14	48	8	8	8	8	48	8	12	24	12	8	40	8	12	8

(158)	**Y**	Bk	G	Bk	G	Bk	G	Bk	Az	Bk	B	G	**R**
	4	24	4	4	4	4	32	6	6	6	24	12	4

(159)	**B**	K	R	K	R	K	R	W	R	G	R	K	G	K	R	W	R	K
	2	12	2	2	2	2	12	2	4	6	4	2	10	2	4	2	4	2
	G	K	R	G	R	W	R	K	R	K	R	K	**G**					
	10	2	4	6	4	2	12	2	2	2	2	12	2					

(160)	**A**	K	A	G	K	**G**
	2	12	2	14	2	14

Over the past century or more several setts have been used bearing these names. Within recent years (157) has been accepted as the tartan appropriate to the Inneses of the Moray district, and (158) as the tartan of the MacInneses of the West; though there is no historical connection between these two clans, the similarity of the names is accompanied by a similarity in the tartans, so that these were formerly treated as Dress and Hunting setts without distinction of name.

An alternative red tartan (159) is given in *The Baronage of Angus and*

The Mearns (1856) and the dark tartan (160) is taken from a miniature of Georgina Innes of Edingight.

161 INVERNESS

R	B	W	B	G	Bk	G	**R**
144	12	4	22	4	4	4	36

In the first edition of *The Setts of the Scottish Tartans* a version of the Inverness tartan was presented, though with reservations. That version derived from the plate James Logan used in his *Scottish Gaël* to illustrate his method of recording tartan setts. Unfortunately, as in other publications, different copies of his book showed differing colourings, and in none were these colours clear, so that the strip we showed was no more than a compromise.

The earl with whom the tartan originated was Augustus, son of George III; he lived from 1773 to 1843. A portrait of him in Highland Dress came to our knowledge in 1966, and we hoped that inspection of this would remove our uncertainty. The portrait proved to be dark in tone, and the colours indeterminate; also, there was a material difference in the structure of the sett, in that the broad band adjoining the main red ground was missing.

Since then, however, a specimen of tartan has been found in the National Museum of Antiquities, attached to a letter dated 19th Nov. 1829, in which it was stated that 'this pattern is made for the Earl of Inverness'. (He would then be aged 46). This specimen is very slightly smaller in its measurements than is specified in Logan's plate, but the structure and proportions are precisely the same; and the colours are quite unambiguous.

In more recent times a variant on this tartan has been produced with a blue ground under the name of 'Duke of York'. This was first worn by King George V while Duke of York and Earl of Inverness, and later, in 1930, by King George VI when he in turn held the titles. The count, supplied to us by the makers, is as follows:

162

B	R	W	R	Y	B	Y	**B**
244	22	8	30	8	12	8	60

Another variation on the Earl of Inverness' tartan changes black to blue, blue to black and green to yellow; it is named 'Princess Elizabeth'.

163, 164 JAHORE

(163)

B	K	B	Y	**K**
40	10	36	52	12

(164)

N	W	G	N	**Y**
114	10	40	10	20

The first pattern was produced in the 1930s for the Jahore Regiment by Andersons' of Edinburgh; it follows a well-known *Vestiarium* theme. The second, though of the same name, is unrelated and its origin is unknown. It may, perhaps, have been a competitor for the Regiment's choice. Neither can be regarded as the Jahore District Tartan.

165 JOHNSTON

Y	G	Bk	G	B	BK	B	**Bk**
6	4	2	60	48	4	4	4

This tartan of one of the great Border clans is first found in the *Vestiarium Scoticum.* There was at one time a prominent family of Johnston in Strathspey, which may in part account for the tartan.

166 JUBILEE

G	A	G	A	G	R/Y	G	A	**G**
6	24	8	12	44	6	44	48	6

The provenance of this design is not recorded but it is perhaps to be associated with the silver jubilee of King George V. A relationship to HUNTING STEWART is evident.

167 KEITH and AUSTIN

Bk	G	B	Bk	**B**
4	18	8	8	8

D. W. Stewart writes:

> Despite the uncertainty concerning the origin of this design, it is included in every complete early collection, like that of the Highland Society of London, of the late Dr Skene, of Messrs Ogilvy & Co. and of Messrs Romanes & Paterson. The last mentioned firm has supplied it from the early years of [the nineteenth] century to various families of Keiths and Austins, including the house of Keith-Falconer, Earls of Kintore ...

See also 'No. 75 or Austin', page 178.

168 KENNEDY

R	G	B	Bk	B	Bk	B	Bk	B	G	Cr	G	Cr	G	Y	G	**Bk**
4	48	8	6	6	6	6	6	8	24	2	4	2	6	2	4	4

McIan renders the colours and proportions of the KENNEDY with unaccustomed care. D. W. Stewart writes concerning it:

> The tartan seems to have been first worn by Kennedy families in the Lochaber district

... The design has been accepted by the Kennedys in Carrick, many of whom adopted it [in the eighteenth] century as an emblem of their Jacobite sympathies... the single red stripe is scarlet, and the two fine lines are crimson; but manufacturers, to save themselves trouble, have been accustomed to vitiate the design by failing to mark this distinction. It is noteworthy that the tartan bears little resemblance to any other Lochaber design of ancient date, and the Kennedys, while generally allied with the Camerons, have ever maintained their own colours ...

169 KERR

Bk	R	Bk	R	Bk	G	Bk	G	Bk	**G**
8	4	2	56	28	6	2	4	2	40

This example of a *Vestiarium Scoticum* tartan is reminiscent of the Stewart of Athol (404); a drawing of the latter was one of several prepared for that work, but not reproduced therein. The Kerrs were a Border family, and the similarity of the tartans has no significance.

There is a hunting tartan in which navy blue is substituted for red.

170 LAMONT or LAMOND

B	Bk	B	Bk	B	Bk	G	W	G	Bk	B	Bk	**B**
6	2	2	2	2	8	8	2	8	8	8	2	2

The Clan Lamont was one of the many clans subjected to a process of absorption by the Campbells; and the tartan now worn by the Lamonts is like that known as Campbell of Argyll (57), except that the lines centred on the green are white only.

Logan lists this design, and the *Vestiarium Scoticum* reproduces it without departing from the accepted pattern beyond refining the proportions. This is unusual, for most of the previously known tartans reproduced there show some alteration in the scheme.

The relation of the Lamont tartan to that of the Forbeses has been discussed in connection with the latter.

171 LASTING SETT

W	R	A	R	W	R	W	P	W	P	W	G	W	Y	W	P	W	Y
4	6	4	6	8	38	4	14	4	14	4	38	4	8	4	8	4	8
W	A	W	P	**W**													
4	12	4	14	4													

Another early Wilson plaid pattern giving six half setts to 19 inches in the 600 reed.

172 LAUDER

R	G	Bk	G	B	**G**
4	30	8	6	16	6

Sir Thomas Dick Lauder was one of the 'particular friends' of the Sobieski brothers, who sponsored the MS from which the *Vestiarium Scoticum* was prepared. This tartan, otherwise unknown, appears in that work.

LEITH — see HAY

173 LENNOX

LR	DR	LR	DR	Myrtle	W	**Myrtle**
4	2	20	4	20	2	4

D. W. Stewart reproduced this design from one of two known copies of a lost portrait dating from the sixteenth century, and claimed to represent the Countess of Lennox, mother of Henry Darnley, second husband of Mary Stuart. This would seem to be the evidence on which the tartan has passed into currency as the Lennox district tartan. It may be that the attribution is a correct one; yet the supporting evidence is slender. The Countess was Lady Margaret Douglas, wife of Matthew Stewart, Earl of Lennox, and daughter of the Earl of Angus. The tartan might equally well have been put forward as a Douglas, a Stewart, or an Angus.

The presence of two shades of scarlet is unusual.

174, 175 LESLIE

(174)	**R**	B	Bk	W	G	**Bk**
	4	16	16	2	16	2

(175)	**Bk**	R	B	R	Bk	Y	Bk	**R**
	2	64	32	8	12	2	12	8

The darker, and older, of these two quite dissimilar tartans is shown by Smibert and by the Smiths. It should be compared with the Colquhoun (80). The Dress tartan (175) is from the *Vestiarium Scoticum*, and seems to be a development of the DRESS BRODIE (34).

176, 177 LINDSAY

(176)	**Cr**	B	Cr	B	G	B	G	B	**G**
	6	4	48	16	4	4	4	4	40

(177)	**R**	K	R	C	G	K	G	K	**G**
	4	2	20	10	2	2	2	2	24

The scheme of the LINDSAY (176), a *Vestiarium Scoticum* tartan, is that of the STEWART OF ATHOL (404), but the black in the latter is here rendered in blue; in this resembling in part the CHISHOLM (71) shown in the same work.

A somewhat similar design (177) appears in *The Baronage of Angus and The Mearns* (1856).

178 LIVINGSTONE

R	G	R	G	R	Bk	R	Bk	R	**G**
16	4	40	32	8	2	4	2	8	24

The Livingstones are variously associated with the Buchanans, the MacDougals, and the Stewarts of Appin, but the tartan does not resemble that of any of these clans. It does resemble a MACDONELL OF KEPPOCH (213); the main difference is that the centre of the design is a solid band of green, where the KEPPOCH has two narrow green bands.

179, 180 LOCHABER

(179)	**G**	K	R	K	G	K	R	B	A	**G**
	8	2	4	2	66	70	4	66	4	8

(180)	**B**	A	B	R	B	R	**B**
	8	4	64	4	140	4	12

The count (179) appears in the Key Pattern Book as one of the "Old superfine tartan setts" for the 600 reed and may have originated as a 'Fencibles' tartan. There are six half setts to the width, the sixth large black mark being increased to 100 threads as a selvage mark.

The second count (180) is reputed to date from 1707 and is named 'OLD LOCHABER'.

181, 182 LOGAN or MACLENNAN

(181)	**Y**	Bk	R	G	Bk	B	R	B	R	B	**R**
	4	2	2	32	24	32	4	4	4	6	12

(182)	**B**	R	G	R	B	R	**B**
	2	6	18	6	2	6	18

D. W. Stewart, in *Old and Rare Scottish Tartans,* gives reasons for regarding the design (182) usually known as a Skene tartan as in fact a LOGAN, it being so named in several early collections. It has also been found under the name of Rose. In some early examples the main blue band is only about two thirds as wide as the green, and this could be regarded as a more pleasing arrangement.

The tartan generally used (181) is quite different, and follows the count given by J. Logan in 1831. The group of five red lines is often to be seen with the lines equally spaced, and even of equal width. The earlier arrangement here shown is preferable.

Logan (182) was a popular pattern early in the nineteenth century and Wilsons' played several variations upon the basic design. There was 'Dark Logan', which had black in place of blue (which was actually purple), bottle green and rose, 'Light Logan', with the second and third red stripes in rose and 'Logan with Yellow' in which the narrow purple stripes were rendered in yellow. All were made in various widths and various sizes of sett, sure indications of a 'fancy' pattern.

183 NEW LOUDEN

R	W	Lt drab	Lt blue	Dk lt blue	LD	W	Olive G
100	4	10	4	4	10	4	24

W	Lt pink	Dk pink	R	K	R	DP	LP	W	**LD**
4	4	4	10	4	10	4	4	4	18

This pattern appeared among the Wilson patterns about 1840 and has been claimed, though apparently not adopted, as a Campbell tartan. It is quite unlike any other contemporary Wilson tartan and this, coupled with the large number of colours (and rather off-beat colours at that) employed leads me to consider that it *may* be the 'lost' tartan planned for Lord Loudoun's Highland regiment some hundred years earlier resurrected as a 'new' pattern when the demand for new tartans became acute. No 'old' Loudoun tartan is recorded but if there is any merit in the suggestion that would have been the original regimental tartan and would have sunk into obscurity when the regiment was reduced.

184 LORD LOUDOUN'S HIGHLANDERS

R	K	B	K	G	Y
8	4	48	40	40	6

Lord Loudon's Highland regiment was raised in 1745, took part in the Rout of Moy and was disbanded in 1748. It has been generally supposed that the tartan worn by the regiment was the anachronistally named

'Government or Universal' pattern but in 1979 Ruairidh MacLeod made the important discovery, in the Huntington Library at Los Angeles, of a piece of sergeants' plaiding 'sent to Lord Loudoun for his Highlanders' in 1746, when they were already in the Netherlands. The thread count is taken from Ruairidh MacLeod's colour slide of the fragment. Plate 2 (a).

185-189 MACALISTER

(185)

R	LG	DG	R	Az	R	W	R	Az	R	DG	R	W	R	Az	R
16	2	4	4	2	2	2	2	2	4	6	2	2	12	2	2
DG	R	Az	R	Az	R	DG	R	Az	R	W	R	B	R	W	R
24	2	2	32	2	2	24	2	2	12	2	2	8	2	2	4
DG	LG	R	LG	DG	R	W	R	B	R	W	**R**				
6	2	4	2	6	6	2	2	4	2	2	16				

(186)

R	Az	R	G	R	Az	R	G	R	Az	R	Az	R	G	R	Az	R	B
8	2	2	12	24	2	2	36	2	2	64	2	2	36	2	2	24	16
R	G	R	G	**R**													
16	16	8	16	64													

(187)

B	R	W	R	DG	LG	R	LG	DG	R	W	R	B	R	W
20	4	4	6	24	4	16	4	24	20	4	4	32	4	4
R	A	R	DG	R	A	R	A	R	DG	R	A	R	W	R
44	4	4	88	4	4	128	4	4	88	4	4	48	4	4
DG	R	A	R	W	R	A	R	DG	LG	**R**				
24	8	8	8	4	8	8	8	24	4	64				

(188)

R	G	Y	R	Y	G	R	B	R	A	R	G	R	A	R	A	R
48	12	4	8	4	12	12	12	24	4	4	32	4	4	48	4	4
G	R	A	R	G	R	A	R	A	R	G	Y	**R**				
32	4	4	24	8	4	4	8	4	4	12	4	16				

(189)

R	P	R	P	R	G	R	P	R	G	R	G	R	**G**
24	18	208	12	12	88	12	12	48	24	24	24	12	76

In its complexity, though not in detail, this tartan (185) resembles the MacDonald of Staffa (205), and it may be regarded as belonging to the MacDonald group.

The relative proportions of the colours are more extreme in Logan's count than in the Smith illustration (185), and there is a material difference in the designs at one of the turning points of the pattern. The McIan drawing clearly indicates the more extended design shown by the Smiths, and it is evident that Logan's count is short by mistake. It remains short in the M'Intyre North count.

James Grant omits the light green lines. The employment of two shades of green would be exceptional in an old tartan, and it may be that in some early specimens the green had bled into what was originally a white line. In old woollen fabrics white is something of a courtesy title, and the off-white will tend towards green, blue, or yellow, or some pale indeterminate colour. In the present design the light green occurs only in contact with a dark green stripe.

The second sett, so much simpler than the former, is that of a specimen in a collection made at the beginning of the nineteenth century. It differs mainly in the omission of the white and light green lines. Whether it should be regarded as the prototype, or as a simplified variant, it is impossible to say; the former, more probably. Support for this surmise is found when we compare this sett with our first three MacDougal setts. It forms a link between these MacDougal setts and the more elaborate MacAlister sett, and it may well have been their common source. Indeed, the MacAlister (185) departs further from it than do the MacDougals. That it was not named by the collector merely in mistake is shown by the presence in the same collection of a named MacDougal tartan, our MacDougal (228).

By comparison with (185) Logan's count (187) is considerably extended while (188), taken from a late nineteenth century pattern book of Meyer and Mortimer, the London tartan merchants, is curtailed. This does not necessarily indicate that these three are different patterns. It has not been unusual in the past for a sett to be reduced by simply leaving a part out!

A much simpler design (189) recorded by MacGregor Hastie is known as MacAllister of Glenbarr.

190 MACALPINE

G	B	Y	Bk	G	Bk	G	Bk	G	Bk	G	Bk	W	Bk
2	8	2	8	2	2	12	2	12	2	2	8	2	8

The tartan called MacAlpine is the same as the Hunting MacLean (272) except that alternate white lines are made yellow; this results in an asymmetrical design.

It is curious that this should be a green tartan, since the other tartans of Siol Alpin are red. The Clan MacAlpine belongs rather to mythology than to history, and the choice of design must be regarded as of recent date. It has been suggested that the Rob Roy (242) would have been a more appropriate choice.

191 MACARTHUR

Y	G	Bk	G	Bk
6	60	24	12	64

Though the MacArthurs as a clan were of the Campbell stock, families of them were at one time and another linked with the MacDonalds, and the

MacArthur tartan has the same basic form as the MacDonald, Lord of the Isles (207). The MacIver tartan (249) has the same black and yellow elements, but on a red ground, and the MacIvers also dwelt in the Campbell country; indeed, the MacArthur might be taken for a Hunting version of the MacIver. The tartan is first recorded in the *Vestiarium Scoticum.*

192-195 MACAULAY

(192)	**Bk**	R	G	R	G	W	G	**R**
	4	36	12	6	18	2	18	6

(193)	**Bk**	R	G	R	G	**W**
	4	32	12	6	16	2

(194)	**R**	G	Bk	G	Bk	W	Bk	**G**
	4	24	8	16	32	2	32	12

(195)	**R**	B	G	B	R	B	G	K	**W**
	192	2	48	2	20	2	24	2	8

In Logan's count for the MacAulay (192) he includes a complete repeat of the design, thus leaving no doubt about the version he was recording. This is the design used by McIan. Yet it appears in the Smith work under the name of Comyn. The question of how this came about is discussed in the notes on the Comyn tartans (83). Apart from the McIan-Logan work of 1843-9, no illustration of a MacAulay tartan appears before the one in James Grant's book (1886), where we find a shortened version (193). This shorter version tallies with the count published by M'Intyre North in 1881 as having been given him by Logan; the difference in the counts consists in the omission of four lines from the table of colours, and could have resulted from a slip on the part of a copyist. (Such slips are fascinatingly easy to make.) On the other hand, the manufacturers, finding Logan's MacAulay tartan to have been called Cumming in the Smith work, may have decided that Logan was wrong, and amended the design for him, M'Intyre North following suit. Encouragement to make the change could have been derived from the fact that the shortened version begins to resemble the MacGregor tartan (241), and the southern MacAulays were at one time identified with the MacGregors. The modern Hunting MacAulay (194) conforms to Logan's early design.

The Baronage of Angus and The Mearns (1856) gives a version (195) of the MacIntyre North count that still more nearly resembles the MacGregor.

196-198 MACBEAN

(196)	**R**	W	B	Az	W	Az	B	W	Bk	G	Bk	W	R	Cr	G	Cr	R	W	**G**
	48	2	4	2	2	2	4	2	2	12	2	2	4	4	2	4	4	2	6

(197)	**P**	R	P	R	G	R	**P**
	6	38	26	10	42	16	6

A curiously elaborate sett (191) for a minor sept of Clan Chattan. McIan has a drawing of a figure representing a MacBean and wearing the CLAN MACKINTOSH (260); apart from this there is no early illustration of a design appropriate to the MacBeans. Towards the end of the nineteenth century the MacBean chief was wearing the Mackintosh tartan with the addition of a black line centred on the red ground (197); he did not recognise the present design.

An almost identical tartan was in production much earlier in the century under the name of Birral, and something very like it appears in the hose worn by McIan's figure of a MacBean; this may explain its later adoption.

Since the above was written a slightly different version of the pattern was registered with Lyon Court under the name of MacBain; the difference occurs at the part adjacent to the red ground. The count for this sett is as follows:

(198)	**G**	W	R	Cr	G	Cr	R	W	Bk	G	Bk	W	Az	Bk	W	Bk	Az	W	**R**
	20	4	10	10	4	10	10	4	4	24	4	4	10	4	4	4	10	4	120

The 'black line' tartan (197) was first noticed by D. W. Stewart in *Scottish Notes and Queries* for July/August 1892, where the date of its use is given as 1872. This caused the initial assumption that the design was a Victorian affectation in honour of Gillies MacBean of the '45 but the subsequent discovery of a specimen revealed first that the overcheck is blue, not black, and second that the proportions are significantly altered from early specimens of Mackintosh, the secondary red pivot being widened at the expense of the adjacent green bars. Both these would be likely to be the work of a designer-weaver rather than of a factory, so the design is likely to be authentic. The blue was probably purple.

199 MACBETH

B	Y	Bk	Y	Bk	W	Bk	G	R	Bk	R	**W**
72	8	12	2	2	2	2	16	12	2	6	2

This is a modern variant on the ROYAL STUART (406). The complete band of pattern remains as in the STUART, except that the blue stripe at the edge becomes yellow; the large expanse of ground between the bands changes from red to blue.

Probably the tartan was produced first, and then the name bestowed, from its anciently royal associations, as a label.

200, 201 MACCALLUM

(200)	**Bk**	B	Bk	G	Az	Bk	G
	2	12	12	8	2	4	16

(201)	**Bk**	B	Bk	G	R	G	**Bk**
	2	12	12	12	2	12	12

When reproducing our first design, D. W. Stewart wrote:

Well-nigh forgotten and rarely encountered, save in the old pattern-book or in the tartan collector's museum, this design is early, though its origin cannot be fixed with any certainty. It has been supplanted by a comparatively modern pattern, known commonly as the Malcolm but occasionally as the MacCallum, which is the ancient form of the name. The new scheme has [1893] existed some forty or fifty years at least, as the Editor has received from a lady in Skye a specimen in a portion of a silk dress her family has owned for about that period without knowing the name of the tartan. In the collection of the Highland Society of London (1822), in that at Moy Hall, and in every other important repository of the kind, the MacCallum as here illustrated is ranked, and the Malcolm is wanting. It is believed that the family, having lost trace of the old sett fifty or sixty years ago [*i.e.*, 1832-43], had the modern design prepared from the recollection of old people in Argyllshire; but, as has frequently happened in similar circumstances, the recovery of the original design shows that considerable deviation had been made.

Three tartans have to be considered in connection with the names MacCallum and Malcolm. The one given by D.W. Stewart (200) may be accepted as the most ancient. We are left with two comparatively recent designs. The Smiths give only one, naming it MALCOLM (322); it is asymmetrical, containing a light blue line accompanied by a yellow line always in the same order. The other, usually called MACCALLUM (201), has a structure common to several tartans of doubtful antiquity; in this case the light lines of the pattern are red. Some editors have described the ancient MACCALLUM as being of this structure but with the lines in light blue — a quite misleading description.

Whichever of the two later designs is the one to which D. W. Stewart referred as being 'recollected', both show a more than considerable deviation from the original form.

202 MACCOLL

G	R	G	R	B	R	B	R	B	R	G	R	B	**R**
8	2	2	24	2	2	6	2	2	4	16	2	2	24

It is odd that while Logan was able to give setts for the MUNRO (343) and the DALZELL (92) which closely resemble this, he knew so little of any MacColl tartan that in the McIan-Logan work the Clan is represented by a figure in the costume of Charlemagne. No MacColl tartan is represented in any early work on the subject. The MacColls derive from the MacDonalds, and this has all the appearance of being in fact a MacDonald tartan. It is almost identical with a sett in production by Wilson's about 1800 entitled Old Bruce, but with the addition to the latter's plain red ground of the MacDonald motif in green.

203 MACCOUL

C	R	B	R	G	R	G	C	R	C	B	R	G	R	G	R	C	**R**
8	72	2	4	24	24	24	12	4	12	24	8	4	8	4	4	4	24

This tartan first appears in the manuscript for the Smith brothers' (Mauchline) work.

204 MACCRAIG

C	A	G	R	K	G	B	R	**G**
16	8	56	8	56	8	56	8	16

Originally from Lochaber, the count is taken from a specimen said to have been taken to Scandinavia after Culloden and thence to the U.S.A.

205-227 MACDONALD

(205)	**R**	G	R	G	R	G	R	G	R	G	B	G	B	R	G	R
	32	2	2	2	2	2	2	2	12	2	2	12	2	2	2	8
	G	R	B	R	W	R	G	W	G	R	G	R	G	R	**W**	
	2	2	8	8	2	8	8	2	[illegible]	2	2	12	2	16	2	

(206)	**W**	G	Bk	G	Bk	G	Bk	B	**R**
	8	60	2	2	2	6	24	20	6

(207)	**Bk**	R	G	R	**G**
	4	36	4	10	32

(208)	**G**	W	G	W	B	W	B	W	B	W	B	W	**B**
	48	2	4	4	4	2	24	2	4	4	4	2	24

(209)	**G**	R	G	R	G	Bk	R	B	R	B	R	**B**
	16	2	4	6	24	24	2	24	6	4	2	16

(210)	**B**	R	B	R	B	R	Bk	G	R	G	R	G	**W**
	16	2	4	6	24	2	24	24	6	4	2	8	2

(211)	**B**	R	B	R	Bk	G	R	G	R	G	**W**
	16	8	24	2	24	24	6	4	2	8	2

(212)	**G**	R	G	R	G	W	Bk	R	B	R	B	R	**B**
	16	2	4	6	24	2	24	2	24	6	4	2	16

(213)	**R**	B	R	G	R	B	R	B	R	G	**R**
	4	2	28	24	16	2	4	2	12	4	16

(214)	**R**	Bk	R	Bk	R	Bk	R	G	R	G	R	G	R	G	**R**
	12	2	2	2	48	2	2	48	24	4	4	4	4	8	48

(215)	G	R	B	R	B	R	G	R	**B**
	4	4	2	48	12	6	24	8	2

(216)	**R**	W	B	W	R	LG	G	LG	R	LG	G	LG	R	W	B	W
	32	2	12	2	8	2	12	2	8	2	32	2	48	2	64	2
	R	W	B	W	**R**											
	12	2	12	2	32											

(217)	G	R	G	R	G	R	B	R	G	R	**G**
	12	4	2	48	4	4	12	4	4	6	36

(218)	**R**	G	Y	R	W	G	Y	G	**Y**
	6	6	2	36	2	42	2	2	6

(219)	**R**	B	R	B	R	K	G	R	G	R	G	R	G	W	R	B	R
	48	12	12	12	12	8	12	12	12	56	12	12	52	12	52	48	10
	G	R	G	R	K	G	K	R	G	R	G	R	G	R	G	R	G
	10	56	10	10	2	60	2	10	10	48	12	8	12	8	12	8	12
	R	B	**R**														
	52	12	60														

(220)	**K**	G	R	G	R	G	R	G	R	**K**
	8	4	4	4	32	4	4	4	4	6

(221)	G	R	G	R	W	B	R	G	R	B	**R**
	4	8	2	64	2	16	8	56	2	2	12

(222)	G	*	C	G	C	A	B	C	G	C	B	*	**C**
	8	2	8	4	96	2	26	12	80	4	4	2	12

(223)	**B**	A	R	B	R	W	R	G	R	B	**W**
	6	2	60	64	6	2	6	52	60	6	2

(224)	**B**	W	R	G	R	W	R	B	R	W	B	W	R	B	R	W	R
	10	4	52	42	10	4	10	52	52	4	10	4	52	52	10	4	10
	G	R	B	**W**													
	42	52	10	4													

(225)	B	W	R	B	R	W	R	G	R	W
	10	4	52	56	10	4	10	56	52	4

(226)	**B**	K	B	K	B	K	G	R	G	R	G	K	W	K	G	R	G
	48	8	8	8	8	44	28	8	8	8	16	2	12	2	16	8	8
	R	G	K	B	R	B	K	B	W	B	K	B	K	B	K	**B**	
	8	28	44	36	48	36	44	48	12	48	44	8	8	8	8	48	

(227)	**B**	R	B	R	K	Y	G
	10	2	10	20	14	2	18

There is general agreement in naming the dark tartan comprehensively known as CLAN MACDONALD (209); this was the only MacDonald sett given by Logan. But when we come to the Glengarry and Clanranald divisions of the Clan there is some confusion. The Clan tartan, with the addition of one white line, is now usually styled MACDONELL OF GLENGARRY (210). A similar pattern, (211), with two fine red lines removed, first appears in the *Vestiarium Scoticum*. It was there named Clanranald, and we have now adopted this name in preference to that of Glengarry used in our first edition. The latter name we consider to be a misnomer on the part of the Smiths, resulting from their specimen having been supplied by a Miss MacDonell of Glengarry, who seems not to have noticed the alteration from (210). Then there is the design in which the CLAN MACDONALD has the addition of two white lines; the Smiths, followed by James Grant, name this the CLANRANALD (212); it seems to be the design used by McIan for the kilt of his figure of a MacDonald of Glencoe. A further example is the GLENGARRY (217).

The MACKEANE, or MACIAN (252), stated by D. W. Stewart to appear in a portrait of Alstair Ruadh of Glengarry, is sometimes known as MACDONALD OF ARDNAMURCHAN, or MACDONALD OF GLENCOE. It was the McIan branch of Clan MacDonald who were massacred at Glencoe in 1692.

Raeburn's famous portrait of Col. Alastair MacDonell of Glengarry shows, none too clearly, a tartan that might be described as a blend of GLENGARRY (217) and OLD STEWART (401). Such, at least, is the impression it gives, though this may be due merely to Raeburn's carelessness in rendering the former tartan.

A quite distinctive tartan appears in the *Vestiarium* and in Smibert, called MAC DONALD OF THE ISLES (206), but it is doubtful if it is older than the former work. Though fine black lines are shown as being in the green band, they might alternatively, so far as the description in the text is concerned, have been put in the blue band.

Early last century there was manufactured, and given distinguished patronage, a tartan called by the Smiths MACDONALD OF SLEAT, LORD OF THE ISLES. In *Old and Rare Scottish Tartans* D. W. Stewart drew attention to the fact that this was a defective rendering of the tartan, MACDONALD (207) shown in a painting at Armadale Castle. In *The Costume of the Clans,* by the brothers John Sobieski and Charles Edward Stuart (1845) there is a representation of the figures from that painting; not only was the black line omitted, but the narrower stripes are rendered in blue instead of green. Several other plates in *The Costume of the Clans* show tartans attributed to the MacDonalds, but these cannot be accepted as authentic. Yet the presence of the black line in the Armadale portrait is no proof that it had always been included; extant specimens without the line show that its omission was customary about the beginning of the century, so that we cannot charge the brothers Stuart with having caused its exclusion.

Another Armadale Castle painting is the authority for the LORD OF THE ISLES: HUNTING (208), first brought to public notice by D. W. Stewart. This is unlike any other tartan, yet unmistakably a MacDonald.

Three designs are here given for MAC DONELL OF KEPPOCH. The first (213) was copied by D. W. Stewart from a relic of 'the '45', a plaid given by Keppoch to Prince Charles Edward. The same circumstantial story is told of a tartan (214) illustrated by McIan, of which our colour-strip is a fair rendering. Judging by the relics, many plaids must have been given to and received from the Prince by his admirers. One of these gifts from the Prince was bestowed on a member of Clan Robertson, and the design is numbered (434) in our list. It would seem that McIan, having heard and confused the two stories, mistakenly used this 'ROBERTSON' to illustrate his figure of a MacDonell of Keppoch. D. W. Stewart states that there were several variations on the scheme he gives, all attributed to the MacDonells of Keppoch, but the 'ROBERTSON' (434) differs too much to be properly classed as a variant of KEPPOCH (213); moreover, the Robertson legend is inconsistent with that told of Keppoch's gift. It is still possible that the 214–434 tartan had belonged to MacDonell of Keppoch but the only positive evidence for this is McIan's attribution which depends on the story related of the previous tartan. But for the existence of the ROBERTSON' fragment, we might have been tempted to assume that McIan's drawing was a poor rendering of the KEPPOCH (213) rather than a probably mistaken attribution of the 'ROBERTSON'.

Our third MACDONELL OF KEPPOCH (215), while supported by a considerable authority, so closely resembles the CLAN MACKINTOSH (260) as to lay the present attribution open to doubt. A composite MacDonell-Mackintosh tartan does not consist well with the long story of inter-clan strife.

The Smith work was the first to show the highly complex MAC DONALD OF STAFFA (205). James Grant gives for MAC DONALD OF STAFFA a very similar design, one now known to have been in production by the Wilsons of Bannockburn before 1820.

THE MACDONALD OF BOISDALE (216), a tartan hitherto not illustrated, is represented among the early collections. The MacDonald motif here takes an unfamiliar form, in red on a blue ground, with white lines interposed. James Logan, discussing the Clanranald tartan, adds: 'MacDonald of Boisdale has a family tartan of a red pattern, with several colours agreeably varied'. The pattern, though in no way odd, is quite distinctive.

Our final MacDonald tartan (218) carries an interesting story. It is taken from the only remaining fragment of a waistcoat that had been given by MacDonald of Kingsburgh to the fugitive Prince Charles Edward during his wanderings after Culloden. Too bright for his purpose, the latter exchanged it with one Malcolm MacLeod. MacLeod, before his capture by the Government forces, hid the waistcoat in the cleft of a rock. Released more than a year later, he returned to search for it, and found that only a small portion had survived undamaged by exposure. This precious relic eventually came into the possession of the Advocates' Library, Edinburgh.

There is little to be added to the original commentary but it should be noted that there is a Lyon Court record of the MacDonald of Clanranald tartan (212) for which the count is as follows:

B	R	B	R	B	R	K	W	G	R	G	R	G
12	4	4	6	24	4	22	4	22	6	4	4	12

In the original fragment of the MacDonald of Kingsburgh tartan, preserved in the back cover of the manuscript of Bishop Forbes' *Lyon in Mourning*, the colours are much darker than those shown by D. W. Stewart (and copied ever since) being approximately deep rose red and dark bottle green. An error such as this — and others may be suspected — can only throw doubt on all D.W.S.' claims for accuracy in his matching of colours.

We have seen that it was normal for weavers to copy one from another with small variations and in the light of this knowledge need not be surprised that No. 215 bears so close a resemblance to Mackintosh. The version given by Bain and by the Johnston two-volume work of 1906 has a line of two threads of light blue between B12 and R48.

The Key Pattern Book gives a plaid pattern entitled "Donald of Staffa's Sett" (219) which is somewhat more elaborate than No. 205; it is for the 600 reed and has two half setts to the width of 25 inches.

A pattern (221) somewhat similar to No. 210 and named MacDonell of Keppoch is taken from a plaid, claimed to be from the 17th century, at the West Highland Museum, Fort William. Other relics to be found there are part of a plaid belonging to Flora MacDonald (226) and a fragment found in Glencoe (222). In this, the colour marked with an asterisk has been interpreted as pink or old gold, while the light blue line has been given alternatively as white. Some of the old dyes did bleed into adjoining stripes and there are numerous complaints from regimental quartermasters about this occurring in diced hose, and it is probable that all these fine lines were originally white.

J. G. Mackay (*The Romantic Story of the Highland Garb and the Tartan*) claims antiquity for the red Clanranald tartan (220) which certainly has the quality of simplicity.

'Flora MacDonald' (227) is but a named fancy pattern which came from Wilsons' about 1847.

In or about 1772 Alexander MacDonald of Glenaladale and his son,

Capt. John, emigrated to Canada and portions of plaids taken with them have survived in Prince Edward Island. No. 223 is said to have been worn by Alexander at the time of Culloden and the other, (224) attributed to Capt. John, is clearly related. The "GLENFINNAN" tartan (225) also called MACDONALD OF GLENALADALE and originally used by the National Trust for Scotland at its Glenfinnan Centre may have been derived from either of these but it has somehow become a non-reversing sett in the process.

228-233 MACDOUGAL

(228)	**Az**	Cr	R	G	R	G	R	B	Cr	R	Cr	G	R	G	R	B	R
	2	24	8	144	16	8	16	36	24	8	24	36	36	36	16	8	144
	Cr	R	**Az**														
	12	8	2														
(229)	**Bk**	R	G	R	G	R	B	R	W	R	W	R	G	R	G	R	Bk
	2	8	16	4	2	4	8	4	2	2	2	4	8	6	8	2	2
	R	W	R	?													
	16	2	?														
(230)	**Az**	Cr	W	R	G	R	G	R	B	Cr	W	R	W	Cr	G	R	G
	2	4	2	2	12	4	2	4	6	4	2	2	2	4	6	6	6
	R	B	R	Cr	W	R	**Az**										
	2	2	12	4	2	4	2										
(231)	P	G	B	P	R	G	R	G	R	G	**R**						
	8	16	12	16	12	4	4	4	48	2	6						
(232)	A	C	R	G	R	G	R	P	C	R	C	G	R	G	R	P	**R**
	2	12	8	50	10	6	10	24	16	6	16	24	24	24	6	6	60
(233)	C	R	G	R	G	R	B	C	R	C	G	R	G	R	G	R	C
	4	4	72	8	4	8	24	12	4	12	24	24	24	4	2	72	8

Though Logan gave a MacDougal design in 1831, the manufacturers seem to have remained in doubt about the details of this tartan (228); yet the general scheme remains much as Logan set it out. Logan's count is defective in that it begins at an odd part of the design, but this does not account for the variation. In our count, we have followed an early specimen, but for most purposes this will require modification.

The Smibert version (229) has no crimson, and white or pale blue lines have been introduced. The Smiths use crimson, and show still more white lines (229). James Grant's version seems to follow the Smith, though the white lines become light blue. Unfortunately, neither in the Smith nor in the

Smibert plates is sufficient of the pattern shown to make the repeat quite explicit, and in the latter case we have left off where Smibert did.

The *Vestiarium Scoticum* gives a quite different design (231); the plate differs considerably from the text in the matter of colour, and we have followed the text.

Wilsons' 'MACDOUGALL TARTAN' is generally similar to No. 230 but has pink in place of white, rose instead of crimson and purple for blue (see Appendix F). A specimen (232) found in the Queen Street museum in Edinburgh follows No. 228 but the main red area is approximately halved and the rose and light blue lines at the pivot are omitted. Logan's count is given (233) for comparison with these two (see Appendix F).

234-236 MACDUFF

(234)	**R**	Bk	R	G	Bk	Az	**R**
	8	2	8	12	8	6	16

(235)	**R**	Bk	R	Bk	B	G	**R**
	8	4	48	12	12	32	6

Though the MacDuffs, Earls of Fife, have always played a prominent part in Scottish affairs, the Clan MacDuff was not conspicuous in the more recent periods of clan history.

It will be observed that the MacDuff tartan, first recorded by Logan (234), is substantially the ROYAL STUART with the white and yellow lines removed. Whether this indicates it as the source of the STUART, or represents a more recent reminder of the early and prolonged association of the Earls of Fife with the Crown, remains to be determined. Some early specimens employ a dark blue.

The MacDuff tartan (235) appearing in the *Vestiarium Scoticum* contains the same elements, but rearranged. There is a modern Hunting design, based on Logan's, but with brown for red. A simple setting for this would be:

(236)	**Brown**	R	Br	G	Bk	B	Br	**R**
	16	2	16	16	16	16	16	4

237 MACEWEN

Y/R	Bk	G	Bk	B	Bk	**B**
4	2	24	24	24	2	4

By the sixteenth century the MacEwens were a broken clan, absorbed or scattered by the Campbells. The tartan resembles the CAMPBELL OF LOUDOUN (59), with the difference that the white line of the latter is, in the MACEWEN, red.

238, 239 MACFARLANE

(238)	**R**	Bk	G	W	R	Bk	R	W	G	P	Bk	R	W	**G**
	84	2	24	4	6	2	6	4	4	24	8	6	8	6

(239)	**Bk**	W	Bk	**W**
	14	12	2	12

Broken as a clan centuries ago, and dispersed from their lands about Arrochar, it is unlikely that the MacFarlanes would have retained so complex a tartan (238) as now bears their name from any very early date. Logan lists the design, and it is reproduced with slight modifications by Smibert and the Smiths. It has a remarkable likeness to the MACPHERSON (297) shown by the Smiths, but there was no connection between the clans.

The *Vestiarium Scoticum* contains a design (239) as simple as the other is variegated. In one early collection the only tartan under this name is that now known as the MENZIES (331).

Early Wilson counts specify purple or light purple where blue is now used; light purple is likely to have been an intermediate shade between the zinc grey of the Mackintosh tartan (page 129) and full purple which was made from indigo with a touch of madder. The hunting tartan changes the main red area to green. The count (238) for the red tartan was registered at the Lyon court in 1957. Its resemblance to No. 292 is more than skin deep; change blue to purple, yellow to white and white to green and, except for the overcheck on the red ground, No. 238 becomes No. 297.

240 MACGILLIVRAY

R	Az	B	R	Az	R	B	R	G	R	Az	R	**B**
8	2	2	64	4	4	24	4	32	8	2	8	4

A characteristic Clan Chattan tartan. The MacGillivrays were strong not only in Strathnairn, but also in Morvern, and the light blue lines are found in many designs of these and intervening territories. Logan and the Smiths both give this tartan, but Logan's count, as so often, produced a rather attenuated sett, and the Smith proportions have been used for our illustration.

241-242 MACGREGOR

(241)	**R**	G	R	G	Bk	**W**	(242) **R** = **Bk**
	72	36	8	12	2	4	

From Logan onwards there is little variation in the MacGregor as shown in works on tartan; the *Vestiarium Scoticum,* differing as usual, omits the black lines, but the difference is a small one.

In a footnote dealing with the Rob Roy (242) (Plate 11 (a)), D. W. Stewart writes:

> Why the simple red and black check receives the title of Rob Roy is something of a mystery. In *Authenticated Tartans of the Clans and Families of Scotland* (Smith: Mauchline, 1850), it is asserted, and the statement is repeated in *The Tartans of the Clans of Scotland* (W. & A. K. Johnston: Edinburgh, 1886) without attempt at verification, that three genuine portraits of Rob Roy represent him as wearing it; but these and other so-called Rob Roy portraits — be their value what it may — afford no sanction whatever for the design. The Editor is not aware on what authority the portraits are classed as Rob Roy. He has seen seven paintings, including the three above referred to, in which the figure is identical, all known as Rob Roy, and in each a separate pattern appears, none of them showing the simple red and black check. The tartan is accepted by sound authorities as the old MacGregor clan pattern. There are fine examples of it in a collection of tartans made by the Highland Society of London in 1816-17, labelled and sealed 'The MacGregor Tartan for undress ordinary clothing. The Seal of Arms of Sir John MacGregor Murray of MacGregor, Baronet. *(Signed)* John M. Murray'.

Nevertheless, in another collection made at the same period both the Rob Roy and the MacGregor (241) appear, and under these names. The latter may have been regarded as a Dress tartan, of relatively recent adoption.

The *Vestiarium*, while illustrating only the MacGregor (241) speaks of two others; one, as used by the MacGregors of Glen Strae, which lacked the white stripe but had a green stripe centred on the red ground; and one, used about Balquhidder, which had its only white stripe in the position of the green of the Glen Strae variant.

Considering the history of the Clan MacGregor, it would be surprising to find that any authentic early tartan of the clan had survived. The Rob Roy is the most primitive of all tartans; yet it may be for that reason that the pattern was adopted at a comparatively late date to replace a disused earlier clan pattern. Whatever its origin in respect of the MacGregors, it is the oldest pattern we know the MacGregors to have used.

In the Sobieski work, *The Costume of the Clans*, three figures from alleged portraits of Rob Roy are shown, wearing tartans not now in circulation. In the third of these the hose alone are of tartan, the kilt and plaid being a solid scarlet. We can only remark that Rob Roy himself tempered his audacity with a measure of discretion.

No. 241 appears in the Key Pattern Book under the name of 'MacGregor Murray tartan' and seems not to have become 'MacGregor' until Sir John himself re-adopted the old name.

243, 244 MACINROY

(243)	**W**	G	R	B	R	B	R	K	G	**K**
	8	8	68	8	8	68	8	36	68	12

(244)	**B**	G	B	G	B	G	K	R	G	R	G	**R**
	20	2	4	6	32	2	32	32	6	4	2	20

The MacInroys are near neighbours to the Robertsons so it is but to be expected that the MacInroy of Lude tartan (243) should have some points in common with the Robertson. It dates from about 1825. In 1826 Adriana MacInroy of Lude married General Sir John MacDonald of Dalchosnie and Dunalastair; it is possible that the sett (244) taken from the manuscript copy of the Smith brothers' book, celebrates this union. The sett is MacDonald with red and green reversed.

245-248 MACINTYRE and GLENORCHY

(245)	**Bk**	G	R	B	R	G	R	Az	B	R	G	R	Bk	**G**
	4	4	6	36	4	12	8	2	12	6	36	6	4	4

(246)	**Az**	R	G	R	B	R	G	R	B	R	G	R	B	R	**Az**
	2	4	4	8	32	4	2	8	2	4	32	8	4	4	2

(247)	**W**	G	B	R	B	**G**
	8	64	24	6	24	8

D. W. Stewart writes of the GLENORCHY (245):

> Wherever authentic records of tartans are preserved this design appears, generally as MacIntyre and Glenorchy, though occasionally as Glenorchy alone. It seems to have partaken of the nature of a district tartan, for the locality whence the title is taken was only partly occupied by the MacIntyres, who appear never to have attained the strength of a clan. No MacIntyre arms are matriculated in the Lyon Register. They are found, however, in Burke's *General Armoury*, and the individual contributing them evidently regarded his family as a sept of the MacDonalds. The pattern in the illustration occurs in the collection of the Highland Society of London (1822), and in reproductions made in Edinburgh about 1820 from examples of ancient designs procured in the Highlands near that time. In a collection formed in 1790 there is a scheme differing very slightly from the present illustration.

The tartan shown by the Smiths as MACINTYRE (246) (they say they had some difficulty in obtaining a specimen) is clearly related to our first design, though differing in detail. This is now known as MacIntyre of Whitehouse. The third (247) is from the *Vestiarium Scoticum*, and has gained currency as the MacIntyre tartan, being reproduced as such by James Grant and several later editors.

McIan's figure of a MacIntyre wears a plain purple kilt, the explanation given being that James Boswell observed a MacLeod so clad during his visit to Skye in 1773.

A variant of the Glenorchy design, very similar in quality but more extended in the repeat, is the following, found in one of the early nineteenth century collections, where it is described as 'Cumming, Glenorchy':

(248)	**G**	R	B	Az	R	G	R	B	R	B	Az	R	B	R	G	R	Az
	66	6	24	2	16	24	6	40	6	6	2	6	40	6	24	16	2
	B	R	G	R	**B**												
	24	6	44	6	6												

Shortened versions of this have recently been woven, but the full sett is worth preserving where the web can be wide enough and the repeats are sufficient in number to show its individual character. The attribution to the Cummings is a questionable one, though Smibert adopted it.

The count (247) was registered at the Lyon Court in 1955. With the green pivot changed to yellow, this tartan is sometimes known as Inglis.

249 MACIVER

W/Y	R	Bk	R	**Bk**
2	24	4	4	32

The lands of the MacIvers and the MacArthurs were on opposite shores of Loch Fyne, and their tartans differ mainly in the colour of the ground; the MacIver is a Dress and the MacArthur a Hunting version of the same pattern.

The similarity of the pattern to the basic red MacDonald (207), and the absence of any other such pattern in the Campbell country, lead us to look for contacts with the MacDonalds, but without much success. While those who remained in the Campbell country were absorbed by the Campbells, and took their name, others seem to have migrated northwards, settling in Lochaber, Glenelg, Wester Ross and Lewis, retaining the name of MacIver. There is little evidence to account for the tartan, and it may be of comparatively recent adoption. McIan shows for MacIver a figure clad in the Leine-chroich, or Saffron Shirt.

250, 251 MACKAY

(250)	**Bk**	G	Bk	G	Corbeau	**G**
	6	28	28	4	28	6

(251)	**R**	B	Bk	B	Bk	**B**
	2	32	12	4	12	4

The tartan of the MacKays (250) resembles that of their neighbours the Gunns (148), but the line centred on the ground is black, not red. The inner stripes of the design are often rendered in blue; but Logan, in his list, carefully described the colour as 'corbeau', defined by the *O.E.D.* as a very dark green, verging on black.

The *Vestiarium Scoticum* scheme (251) is the same, but the colours differ.

The colour that Logan describes as 'corbeau' is specified by Wilsons' to be purple. The pattern known as MACKAY OF STRATHNAVER derives from a plaid said to have been taken to Canada at the time of the Sutherland Clearances. It is a complex sett comprising squares of colours separated by fine red lines, the colours in order of appearance being Green, Black, Dark grey, Mid-grey, Brown, Light brown, Fawn, Cream, Light brown, Brown, Mid-grey, Dark grey, Black and Green. The pattern reverses about the green stripes and a representative count is 38 threads to the large squares and 2 to the red lines.

252 MACKEANE or MACIAN

Y	Bk	R	Bk	R	Bk	**R**
4	2	24	16	8	16	8

Concerning this tartan D. W. Stewart has a note of especial interest. He writes:

> The *Vestiarium Scoticum*, already acknowledged as the earliest and the most elaborate illustrated publication on tartan designs, was edited by the late John Sobieski Stuart from a MS. stated to belong to the sixteenth century. The MS. was printed and published in 1842, with plates executed from drawings by Charles Edward Stuart, the editor's brother. Of course the drawings are but a development of the descriptions in the MS. It need scarcely be added that the volume is now rare and costly. The MS. was transcribed and illuminated in 1829 by Sir Thomas Dick Lauder, for whom Charles Edward Stuart prepared a series of drawings which included several tartans not illustrated in the published work. One of these is here reproduced, and Sir Richard Urquhart, Knycht, the reputed author of the MS., thus describes it: 'Mackeane hethe four stryppes of Blak upon ain scarlett feilde, and upon the scarlett sett ain spraig (sprainge) of yellow of saxteen threidis, havand thereto ain bordure of Blak of twa threidis'. The Maclans, whose name is variously spelt in the early clan rolls and elsewhere as M'Kane, McCoin, MacNoin, Clanayioun, &c., were a branch of the Clan MacDonald. That the use of the design was not confined to this branch is evidenced by a contemporary portrait of Alastair Ruadh of Glengarry (who was prominent in the '45), in which he is depicted in this tartan.

This and the MacQueen tartan (306) are obviously reversals one of the other. Although the MacQueens claim Sweyn as the founder of their name, the two names have nearly a score of spellings between them, and it is not always clear at sight to which clan these spellings refer. From the fifteenth century the MacQueens came to prominence as a sept of Clan Chattan, and were signatory to the Bond of 1690; but both they and the MacKeanes derived from the MacDonalds.

In view of the number of other tartans in the *Vestiarium* which have the same scheme, one is tempted to wonder whether the correspondence of this one to the portrait of Alastair Ruadh is anything more than a fortunate coincidence. The tartan is sometimes known as MacDonald of Ardnamurchan, or MacDonald of Glencoe.

253 MACKELLAR

G	W	G	Y	G	W	G	K	A	B	**W**
64	4	4	6	4	4	4	32	4	32	6

MacKellar is an Argyllshire name and one might expect a less elaborate version of the blue, black and green tartan common in the Campbell country. Its origin is unknown to me.

254-256 MACKENZIE

(254)	**B**	Bk	B	Bk	B	Bk	G	Bk	W	Bk	G	Bk	B	Bk	**R**
	24	4	4	4	4	24	24	2	4	2	24	24	24	2	4

(255)	**B**	Bk	B	Bk	B	Bk	G	W/R	G	Bk	B	Bk	**B**
	36	4	4	4	4	12	36	4	36	12	36	2	8

(256)	**B**	R	W	R	W	K	G	K	W	K	G	K	B	K	**R**
	36	6	6	6	6	38	36	4	6	4	36	38	34	4	6

The regimental tartan of the Seaforth Highlanders, who were raised in 1778 by MacKenzie, Earl of Seaforth, has the same scheme as the Athol Murray (348), the difference being that the outer of the three red stripes of the latter are, in the MacKenzie, white. The design (255) given in the *Vestiarium Scoticum*, also based on the Black Watch, differs in the distribution of the red and white lines.

What tartan the MacKenzies may have worn prior to 1778 we do not know; very possibly it was a red one.

No. 256 appears in the already mentioned manuscript note book as "71st Regt., Drummers' Plaids"; MacGregor Hastie states it to have been used by pipers and drummers. The colour strip is shown at Plate 4 (j).

It is probably not widely known that *c.*1827 the regimental children of the 78th depot were dressed in tartan the boys in 78th tartan with hose of medium-size Rob Roy and the girls in frocks of Wilsons' No. 248 which is not listed in the Key Pattern Book.

Stewart refers to a possible red MacKenzie tartan. I regard this as *probable*; it *ought* to bear a noticeable likeness to Ross or MacRae.

257 MACKINLAY

B	Bk	B	Bk	G	Bk	R	Bk	G	Bk	B	Bk	B	Bk	**B**
4	4	16	12	16	2	4	2	16	12	4	4	4	4	12

This tartan is almost identical with that given by Logan for Murray (347) but the resemblance is without significance. The tartan is probably of recent adoption.

258, 259 MACKINNON

(258)	**W**	R	P	G	R	G	B	R	G	R	B	G	R	**P**
	4	8	4	16	32	4	8	4	32	12	4	4	6	4

(259)	**Bk**	R	G	R	G	R	**W**
	2	36	24	4	24	36	2

The designs given in successive works on tartan exemplify some of the changes to which tartans have been subject, despite efforts to stabilise them. In Logan's count there is a group of three white lines and one isolated white line. This single line, and the two outer lines of the group, become, in Smibert, pink; in the Smith version, crimson; and James Grant makes them black, which is the rendering adopted in most of the recent works. Smibert's pink lines have the appearance of an attempted erasure, as if they were intended to be white. When we turn to Mclan's drawing we find the outer lines of the triple group are black, but the isolated line remains white. Thus we have five versions in five important works. Examination of a specimen dating from before Logan's time shows these variable lines to have been then a light shade of blue. The Clan tartan now worn by MacKinnons, as authorised by the Chief, has these light blue lines rendered in purple.

The *Vestiarium Scoticum* gives an altogether different tartan (259). The modern Hunting MacKinnon is based on this; it consists of equal broad bands of green and of brown; single green and white lines are centred on the alternate brown bands, and a red line on each green band.

Both the authorized sett and the hunting tartan were registered at the Lyon Court in 1960.

260-264 MACKINTOSH

(260)	**R**	B	R	G	R	**B**
	48	12	6	24	8	2

(261)	**R**	Bk	W	G	W	Y	R	Bk	R	Y	W	Az	Bk	R	Y	**W**
	48	2	2	12	2	4	4	2	4	4	2	12	4	6	6	2

(262)	**R**	W	R	Bk	G	**R**	
	10	4	56	24	32	6	
(263)	Y	G	B	R	G	R	**B**
	4	24	12	6	24	8	2
(264)	**R**	LG	R	LG	R	LG	**W**
	2	28	2	2	28	2	2

This (260) (Plate 12 (b)) is one of the few ancient tartans too well authenticated to admit of doubt or question. True, the *Vestiarium Scoticum* offers an alternative (262), but it is not acceptable as such.

Logan writes, in *The Scottish Gaël*: 'The chief also wears a particular tartan of a very showy pattern', and the Smiths illustrate it, claiming that it had been in use for many generations (261) (Plate 15 (c)). This is now alternatively known as Clan Chattan (Plate 12 (f)); and, with a white line on the red ground, as Clan Chattan Chief. The simple Clan pattern is the basis of many other tartans, all more or less associated with Clan Chattan. What is also possibly a Mackintosh tartan (432) is shown later.

The Hunting Mackintosh (263) is a recent arrangement.

Logan's 'showy' pattern was acknowledged by the then Chief, Sir Aeneas Mackintosh (describing himself as 'of that Ilk' instead of the more usual 'of MacKintosh') as the Clan tartan in 1816. Wilsons' made either version without distinction as "Mackintosh tartan" and it was not until 1947 that these were registered at the Lyon Court as Clan Chattan and Clan Chattan (Chief). At that time the counts were being recorded in the old one-eighth inch units and ran, for the Chief's tartan, $\frac{1}{2}$W, 15R, 1B, $\frac{1}{2}$W, 8G, 1W, $1\frac{3}{4}$Y, $1\frac{3}{4}$R, $\frac{1}{2}$B, $1\frac{3}{4}$R, $1\frac{3}{4}$Y, 1W, 8Az, 2B, 2R, 3Y, 1W, and for the Clan tartan $30\frac{1}{2}$R, 1B, $\frac{1}{2}$W, 8G, 1W, $1\frac{3}{4}$Y, $1\frac{3}{4}$R, $\frac{1}{2}$B, $1\frac{3}{4}$R, $1\frac{3}{4}$Y, 1W, 8Az, 2B, 2R, 3Y, 1W. In this instance 'B' signifies Black and 'G' Green and the patterns repeat in reverse, the end stripes having to be doubled.

The Wilson version uses a purplish grey instead of light blue (light purple in one later count) and first appears, without the white overcheck on red, under "Superfine Tartan Patterns" in the Key Pattern Book.

Two counts are given (for six half setts, 25 inches wide for the 600 reed) and are worth quoting in full.

		New method
Scarlet	90	94
Black	6	6
White	4	4
Green	40	42
White	4	6

Yellow worsted	4	—
Yellow silk	6	6
Scarlet	10	10
Black	4	4
Scarlet	10	10
Yellow silk	6	6
Yellow worsted	4	—
White	4	6
Gray	40	42
Black	14	14
Scarlet	14	14
Yellow silk	16	16
Yellow worsted	4	—
White	4	4
	284	284

These are centre-to-centre counts and in setting up the loom the pivotal stripes are doubled.

A relic of Culloden (264) is preserved in the Provost MacBean collection in Inverness Museum. The green is very pale and the red a rose shade.

The Mackintosh recounts the story told to him that the hunting tartan was invented between the wars by a manufacturer wanting a 'softer' looking Mackintosh tartan than that produced by the rather harsh colours of the day. The Chief's wife, seeing it on sale in Inverness, thought it looked terrible and should be suppressed, so she bought the entire stock but this, unfortunately, only stimulated production and by 1948 so many Mackintoshes were wearing it that the present Chief's father legitimised the tartan by registering it at the Lyon Court.

265-267 MACLACHLAN

(265)	Y	W	Bk	G	Y	W	**R**						
	6	4	32	32	6	4	48						
(266)	**R**	Bk	R	Bk	R	Bk	B	G	B	Bk	R	Bk	**R**
	32	4	4	4	4	32	32	6	32	32	32	4	4
(267)	Y	Bk	Y	Bk	Y	Bk	Y	**Bk**					
	12	4	48	12	4	42	4	12					

When illustrating our first design, D.W. Stewart wrote;

> The accompanying tartan is one of two ancient designs bearing the same name. It figures in all the collections formed in the early years of the [nineteenth] century, and

an excellent example (the precise date of which, however, is unknown) has been procured from Messrs Romanes and Paterson. The other design, to be found in a collection made in 1790, is shown in an ancient piece of hard tartan with a simple check in red and green about five-eighths of an inch square in the Editor's possession. In the *Vestiarium Scoticum* the MacLachlan is depicted as a brilliant combination of yellow and black, being the sett in use by the present McLachlan of MacLachlan. The clan generally use a red and dark blue design, which cannot be traced further back than 1850 to the Smiths' and Smilbert's works. The existence of the tartan illustrated appears to have been generally overlooked by the clan, a fact greatly to be regretted, as it is one of the finest of the old clan setts. That the illustration represents an early and authentic clan pattern of the MacLachlan cannot be doubted, for it is the only example occurring under that name in the collections of the Highland Society, the Campbells of Craignish, The Mackintosh of Mackintosh, and many others ...

The tartan described as first known in 1850 is to be found in Logan's work of 1831, and what is presumably intended for the same appears in McIan's drawing. It would thus seem that the tartan (266) was in use nearly a generation earlier than D.W. Stewart supposed.

268 MACLAREN

B	Bk	G	R	G	Bk	Y
48	16	16	4	16	2	4

The MacLaren differs from the Ferguson (117) only in having a yellow line where the latter has a white. They share the unusual feature of an unbroken band of blue.

The present tartan appears under this name in McIan's plate for Clan MacLaren. The Wilsons of Bannockburn were producing it before 1820 — but only under the name of 'Regent'. The Regency ended when George IV succeeded to the throne in that year, the name of the tartan then becoming outdated; but production of the sett continued, as we know from specimens attached to customers' orders for more. Writers of the period tell us that the demand around 1822 for Clan tartans exceeded the authentic supply, and that not only were new setts invented but pre-existing ones acquired new names. Our present tartan may have been one of the latter; no older MacLaren has come to light.

The sett is usually seen with the red lines central on the green, and they are so in a specimen sent to the Wilsons with an order dated 1821. Yet the Wilsons' own count shows these lines displaced outwards from the centre, and they are so in a specimen of 1822. This displacement may have continued up to James Grant's time, for his plate shows it; but, strangely enough, it appears only in one way of the tartan, leaving us in doubt which form he intended to represent, since it could hardly be both.

269, 270 MACLAINE OF LOCHBUIE

(269) **R** G Az **Y**
64 16 8 2

(270) **B** R **B** Bk **Y**
64 6 8 2 6

The Hunting tartan (270) is modern, but the other dates at latest from the eighteenth century, and is found in many early collections. It was first published in James Grant's work, in 1886. D. W. Stewart points out that the use of so much light blue is unique among old tartans.

271, 272 MACLEAN OF DUART

(271) **Bk** R Az R G Bk W Bk Y Bk Az **B**
2 4 2 24 16 2 2 2 2 6 2 8

(272) **Bk** G Bk G Bk W Bk G
2 32 4 4 12 2 12 6

The version given by Logan and by Smibert has an undifferentiated light blue band at the centre of the design, but the Smiths reject this as an innovation, and show a band of dark blue flanked by light blue lines (271). It is the latter form that is now in general use.

The Key Pattern Book allows the alternatives of plain light blue and either grey or 'drab' with light blue edging at the centre of the pattern.

Comparison of the MacLean with the Royal Stuart (405) reveals that the one is an inversion of the other. The succession of colour is the same in order, and much the same in proportion, in the two tartans, but the direction has been reversed. The triple arrangement of lines, in black, white, black, at the centre of the Stuart, has been moved to the centre of the red ground, where they are rendered as light blue, black, light blue. So close is the association that we find Logan's count for the MacLean differs from the more modern rendering of the widths of the yellow and white lines in the same way as his count for the Royal Stuart does — the outer white lines are much wider than the near-by yellow lines. This peculiarity is also found in the Smith version of the Prince Charles Edward (407). This MacLean tartan was at one time worn by many of the name of Wallace.

Much has been made of the documentary evidence for the antiquity of the Hunting MacLean (272). While this establishes the production by MacLeans of cloth, white black and green in colour, as early as the sixteenth century, there is nothing in that evidence to indicate the nature of the design, supposing the three colours to have been woven together into a tartan. This last point, the weaving of a tartan in these colours, is claimed proved by the existence of this HUNTING MACLEAN tartan. Unfortunately, the first appearance of the design was in the *Vestiarium Scoticum*, where the documentary evidence referred to was also first quoted. It is open to suspicion that the tartan was invented to fit the evidence, and that the evidence was then produced to support the tartan. Whatever the truth may be, the documentary evidence, while certainly supporting the claim to antiquity made for the tartan, equally certainly does not establish it. It would indeed be wonderful to have an unquestionable clan or district tartan of as early a date as 1587. For that very reason we would require more and better evidence than the present case affords.

MACLENNAN — see LOGAN

273-275 MACLEOD

(273)	**R**	Bk	G	Bk	B	Bk	**Y**		
	6	4	30	20	40	4	4		
(274)	**R**	Y	Bk	Y	**Bk**				
	2	24	16	2	16				
(275)	**K**	Y	K	R	K	Y	R	Y	**K**
	2	4	8	2	8	4	2	24	2

This design (273) (Plate 12 (a)) appears in early collections, and it was recorded by Logan and by Smibert; yet, according to the Smiths, the correct tartan of the MacLeods was the MACKENZIE (254). Logan, writing for the McIan work, was aware of this widely held opinion, and, while explaining it, also deplored it. The present tartan has now returned to favour.

The tartans shown for the first time in the *Vestiarium Scoticum* do not display great originality of design, but many of them show courage in the choice of colour. This well-known example (274) is mentioned by Sir Thomas Dick Lauder in a letter written to Sir Walter Scott in 1829: 'MacLeod has got a sketch of his splendid tartan, "three black stryps upon ain yellow fylde," &c' (Plate 11 (d)). This sketch was supplied by one of the brothers Hay, or Stuart, who were responsible for the *Vestiarium*, several years before publication, MacLeod being one of their 'particular friends'. No prior record of this tartan exists. A contemptuous critic of the *Vestiarium* has likened the design to that of a horse-blanket.

I do not regard the resemblance between the dark MacLeod tartan and that of Lord Loudoun's Highlanders as being entirely fortuitous. Loudoun's was a largely MacLeod regiment and MacLeod's piper, Donald Ban MacCrimmon, was the only casualty of the Rout of Moy. When Clan tartans became fashionable it would have been but natural for MacLeods to take the regimental tartan and reverse the overchecks.

There are two black and red versions of the *Vestiarium* sett which may have been inspired by the portrait of Norman MacLeod. One has the straightforward change of red for yellow, with a black overcheck on the (now) red ground and the other has black for yellow and red for black, the red overcheck remaining on the black square. A much more plausible yellow tartan appears in another Dunvegan portrait, that of John Norman, 24th Chief, who is pictured holding what seems to be a snuff-box of Mauchline ware. Ruairidh MacLeod extracted the sett (275) from this in 1977. It may be an alternative Sobieski confection or the inspiration for the *Vestiarium* design; it is certainly the more convincing of the two.

276-278 MACMILLAN

(276)	**R**	Y	R	Y	R	Y	R	Y	**R**			
	2	16	4	16	6	4	24	2	6			
(277)	**R**	G	R	G	Bk	Y	Bk	B	Y	**B**		
	2	16	4	16	8	4	8	24	2	6		
(278)	G	K	G	K	G	K	C	G	Y	K	Y	K
	4	2	36	2	4	2	24	8	12	2	12	2

The scheme of the red and yellow MACMILLAN (276) is the same as that of the WEMYSS (423), and similar to that of the HUNTING MACLEAN (272), though the fact may not at first be obvious; these two first appear in the *Vestiarium Scoticum*.

There is a tartan sometimes called the MACMILLAN ANCIENT (278). This resembles the BUCHANAN (40), and derives from one of McIan's drawings; but as in the McIan-Logan work the MacMillan tartan is stated to be identical with the BUCHANAN, the making of a distinction between the two is pointless.

The modern Hunting tartan (277) results from the super-imposition of red and yellow lines from the red-yellow design (276) on the conventional blue, black, and green basis of so many of the dark tartans. The device is ingenious and the result satisfactory.

279-281 MACNAB

(279)	G	Cr	G	Cr	G	Cr	R	Cr	R	Cr	G	Cr	**G**
	16	2	2	2	2	12	16	2	16	12	14	2	2
(280)	**Cr**	G	Az	G	**R**								
	48	2	2	4	48								
(281)	**Bk**	R	Cr	G	Cr	R	**G**						
	2	24	4	8	4	4	12						

The structure of the usual MacNab tartan (279) is identical with that of the

Black Watch (20); but, by a translation of colours, the most subdued of tartans becomes one of the most striking. The colour changes are: black to crimson, blue to green, and green to scarlet. Inspection through a green filter reveals the Black Watch structure very clearly. Logan records the pattern. The design (280) given by Smibert and the Smiths (the latter saying that it was made for the then Chief), is to be found in the hose worn by the figure in Mclan's drawing, where it is included as being 'of an old pattern, reckoned appropriate to this clan'.

The *Vestiarium Scoticum* contains yet a third design (281); all three are remarkable for their extensive use of a combination of crimson and scarlet.

Wilsons' regarded No. 280 as the genuine MacNab tartan and this was the pattern that they supplied to James Logan.

282 MACNAUGHTON

Bk	Az	R	Az	Bk	G	R	Az	**Bk**
2	2	32	16	24	32	32	2	2

The MacNaughton tartan closely resembles the MacDuff (234), but the resemblance has no apparent significance.

The fine lines are the subject of a curious error, which may have originated in one of Mclan's drawings. Logan and the Smiths record the design correctly: Smibert has a slight error; but in Grant's illustration these lines are shown correctly only in one way of the tartan, the other having a plain azure stripe. At least four subsequent books reproduce this oddity, which cannot possibly be correct. The slavish copying of obvious error vitiates much of the literature of the tartans.

Wilsons' made this pattern with Black/Blue/Black pivots (instead of Blue/Black/Blue as above) under the name 'Montrose'.

283-287 MACNEIL

(283)	**Y**	Bk	G	Bk	B	R	**W**
	2	6	30	28	32	4	2
(284)	**Y**	Bk	G	Bk	B	**W**	
	6	4	24	24	28	6	
(285)	**Y**	Bk	G	Bk	Smalt	**W**	
	2	10	24	24	24	2	
(286)	**Bk**	B	Bk	G	W	G	**B**
	4	12	12	12	2	12	8

(287)	**W**	G	Bk	G	B	G	B	R	**B**
	8	4	2	48	12	12	40	2	12

An unfamiliar design (283) for MacNeil is given by D.W. Stewart in *Old and Rare Scottish Tartans*, where he describes it as the oldest of several known Clan MacNeil tartans. The usual pattern (284) is a modification of that recorded by Logan (285), which is notable for the massive black enclosure of the yellow line, as in our first sett. Where we have blue, Logan describes the colour as 'smalt'. The fourth arrangement (286) is known as the MacNeil of Colonsay; it is probably of later date than the previous tartans.

The *Vestiarium Scoticum* provides a pattern (287) that has not been generally adopted (see Blairlogie).

288-293 MACNICOL or NICOLSON

(288)	**R**	G	R	Bk	R	Az	R	G	R	Bk	R	**G**
	12	2	12	8	2	2	2	16	12	2	12	2

(289)	**G**	R	G	R	K	B	K	R	G	R	**K**
	4	16	24	4	8	2	16	16	4	16	4

(290)	**R**	G	R	K	B	K	R	G	R	K	**R**
	32	8	32	32	4	12	8	60	32	8	24

(291)	**K**	R	G	R	G	R	K	A	K	R	G	R	**K**
	4	16	4	16	28	4	12	2	14	16	4	16	4

(292)	G	R	K	A	K	R	G	R	K	R	G	R
	20	2	8	2	10	12	3	12	2	12	3	12

(293)	**B**	K	G	K	G	K	B	R	K	R	G	K	Y	K	W	K	**G**
	20	4	4	4	4	4	16	10	18	10	20	4	4	4	4	4	20

The figure McIan supplies for MacNicol is that of a woman wearing a small tartan shawl. Logan says quite definitely of the MacNicols that 'as we have never met with a tartan peculiar to them, it is probable they adopted that of their superiors' — the MacLeods. Cloth has been woven purporting to show a correct sett, but the sett seems intended for that appearing in McIan's drawing, where no such claim is made for it. The drawing admits of many interpretations; the sett given here is one such reconstruction, and should not be regarded as that of an authentic MacNicol tartan; other versions are to be seen. The appropriate tartan for the MacNicols and the Nicolsons would be a MacLeod tartan.

Of the 'many interpretations' referred to above, No. 289 'MacNicholl' is from the Smith brothers' manuscript and No. 290 'McNicol' is from the records of the now-defunct Inverness Tweed Mill Co., Ltd. It is dated 1869.

'NICHOLSON' (291) came originally from *The Highlander* of 16th September 1876; it was quoted in the *Oban Times* of 9th February 1929 and is attributed to J.G. Mackay. On 14th January of the same year the *Oban Times* gave a non-reversing count (292) of the same name. An entirely different pattern (293) is of unknown provenance.

294 MACPHEE

W/Y	R	G	R	**G**
2	24	4	2	32

A note on the Clan MacPhee or MacDuffie appears in the McIan-Logan work, but no tartan is shown, and the present design seems to be of recent adoption. Whatever the history of the Clan, the tartan is a variant on the red MACDONALD (207).

An old Gaelic saying tells of 'The Stewarts, the race of kings and tinkers', and this may be regarded as the tartan of tinkers and kings, for MacPhee is a name with strong tinker connections and the pattern differs from the Bruce only by the omission of the red overcheck from the large green square.

295-301 MACPHERSON

(295)	**R**	Bk	W	R	Az	Bk	Az	Bk	Az	Bk	Y	G	R	Az	**R**
	2	2	2	24	8	2	2	2	8	12	2	16	24	4	24
(296)	**R**	Bk	W	R	B	Bk	B	Bk	B	Bk	Y	G	R	B	**R**
	2	2	2	8	8	2	4	2	8	12	2	16	12	2	12
(297)	**W**	R	Bk	W	G	Y	R	Bk	R	Y	B	Bk	R	Y	**B**
	2	24	2	2	16	6	4	2	4	6	16	4	6	6	2
(298)	**B**	R	Gy	R	B	R	Bk	R	**B**						
	2	2	16	2	2	2	16	2	2						
(299)	**W**	R	W	Bk	W	Bk	**Y**								
	6	2	60	40	6	18	2								
(300)	**A**	R	Y	R	K	A	Y	R	K	R	Y	G	W	K	**R**
	6	8	18	18	18	72	18	8	2	8	18	72	2	4	320
(301)	**G**	R	Y	P	R	P	R	G	R	P	**R**				
	4	14	4	4	140	72	10	84	4	4	10				

The tartan generally worn as CLAN MACPHERSON (295-6) is sufficiently elaborate to have been classed as a tartan of the Chief. It suggests a mixture the ROYAL STUART with the MACDUFF (234). Two settings of it are shown here, the first being in accordance with Logan's count, the second representing a modern example. Comparison of these two will show the characteristic modern trend towards more compact setts.

During the first two decades of last century the Wilson firm was weaving this tartan, listing it four times in their records up to 1819, with eleven counts in all. They name it 'No. 43' or 'Kidd sett' or 'Caledonian pattern' — usually all three together — but never as MacPherson. They also wove three similar patterns, one of which they named 'Caledonia'. Of these three the one listed as 'No. 155' has recently been illustrated under the name 'Caledonia', and is known to have been worn in Edinburgh in 1822. It is curious then that if the Kidd Sett had for any long time been a recognised MacPherson tartan it should not have been so named, the record of it coming, as it does, among a sequence of clan names. It may be that certain MacPhersons wore it long before about 1820, but a date prior to this at which it was generally recognised as their clan tartan has not been positively ascertained. Early in 1822 Messrs Wilson received a large order for various named tartans, among them 'Caledonia or MacPherson 43', which clearly shows that No. 43 and MacPherson were by that date one and the same, as by implication were Caledonia and Kidd.

A still more Chiefly design (297) appears only in the Smith work, and is there styled 'Clan MacPherson'. It so closely resembles the accepted MACKINTOSH CHIEF (261) both in design and in brilliance that there can be small wonder at its failure to gain popular adoption. An early eighteenth century plaid, associated with the MacPhersons of Crubin, has a design almost identical with this.

The tartan (298) stated by D.W. Stewart to be the earliest known to have been worn by the Clan, is reputed to have been used in two forms — as a Clan tartan with a white ground, and as a Hunting with the ground in grey. The design is doubtless old; but that any clan tartan in general wear for the kilt or plaid would have so much white in it seems highly improbable. The Smiths give a rendering of it, as here, with the grey ground. An alternative white version has red and blue reversed.

The design (299) provided by the *Vestiarium Scoticum* is known as the CLUNY, and sometimes as the DRESS MACPHERSON. It was first worn by the Chief in 1829, when he was supplied with the sett in advance of publication.

Wilsons' No. 43 was acknowledged as the Clan tartan by Duncan Macpherson of Cluny in 1817. It is not known why he preferred it to the same maker's 'MACPHERSON OF CLUNY'S TARTAN' (301) which, from its name, was clearly the choice of *some* Chief of the Clan; possibly it was something to do with the latter's similarity to the red Mackintosh tartan at a time when there was lively controversy over the Chiefship of Clan Chattan.

The Crubin plaid (300) differs only at one pivot from the tartan named here as MACKINTOSH, CHIEF and it seems highly probable that they shared a common source. Wilsons', long before the Smith brothers, made both versions of the latter as 'Mackintosh' and so it is probable that the Smiths' attribution of No. 297 is just a mistake.

Of the other Macpherson tartans listed, the *Vestiarium* sett is now known as DRESS MACPHERSON. At about the time of the *Vestiarium* it was made by Wilsons' under the name 'MAGGIE LAUDER'. With a white pivot (instead of yellow) this tartan is 'MACPHERSON OF CLUNY' and is registered as such at the Lyon Court.

See Plate 15 (a), (b) and (d-h).

302-305 MACQUARRIE

(302)	**G**	R	G	R	G	R	B	R	G	R	G	R	**G**
	4	6	4	104	4	4	56	4	84	4	4	6	4

(303)	**R**	Az	R	B	R	G	**R**
	4	2	32	24	8	32	12

(304)	**R**	Az	R	B	R	G	R	G	R	B	R	**Az**
	2	2	12	6	2	12	2	12	12	2	2	2

(305)	**R**	G	R	G	R	**G**
	32	2	2	2	8	24

Our first design (302) is to be found in a specimen collected about the year 1815, and has not hitherto been illustrated. James Logan provides the second (303). Logan's count is misleading, but reference to Smibert's version shows what was intended. The third (304) comes from the Smith work; they say that its authenticity was unquestioned. The MacQuarrie tartan now most often used (305) is related to the red MACDONALD (207), and is the one illustrated in most of the books from 1886 onwards.

In 1984 the Scottish Australian Heritage Council held a competition for the design of a tartan to be worn by Australian Scots. The winning design, by John Reid, a Melbourne architect, was based upon the tartan of Governor Lachlan MacQuarie and uses the 'colours of the Australian outback'. The count is as follows:

A/W	Pink	Fawn	Pk	F	K	F	Pk	**F**
4	30	20	8	4	4	4	8	100

Pink approximates to red sandstone and Fawn to yellow sandstone.

306 MACQUEEN

Y	Bk	R	Bk	R	**Bk**
2	24	12	4	12	4

A *Vestiarium Scoticum* design, obviously a reversal of the MacKeane (252); possibly suggested by the similarity in the sounds of the names, and the difference in spelling.

307-314 MACRAE

(307)	**G**	R	G	R	B	R	B	R	B	R	B	R	B	R	B	R	W
	20	4	20	18	2	2	4	2	2	18	2	2	4	2	2	18	2
	R	B	R	B	R	W	R	G	R	G	R	G	R	G	R	G	Y
	8	22	4	22	8	2	18	4	8	4	18	10	6	8	6	6	2
	G	R	G	**W**													
	6	6	12	2													
(308)	**G**	R	G	R	B	R	B	R	B	R	B	R	B	R	B	R	W
	8	2	8	8	2	2	2	2	2	8	2	2	2	2	2	8	2
	R	B	R	B	R	W	R	G	R	G	R	G	R	**G**			
	2	8	2	8	2	2	8	2	2	2	8	8	2	8			
(309)	**W**	Bk	P	Bk	Reseda	Cr	Res	Bk	**Res**								
	6	2	30	28	8	4	8	4	28								
(310)	**G**	Bk	G	Bk	G	R	G	Bk	B	W	B	Bk	G	R	G	Bk	**G**
	24	6	24	6	24	4	6	2	6	2	6	2	6	4	24	6	24
(311)	**R**	K	G	W	G	K	B	K	B	K	G	R	G	K	**G**		
	8	6	12	6	6	26	26	6	26	26	12	6	14	6	12		
(312)	**G**	K	G	C	G	K	B	K	W	K	B	K	G	K	**C**		
	52	8	12	8	12	52	52	6	14	6	52	52	52	6	14		
(313)	**B**	R	B	R	G	R	G	R	G	R	W/Y	R	G	R	G	R	G
	30	8	30	48	4	6	4	6	4	8	8	8	4	6	4	6	4
	R	G	R	**G**													
	48	48	8	30													
(314)	**P**	G	P	G	P	G	P	G	W	G	P	G	P	G	W	G	P
	50	12	50	52	10	14	10	52	6	14	58	12	58	14	6	52	4
	G	P	G	P	G	P	G	P	G	P	G	P	G	**P**			
	4	8	4	4	52	4	4	8	4	4	52	50	12	50			

The MacRae tartans have been discussed in connection with the Huntly

(156). It is unfortunate that the two earliest illustrations of the usual MacRae tartan (308) are both faulty. In Smibert the broader green stripes are in pairs, not in triplicate, as they should be; the blue of the tartan prints as a black, as so frequently in Smibert. The Smith plate has a positive error of design towards the edge of it, and it is difficult to see how a tartan set up from it would work out. This error has been repeated in subsequent works, and new ones introduced for good measure.

M'Intyre North prints a Logan count for a dark MacRae which is not found in *The Scottish Gaël*. The order of the colours is not a simple one, but it is identical with that of the Hunting MacRae (309); yet the quantities are very different. The count seems to contain an error; with this adjusted, the resulting tartan (310) looks improbable; made strictly to the count as given, it becomes incredible. It would seem as if Logan or someone else had encountered the relic that D. W. Stewart reproduced, but that at some stage the record had been jumbled. The sett shown by McIan looks like the MacLeod (273).

A tartan occasionally offered as a Dress MacRae is composed of equal bands of sapphire blue and of white, a red line being centred on the white and a yellow line on the blue. Its origin is explained in a reference by D. W. Stewart to an incident in the Clan history; the colours in the tartan are named by him as being those found in a piece of knitting, dating from the end of the eighteenth century, which was said to reproduce the tartan mentioned in the story. The sett is thus an indirect reconstruction of a tartan used for hose, about 1715, by MacRaes of Conchra, Lochalsh.

A tartan (311) clearly related to the Hunting MacRae appeared in the pattern book of Garry & Deas, Perth but a Wilson specimen named MacRae, Hunting, seen in the Smith Institute, Stirling, though after the style of No. 312 is extended to the full Black Watch pattern with a red pivot on a second green stripe. No. 313 was given as the correct sett for MacRae of Inverinate by the late Mrs MacRae of Inverinate.

Wilsons made two interesting patterns named respectively 'Rae tartan' and 'MacCrae Tartan'; 'Rae' was Ross with green for red and all the other stripes in purple; in 'MacCrae' (314) the same treatment was applied to the red MacRae tartan except for the white overchecks which remained.

See Plate 11 (b) and (c).

315-318 MACTAVISH

(315)	**Az**	R	B	Az	Bk	**Az**
	4	24	4	12	12	2
(316)	**R**	A	K	W	K	Y
	8	56	12	24	24	6

(317)	**A**	T	G	A	K	**A**	
	8	56	12	24	24	6	
(318)	G	K	G	B	R	G	**R**
	12	12	12	4	24	4	24

This tartan has recently come into use as being that appropriate to the Thomsons; Thomson is the anglicised form of the name MacTavish. It is not recorded in any of the early illustrated books. Many MacTavishes wear the CAMPBELL OF ARGYLL (57).

'LORD THOMPSON, DRESS' (316) and 'LORD THOMPSON, HUNTING' (317) derive directly from this tartan and both are registered at the Lyon Court. Though commonly known as Dress MacTavish and Hunting MacTavish they are strictly the property of Lord Thompson of Fleet. *The Baronage of Angus and The Mearns* gives an entirely different sett (318).

319 MACTHOMAS

G	Lilac	G	K	B	Magenta	**B**
6	4	44	22	44	4	6

Reputed to be of early eighteenth century origin, this tartan has been adopted by the Clan Society and is registered at the Lyon Court.

320 MACWHIRTER

A	G	K	A	K	Y	K	A	K	R	W	**A**
4	32	4	8	4	8	4	8	4	32	4	4

From the manuscript of the Smith brothers' book. The reason for the marked resemblance to Buchanan is not obvious.

321 MAINE

Designed by Sliomas Gilis of Yarmouth, Nova Scotia — who also designed the Nova Scotia tartan — in 1968. Licensing of manufacturers is in the hands of the copyright holders, the Maine Tartan and Tweed Company, Plymouth, Maine, who are the exclusive agents and to whom requests for the thread count should be addressed.

322 MALCOLM

B	R	B	Bk	G	Bk	Y	Bk	Az	Bk	G	Bk	B	R
2	2	12	12	12	2	2	2	2	2	12	12	12	2

Though the name Malcolm is but a variant on the name MacCallum, it is usual to distinguish this design from the two other MacCallum tartans by calling this alone MALCOLM. It first appears in Smith. Being asymmetrical, it thereby breaks the almost invariable custom in weaving. There is no reason to suppose it of ancient origin.

323 MANITOBA

Y	Maroon	LG	DG	LG	A	LG	A
4	12	2	4	24	2	2	4

One of the earlier Canadian Provincial tartans, this was also the first count issued by the Lyon Office using heraldic colours, though here translated into ordinary terms. The colours given here are as shown on a print supplied by the Department of Industry and Commerce, Winnipeg. The light green is grass green and the dark green is dull.

324 MANX

P	G	Rowan red	Gold	Royal B	A	W
4	12	2	2	6	20	2

The tartan designed by Miss Patricia McQuaid at the instigation of Lord Sempill, to be the Manx National tartan.

325-327 MATHESON

(325)

G	R	G	R	G	R	B	G	R	G	R	G	R	G	R	G	R
16	8	2	2	2	48	16	8	2	2	2	8	16	2	2	2	2
B	G	R	G													
16	16	4	8													

(326)

R	G	R	B	B	Az	G	R	G	R	G	R	G	R
4	4	24	20	6	20	4	4	4	20	24	4	4	

(327)

G	B	G	B	G	B	Bk	G	B	G	B	G	B	G	B	G	B
16	8	2	2	2	48	16	8	2	2	2	8	16	2	2	2	2
Bk	G	B	G													
16	16	4	8													

The design usually worn by Mathesons (325) is that given by the Smiths. It has an irregular and capricious character that leads one to suspect that it was composed from elements of two or more other tartans. The count which M'Intyre North obtained from Logan produces a pattern (326) consisting of an arrangement of part only of the former one, yet this latter sett has an internal harmony lacking in the first. It seems to incorporate the ERSKINE (112). The more recent Hunting sett (327) follows the Smith version in its lay-out. McIan's drawing is so indeterminate that it might be taken to represent either of the two red designs.

328 MAXWELL

R	G	R	Bk	R	G	**R**
6	2	56	12	8	32	6

This is one of the Lowland tartans first displayed in the *Vestiarium Scoticum,* and no other authority for it can be quoted.

329 MELVILLE

K	B	K	G	W	**K**
4	24	26	26	4	8

A Wilson pattern of 1847 or thereabouts giving sixteen half setts to a width of 25 inches.

330-334 MENZIES

(330)	**R**	Az	W	G	**R**							
	10	4	2	10	10							
(331)	**R**	W	R	W	R	W	R	**W**				
	72	8	6	8	12	4	2	24				
(332)	**G**	R	G	R	G	R	G	**R**				
	96	8	4	8	12	4	6	18				
(333)	**Bk**	W	Bk	W	Bk	W	Bk	**W**				
	64	8	4	8	8	4	2	12				
(334)	**W**	R	W	R	W	Cr	R	Cr	R	Cr	R	**W**
	8	2	4	6	48	10	6	2	2	2	40	4

The tartan (330) for which Logan gives a count is possibly the oldest MENZIES we have, but it is rarely seen now. Logan's count seems defective, but a specimen of earlier date, in which the azure stripe is, incidentally, rather a pale green, has been followed in resolving the doubt.

The more usual scheme may have originated as one widely used for hose in its red and white form (331) though it is now popular as a tartan for general use in the Hunting version (332), in which the red and white of the former become green and red. It is also found rendered in black and white (333). Whatever the origin of this design, the Hunting version, as shown by D. W. Stewart, is a tartan of outstanding beauty and simplicity. In its just proportions and economy of means it is a fine example of the weaver's art. Beside it, the red and white form looks raw in more than a small quantity, and, with the black and white, serves to demonstrate how greatly design depends on colour and tone relations.

McIan's drawing represents the red and white tartan (331); the *Vestiarium Scoticum* contains what may be an attempt to improve on it (334).

In the McIan-Logan work it is reported that the red sett had 'attracted attention on the occasion of Her Majesty's late visit, and since become popular'. This would be in 1842.

One early specimen has, attached to it, the name MacFarlane, but it is now invariably accepted as a Menzies tartan.

335-337 MONTGOMERIE

(335)	**Bk**	Reseda	Bk	P	Bk	R	**Bk**		
	8	10	8	56	8	10	8		
(336)	**G**	**B**	G	**B**					
	24	6	2	6					
(337)	**G**	K	G	K	G	K	G	K	**G**
	72	4	6	8	6	4	72	64	12

Reproducing this early tartan (335), D. W. Stewart expresses the opinion that it was probably adopted by the Montgomeries of Ayrshire about the time of the Union of 1707. If this is correct, it must be one of the earliest genuine Lowland tartans we have. It has the rare feature of a plain purple ground.

The *Vestiarium Scoticum* contains an even quieter design (336), three blue stripes on a green ground. Schemes in triple or quadruple stripes are of frequent occurrence in that work. One, given under the name of Elphinstone, differs from this only in having the stripes purple, not blue.

The Highland Society of London Collection has a different pattern (337).

338-340 MORAY OF ABERCAIRNEY

(338)	**A**	N	K	R	LR	G	LR	N	**A**
	6	2	2	16	2	16	2	2	6
(339)	**A**	G	LR	G	LR	**R**			
	4	2	2	8	2	16			
(340)	**B**	LR	G	LR	**R**				
	8	2	8	2	16				

D.C. Stewart extracted patterns from the portrait of James Moray of

Abercairney for the belted plaid (338) and the warp (339) and weft (340) of the coat. Taking threadcounts from pictures is a tricky business and someone else might easily get a different answer.

341, 342 MORRISON

(341)	**Bk**	G	Bk	G	B	**R**
	6	28	28	4	28	6

This is a comparatively late tartan; it was made by adding a red line to the MacKay (250), both clans being found in north-west Sutherland.

In 1967 the following sett was registered at Lyon Court as the Morrison Clan tartan: (342)

(342)	**G**	R	Bk	R	Bk	R	G	W	**G**
	10	64	10	14	10	34	30	8	18

It has a striking resemblance to the Seton (386).

343-346 MUNRO

(343)	**G**	Cr	G	R	B	Y	R	B	R	Y	B	R	G	R	B	Y	**R**
	4	4	4	32	2	2	6	12	6	2	2	6	32	6	2	2	48

(344)	**W**	R	Bk	R	**Bk**
	6	64	36	8	36

(345)	**R**	Y	B	R	G	R	B	Y	R	B	R	Y	B	R	G	R	G
	52	2	2	6	52	6	2	2	6	12	6	2	2	52	6	6	6
	R	G	**R**														
	6	6	104														

(346)	**R**	Y	P	R	G	R	P	Y	R	P	R	Y	P	R	G	C	**G**
	72	4	2	6	82	6	2	4	6	24	6	4	2	74	6	6	8

Logan's count for the Munro is misleading, as it indicates a duplication of the group of three green lines normally centred between the main bands of pattern. Yet this duplication appears in McIan's drawing, and it could be regarded as an improvement in design. What is usually considered the correct sett (343) is shown by Smibert and the Smiths. The Dalzell (92) as given by Logan is almost identical with this, but, in the Dalzell, Logan makes the spaces between the three green lines crimson, not scarlet. The Smiths do this in their plate of the Munro, and it is shown so here. These crimson stripes may, in early specimens, be found rendered in bright pink. The MacColl (202) has a scheme similar to the Munro, but with the yellow lines omitted.

We have remarked on the three-stripe schemes appearing in the *Vestiarium Scoticum.* The Munro (344) provides another example.

As undress this clan wears the Black Watch. Some members have even claimed the Black Watch as an early Munro tartan, on the same grounds as the Campbells.

The Tartan that Wilsons' supplied to James Logan as 'Munro' was known to them as 'George 4th with Yellow' (the customary version had white overchecks) and their comments, subsequent upon publication, imply that Logan's tabulation (345) was a correct rendering of the pattern. However, for 'Dalzell' Wilsons' supplied "Our common George 4th with silk — no pink" and the comments say "the pattern you have given . . . is quite well known to us as the George 4th". In fact, it is an older and different pattern, 'Lochiel Tartan' (346 and Plate 16 (g)) with yellow changed to white and this *did* have rose or pink. We are thus left with one table — Munro — that has been branded as inaccurate and the other — Dalzell — which is demonstrably so; what is clear is that both should be the same, except for the interchange of white and yellow and that there should be no rose or pink infill between the green overchecks. In the absence of an undoubted specimen of 'George 4th' it is impossible to establish the accuracy of Logan's table for Munro; however, the specimens supplied were 27 inches, two whole setts wide, and the abbreviated pattern (343) given by Stewart would make two setts less than 24 inches wide. The full count (345) and Plate 16 (f) would give a width of 32 inches on the loom, so it may be that the red band between the green lines should be halved. See Plate 16 (f) and (g) and Appendix F, including Note 1 at end.

347-349 MURRAY

(347)	**B**	Bk	B	Bk	G	R	G	Bk	B	Bk	B	Bk	**B**
	4	2	12	12	12	4	12	12	2	2	2	2	12

(348)	**B**	Bk	B	Bk	B	Bk	G	R	G	Bk	B	Bk	**R**
	24	4	4	4	4	24	24	6	24	24	24	2	6

(349)	**B**	R	B	R	B	R	B	R	Bk	R	B	R	B	R	G	R	G
	4	2	2	4	8	4	2	2	4	2	2	48	24	4	4	16	24
	R	B	R	**Bk**													
	8	4	4	2													

James Logan, writing in *The Scottish Gaël* about the tartan of the Black Watch, says:

The regular colours are blue, black, and green, but a red stripe in the middle of the former is often introduced. This is said to have been first added by Lord Murray, who commanded the regiment, as the Athol sett . . .

Logan's own count for the Murray tartan (347) shows a red line centred in the green only, whereas the accepted design (348) has an additional red line filling the space between the two black lines that occur in alternate bands of blue. The characteristic feature of the second arrangement lies in this widely spaced group of three red lines. The MURRAY was at one time in general use as a district tartan, and may well have been an Athol tartan before it was called MURRAY. The arrangement given by Logan, and found also in the *Vestiarium,* is sometimes named MACKINLAY (257).

It is interesting to find that in one of the early collections the red line occurs, as in Logan's version, in the green bands but not in the blue, while each blue band has only the central pair of black lines. This is the simplest and possibly the oldest Murray design. In the collection it is described as 'Murray of Athol', and the design (348) is entitled 'Murray of Mansfield'. The Earls of Mansfield were a branch of the Murrays of Tullibardine.

James Grant wrote of the MURRAY OF TULLIBARDINE (349):

> That tartan called the Tullibardine is a red tartan, and was adopted and worn by Charles, first Earl of Dunmore, second son of the first Marquis of Tullibardine ... in 1679 [he] was lieutenant-Colonel of the Royal Grey Dragoons, now known as the Scots Greys ...

It is refreshing to be able to report so specific a claim for the antiquity of a tartan design. The design itself does not give the impression of having been invented as it stands, but rather of one that has grown from simpler forms. It is, of course, a family and not a clan tartan.

It is remarkable that our earliest visual record of this tartan should occur in a portrait of the Chief of another clan. Anyone examining the famous portrait by Allan Ramsay of Normand MacLeod, at Dunvegan Castle, will soon realize, once it is pointed out, that the plaid, although in the same red and black as the other garments, shows in every detail the elaborate scheme of the Tullibardine, but with the blue and green changed to black. A rational explanation appears when we learn that Normand had spent much of his early days among the Murrays, to whom he was related through his mother, and that he had a great affection for them.

The change in the colouring was probably only slight and can be attributed to Allan Ramsay's artistic licence.

350, 351 NAPIER

(350)	W	B	Bk	W	Bk	W	Bk	W	Bk	W	**Bk**
	2	24	8	4	4	8	4	4	4	4	8
(351)	**R**	B	K	W	K	W	R	W	K	W	**K**
	10	72	24	10	10	36	10	16	16	16	36

The NAPIER is a good example of Lowland plaid design, reminiscent of the CLERGY but more secular in colour. The scheme is not so fortuitous as one might suppose at first glance. The arrangement of black and white stripes is made up of three bands close together, of the narrow-wide-narrow theme associated with many MacDonald tartans, these bands being rendered in white on black, black on white, white on black. The remainder of the design does not call for comment.

From failure to realise what the scheme is, weavers sometimes vary the widths of the stripes in such a way as to vitiate it; but it is necessary to remember that whatever may have become of some designs in the course of time, they were never quite irrational in their original conception. Unfortunately, it is not always so easy to decipher the scheme as is the case here.

The tartan of MERCHISTON CASTLE SCHOOL Pipe Band (351) is based on Napier. Merchiston Castle was the home of John Napier, the inventor of logarithms.

352 'NATIONAL'

W	B	R	K	G	Y	B	K	W
4	6	12	16	24	2	8	4	4

A well-intentioned effort by the National Association of Scottish Woollen Manufacturers to produce a Scottish national tartan. It failed to catch on.

353 NEW YORK FIRE BRIGADE PIPE BAND

K	W	G	K	B	A
14	3	42	36	40	10

The count is taken from a specimen provided by Grainger and Campbell, Glasgow. The pattern bears a close resemblance to that of the dark Rose tartan.

354 NEW BRUNSWICK

A	Y	A	DG	LG	DG	LG	DG	LG	DG	A	Y	A	Y	A	DG	
2	2	2	2	4	4	4	4	4	2	2	2	2	2	2	36	
R	T	R	Y	R	T	R	A	Y	N	Y	R	DG	A	Y	A	Y
12	8	18	4	6	18	6	8	6	4	2	32	36	2	2	2	2
A	DG	LG	DG	LG	DG	LG	DG	A	Y	A						
2	2	4	4	4	4	4	2	2	2	2						

The count is taken from a specimen provided by Bonda Textiles Ltd, Yarmouth, Nova Scotia. It does not agree precisely with the Lyon Court count wherein the colours are given as Forest green, Meadow green, Azure, Gold, Beaver brown, Red and Ship grey.

355 NOVA SCOTIA

R	Y	DG	LG	DG	LG	DG	B	**W**
2	4	16	8	4	4	4	40	4

The count is taken from a specimen supplied by Tartan House Ltd, Halifax, Nova Scotia. The two greens are named as representing the evergreen and deciduous trees of Nova Scotia. The sett is registered at the Lyon Court.

356-359 OGILVIE and DRUMMOND OF STRATHALLAN

(356)	**R**	W	Bk	Y	P	Y	G	Y	Bk	R	Bk	R	Bk	R	Bk	Y	G
	8	2	4	4	8	4	12	4	4	4	4	4	4	4	4	8	16
	Y	Bk	R	W	R	W	R	Bk	Y	G	W	G	Y	P	R	Bk	R
	8	4	16	4	16	4	16	4	4	16	4	16	4	4	8	4	28
	W	B	W	R	W	B	W	R	Bk	R	P	Y	G	Y	G	Y	Bk
	2	4	2	28	2	4	2	28	4	8	4	8	12	4	12	8	24
	W	B	W	Bk	R	W	R	W	R	Bk	Y	G	Bk	G	Bk	G	Y
	2	8	2	24	16	4	16	4	16	4	4	28	8	28	8	28	4
	Bk	R	W	R	W	R	Bk	Y	G	W	G	Y	Bk	R	W	R	W
	4	16	4	16	4	16	4	4	16	4	16	4	4	16	4	16	4
	R	Bk	Y	G	Bk	**G**											
	16	4	8	28	8	28											

(357)	**W**	Az	Y	P	R	W	R	W	R	Bk	Y	Az	R	**Az**
	4	10	4	4	12	4	12	4	12	4	10	20	6	20

(358)	**R**	G	Bk	G	Bk	G	Bk	Y	**B**
	8	6	2	6	2	32	16	4	48

(359)	**R**	G	Bk	G	Bk	B	Y	**B**
	6	4	2	48	32	4	2	56

The tartan best known under the name of Ogilvie (356) is one of extraordinary complexity. The count given by Logan is such that even a single repeat of the design, if laid out for the usual 26-inch web, would have to be woven at 64 threads to the inch, thus giving a fabric finer than would at any early date have been normal for the kilt. His specimen may have been a silk plaid or shawl.

It is only since 1812 that the design has carried the name of Ogilvie. Prior to that date, at which the two Houses had become connected by marriage, it was known as DRUMMOND OF STRATHALLAN. Yet at that period there was already in existence the OGILVIE (357), simpler in design, the elements of which go to make up a large part of the Strathallan tartan. The resemblance must be more than accidental, and it is strange that it should seem to forecast the 1812 marriage. No light can be thrown on the early history of these two tartans. McIan's drawing seems intended to represent both of them, his figure wearing a plaid in this DRUMMOND and trews in the bright but simpler OGILVIE (357).

The more elaborate design is sometimes rendered with blue in place of green. In such cases the portions consisting of two black lines on a green ground are usually changed to two red lines on the blue ground, as in the simpler sett (357).

Possibly older than either of these, and more suggestive of a serviceable tartan, is the OGILVIE HUNTING (358). The producers of the *Vestiarium Scoticum* must have been aware of this tartan, but their version (359) differs in detail from the previous one, which is the form found in the early collections. The text would permit the yellow stripe to touch the black, though the plate shows it detached; only single black lines are mentioned.

360 OLIPHANT

G	W	G	B	Bk	**B**
4	2	64	48	8	8

Our only knowledge of this tartan is that it appears in the *Vestiarium Scoticum*. It has not come into general use, and is rarely reproduced.

361 POLARIS

Navy B	K	NB	K	NB	K	G	Gold	K	Royal B	K	Gold
24	4	4	4	4	28	24	4	4	4	4	4
G	K	NB	K	**NB**							
24	28	28	4	4							

Yet another Black Watch variant, this time designed for the crew of the U.S. nuclear powered submarine of the name in 1964.

362 PRINCE EDWARD ISLAND

W	K	G	K	R	K	**W**
4	2	32	24	24	2	4

A Canadian Provincial tartan, simpler and therefore more distinctive than most.

363 RAE TARTAN

P	G	P	G	P	G	P	G	P	G	P	G	P	G	P	G	P
54	12	54	56	10	14	10	56	62	12	62	56	4	4	8	4	4
G	P	G	P	G	P	G	P	G	**P**							
56	4	4	8	4	4	56	54	12	54							

The companion to 'MacCrae tartan' in the Key Pattern Book; it is based directly upon Ross, with green for red and purple for everything else. Both were made with two half setts to a width of 25 inches in the 24 reed. See Plate 13 (e).

364, 365 RAMSAY

(364)	**R**	Cr	R	Bk	W	**Bk**				
	6	2	60	56	4	8				
(365)	**R**	B	R	K	R	W	R	W	K	**R**
	128	8	2	8	24	8	2	8	8	2

Ramsay was one of the names adopted by members of Clan MacGregor when their own was proscribed under successive enactments directed against the Clan. These repressive laws were almost continuously in force from 1563 to 1775. The choice of the early MacGregor tartan as the basis of the Ramsay may be explained by the adoption of the latter name by so many MacGregors. The design has the authority of the *Vestiarium Scoticum*.

As usual, *The Baronage of Angus and The Mearns* gives a different sett (365).

366 RATTRAY

G	K	R	B	R	B	R	B	**W**
142	8	8	18	8	8	72	8	8

A family tartan registered in the 1960s. For a time counts were issued by the Lyon Office in both numbers of threads and eighth-inch units. The Rattray count exposed the weaknesses of the latter method and subsequent counts were recorded in thread numbers only.

367 RITCH SETT

R	W	R	W	R	W	A	W	P	W	P	W	A	W	G	LG	W
12	4	6	4	40	4	12	4	20	4	20	4	12	4	20	8	4
LG	G	W	R	W	R	W	G	W	G	Y	G	W	A	W	A	W
8	20	4	28	4	28	4	6	4	4	4	4	4	8	4	8	4
G	Y	G	W	G	W	R	W	R	W	P	A	W	Y	W	LG	W
4	4	4	4	6	4	28	4	28	4	20	4	4	8	4	8	4
Y	W	A	P	W	R	W	A	W	R	**W**						
8	4	4	20	4	40	4	12	4	28	2						

An 'Old Superfine Tartan sett' for the 600 reed. Three half setts made a web 27 inches wide but for the more usual 9 inch plaiding two half setts, plus 112 threads of the third, were put on. A footnote to the count tells that the sett was named Ritch from the great quantity of silk with which it was usually made. I doubt the truth of this as I have yet to find any order for it 'with silk' and it was probably rather too early for this technique.

368-371 ROBERTSON

(368)	**W**	G	R	B	R	G	R	B	R	B	R	G	**W**		
	2	4	36	4	4	36	4	36	4	4	36	4	2		
(369)	**R**	G	R	B	R	G	R	B	R	G	R	G	**R**		
	2	2	18	2	2	18	2	18	2	2	18	2	2		
(370)	**W**	Bk	B	Bk	G	Bk	R	Bk	G	Bk	B	Bk	B	Bk	**B**
	6	2	24	24	32	2	6	2	32	24	4	4	4	4	24
(371)	**G**	R	B	R	G	**R**									
	2	72	16	4	40	4									

The first positive record of a Robertson tartan, that of the early collections, vouches for the Robertson design (368) with the white line. The more commonly seen design has red in place of the white (369). Logan's count for this is confused in its arrangement, but it shows a feature worthy of special note. It is usual to render in blue the lines flanking the broad blue and green stripes; but according to Logan the line nearest the green stripe is blue, and that next the blue stripe is green. Whether or not this was formerly usual, it certainly makes for balance in the design. A similar alternation is to be seen in the MacIntyre and Glenorchy (246).

In selecting yarns for weaving these two Robertson tartans it is important to have the blue and the green of equal tone value; if one is darker it spoils the symmetry of the pattern.

It is interesting to note that McIan's Robertson drawing, in part, shows the same type of irregularity as does his Buchanan (40). Unlike the Buchanan, the Robertson has survived in its symmetrical form.

The Hunting Robertson (370) or Robertson of Kindeace, is reputed ancient; it was certainly being worn before 1820. It resembles the Athol Murray (348), which it might naturally do, though its use was maintained only by the Robertsons of the North.

The design in the *Vestiarium Scoticum* (371) differs from the foregoing, and is not widely used. Another tartan associated with the Robertsons is discussed in Note (434).

I have referred to the question of tone values under Deas but it may be remarked here that Wilsons' specified Purple — which is dark — and

Green — which is not — for their Robertson tartan. These colours give the appearance of light and dark squares, each with a red centre; if green and blue of equal value are used the pattern becomes a smaller check of red and what the Sobieski brothers called 'minglit'.

372, 373 ROSE

(372)	**Bk**	W	G	Bk	B	**R**			
	8	2	20	20	20	4			
(373)	**G**	R	P	Cr	P	Cr	P	Cr	**W**
	8	64	18	12	4	6	4	24	6

Two tartans carry this name, though it has been given also to the LOGAN (182): the Dress (373), as found in the *Vestiarium Scoticum,* and the Hunting (372), as recorded by James Logan. The white lines do not show well in McIan drawing of the latter. The plate in the *Vestiarium* gives a poor rendering of the colours specified in the text. We have followed the text for colour.

374-377 ROSS

(374)	**G**	R	G	R	G	R	G	R	B	R	B	R	B	R	B	R	B
	36	4	36	36	4	8	4	36	36	4	36	36	2	2	4	2	2
	R	B	R	B	R	B	R	G	R	**G**							
	36	2	2	4	2	2	36	36	4	36							

(375)	**G**	R	G	R	G	R	G	R	B	R	B	R	B	R	B	R	B	**R**
	36	4	36	36	4	8	4	36	36	4	36	36	2	2	4	2	2	36

(376)	**B**	R	B	R	B	R	B	R	G	R	G	R	G	**R**
	4	6	2	56	6	2	6	8	2	2	2	4	24	6
(377)	**R**	G	R	G	Bk	G	Bk	G	LG	G	LG	G	LG	**G**
	2	4	2	24	4	4	4	6	2	2	2	4	8	4

This (374) (Plate 11 (a)) is the plainest of the tartans discussed in connection with the HUNTLY. The version here given may be taken as correct; it differs from the HUNTLY (156) in having no light lines. Logan gives a count for ROSS, but his count stops short. It is illustrated here (375) as a matter of interest, to show such errors can yet produce quite regular tartans. The Smith and Smibert works show the scheme correctly, but when we come to James Grant another major error has developed, and since then the rendering has gone from bad to worse. McIan's drawing has its own peculiar mistakes.

The Ross tartan in the *Vestiarium Scoticum* (376) is quite different in character, but shows an awareness of the traditional sett. The group of three lines, though green in the plate, is described in the text as blue. There is a modern Hunting Ross (377), based on the *Vestiarium* scheme.

378-380 ROTHESAY

(378)	**W**	R	W	R	G	R	G	R	G	R	G	R	G	R	G	R	**W**
	4	2	2	64	4	6	4	8	32	8	32	8	4	6	4	64	4

(379)	**G**	R	B	R	K	R	G	R	K	R	**W**
	4	52	8	4	8	4	16	8	2	2	4

(380)	**R**	W	B	W	K	W	G	R	K	R	**W**
	4	56	8	4	12	4	14	8	2	4	2

This is described in the *Vestiarium Scoticum* as being worn by the Prince of Rothesay, meaning the Royal Prince bearing the title of Duke of Rothesay. It has recently been revived, presumably as a district tartan. Its relationship to the Ross (376) from the same work will be obvious; the designer may have been influenced by the similarity in sound between the names Ross and Rothes. The description of the Rothesay given in the text of the *Vestiarium* (where it is grouped as a Stuart tartan), has little correspondence with the design shown in the illustration of it. Present-day renderings follow the illustration, not the text, and the former has been followed here also. The description in the text is not very explicit; and there is an alternative description, conflicting with the first, and equally confused. This is a particularly marked instance of the discrepancies that exist between text and illustration in the *Vestiarium*.

In what we know as the 'Lauder Transcript' of the *Vestiarium*, 'Stewart of rothsaye' (379) relates to 'Clanne Stewart' and 'Duke of Rothesay' (380) to 'Roialle Stewarte'. Neither bears any resemblance to the *Vestiarium* plate. There is also a Hunting Rothesay tartan based on No. 378 with red and green transposed and the three white lines on every green square.

381 ROYAL CANADIAN AIR FORCE

Maroon	A	K	M	K	A	K	W	K	M	K	M	B	M	B
4	6	1	2	1	14	3	3	2	2	2	2	4	2	6

M	B	**M**
2	6	3

A pattern for tie material to be woven in 2/32s worsted at 32 ends per inch, plain weave, to a 4 inch repeat; it is a variety of the Anderson tartan. The threadcount was provided by the Canadian Department of National Defence and the colours are specified in the Munsell range as:

Dark blue	10PB 1.7/2
Light blue	2.5 PB 5/8
Maroon	10RP 1.7/3

382 RUTHVEN

R	G	R	B	G	**W**
4	2	60	36	30	6

A family tartan, first recorded in the *Vestiarium Scoticum*. Though a white line appears in the plate, the text gives no warrant for it.

383 SASKATCHEWAN

W	K	G	T	Gold	R	Gold	**Y**
4	2	12	22	52	4	2	4

A Provincial tartan registered at the Lyon Court in 1961.

384-390 SCOTT

(384)	**G**	R	Bk	R	G	R	G	W	G	**R**				
	8	6	2	56	28	8	8	6	8	8				
(385)	**W**	Bk	W	Bk	W	Bk	W	Bk	W	Bk	**W**			
	4	2	12	12	4	2	2	2	4	12	12			
(386)	**G**	K	W	K	Y	B	G	K	G	R	G	W	G	**K**
	16	6	6	12	8	24	12	16	24	6	6	6	6	16
(387)	**B**	A	G	**K**										
	28	4	12	4										
(388)	**K**	P	K	A	G	**K**								
	4	14	18	4	16	4								
(389)	**K**	W	K	W	K	W	K	W	K	W	K	**W**		
	124	8	16	4	4	4	4	4	4	4	12	12		
(390)	**R**	G	R	B	R	K	**R**							
	28	102	10	82	10	18	214							

In a letter from Sir Thomas Dick Lauder to Sir Walter Scott in 1829 concerning the Urquhart MS. of the *Vestiarium Scoticum*, mention is made of the tartan (384) attributed to the Scott family. Sir Walter rejected the idea that the Borderers ever had distinguishing tartans, in quite unequivocal terms. But Smibert publishes a design in black and white (385) which, he says, was prepared for his own use by Sir Walter Scott in 1822, and that he wore it, in private, in the form of a Lowland shepherd's plaid.

Opportunity may be taken here to remark that the romantic aspect of the interest shown, since his day, in Highland history and affairs, is in great measure due to Sir Walter Scott. Subsequent writers have improved the perspective and elaborated the detail of the picture he drew of Highland life and character in the eighteenth century and earlier; but it was he who first set before a wide public of readers of English the idea of the Highlands as other than a wilderness inhabited by cut-throat cattle dealers.

The essence of the red tartan (384) is the *Vestiarium*'s MacGregor with the central green stripe and its white overcheck doubled, a predictable relationship between the tartans of the most famous MacGregor and his greatest publicist but not one likely to have occurred if they were really sixteenth century patterns as the Sobieskis pretended. There is a hunting tartan in which the main red area is made in brown with a red overcheck and a dress set with a red band next to the outermost green stripe and white thereafter up to the black overcheck.

The so-called green Scott (386) has been popular but its origin is not recorded; nor is that of another dark tartan (387) exhibited as part of the John Telfer Dunbar collection at the Canongate Tolbooth, Edinburgh.

In the 1840s, Wilsons' enshrined the fame of the author in 'SIR WALTER SCOTT' (388), and later in the century they produced another fancy pattern, BUCCLEUCH (390). Another black and white Scott tartan (389) comes from the Morgan collection.

391, 392 SCOTTISH SCOUTS

(391)	**Mid N**	Dk N	MN	DN	MN	DN	Lt N	DN	LN	DN	MN	DN	**MN**
	22	4	4	4	4	24	24	4	24	24	22	4	4

(392)	**R**	G	B	G	R	G	**Y**
	6	44	32	28	4	12	2

The grey tartan was devised by Lord Glentanar in the 1920s, when he was Chief Commissioner of the Scout Association for Scotland. Based upon the Black Watch tartan, it was intended to be worn by Scottish Scouts who had no family tartan or by troops who wished to wear a uniform tartan. It did not achieve great popularity but in the Spring of 1989, with the light grey changed to white, is being sold as 'DRESS GREY WATCH', which seems to deserve an exclamation mark!

The tartan (392) currently in use for Scottish Scouts is based upon the MACLAREN, in honour of a MacLaren who gave an estate to the Movement. On the blue and green base the strong red overcheck represents the Rover

Scouts, the finer red lines the Scouts and Senior Scouts and yellow the Wolf Cubs.

(393) SETON

R	G	R	Bk	R	B	R	G	W	**G**
4	2	64	8	4	8	8	24	2	12

Though a Lowland family, the Setons had early and close links with the House of Gordon. The tartan is represented in the *Vestiarium Scoticum.*

394, 395 SHAW

(394)	**G**	Bk	B	Bk	B	**R**
	48	4	6	4	16	4

(395)	**A**	K	R	P	R	G	R	**P**
	10	2	60	30	16	60	16	4

This design (394) is used by Shaws, but its standing as a distinctive ancient tartan is doubtful. It derives from McIan's drawing of Fearchar Shaw, who was executed for his part in a mutiny of the Black Watch in 1743. The drawing was made from a painting, and it seems that it was there intended to represent the Black Watch tartan. Logan does not actually name the tartan represented, but in his comment on the drawing says: 'The tartan had at that time a red stripe, which is now omitted, and the pattern resembles that of the Sutherland, but in making up the kilt the blue interval is shown, which gives a sombre hue to the Breacan'. This corresponds exactly with his description of the Black Watch tartan, in *The Scottish Gaël.* The reduction of the usual black stripe to two black lines, seen in the Shaw, arises from McIan's custom of indicating stripes of colour by their outlines, later to be filled in with solid pigment. These outlines show in this as in many other of his drawings; hence the Shaw. Shaws may appropriately wear Mackintosh tartan.

There was never any reason for the tartan to be called Shaw and when the late Chief, Major C. J. Shaw of Tordarroch, matriculated and became the first Chief of the Clan for some 400 years, he had a new tartan (395) designed which reflects the Clan's Mackintosh ancestry. There is a green version, analogous to the Hunting Mackintosh, with R60 in green. Both tartans are registered at the Lyon Court but the colours given are taken from the first specimens of the designs.

396, 397 SINCLAIR

(396)	**R**	G	Bk	W	Az	**R**
	56	32	8	2	12	56

(397) **G** R G Bk W B **R**
4 2 60 32 2 32 4

The usual tartan is that given by Logan (396). The shades of colour in the green and the blue bands are variously represented; James Grant shows a comparatively dark blue, with a light blue for the green. Possibly the latter is intended for reseda.

In the *Vestiarium Scoticum* there is a Hunting sett (397). This will be seen to be a variant on the other. The red ground between the blue stripes has been contracted, and the blue stripes expanded, to produce a red stripe on a blue ground; similarly, the red band contained by green has been contracted to form two red stripes on a green ground. The resultant tartan has the conventional green-black-blue basis; it retains the original white lines, the former red ground being represented only by the red stripes.

It is interesting to compare the SINCLAIR (396) with the MENZIES (330). Smibert, by omitting the black, makes this MENZIES serve for SINCLAIR.

398-400 SKENE

(398) **B** R G R B R **B**
2 6 18 6 2 6 18

(399) **Bk** R G Bk Orange Bk G Bk R Bk B **Bk**
8 6 48 8 6 8 48 8 6 8 48 8

(400) **R** Bk G Bk **Y**
2 4 32 4 2

D. W. Stewart drew attention to the fact that this tartan (398) is named LOGAN in the early collections, and claimed that that was its proper designation. It first appears as SKENE in the Smith work, with the difference that the fine lines are in green, not blue. James Logan, in *The Scottish Gaël*, gives a sett (182) for LOGAN, but not one for SKENE. Yet he seems to have learned of a Skene tartan by the time he wrote for the McIan-Logan work, and was able to supply a count to M'Intyre-North. This (399) seems to be the design McIan attempted to reproduce in his drawing. Yet a third design (400) has been offered as SKENE but is probably merely a misinterpretation of McIan's drawing.

There is a tradition that the Skenes were descended from the Robertsons of Athol, and the design (398) first given by the Smiths has some slight likeness to the ROBERTSON (369).

401-419 STEWART

(401) **G** Bk B Bk G R Bk R Bk R B Bk G Bk G Bk **B**
24 2 4 2 24 4 24 2 24 4 24 2 4 2 4 2 24

(402)	**G**	B	Bk	B	Bk	B	Bk	G	R/Y	G	Bk	G	Bk	**G**
	4	6	2	2	2	2	8	24	4	24	6	4	12	4

(403)	**G**	R	Az	B	R	G	R	B	R	G	R	G	R	Az	B	**R**
	4	4	2	4	48	4	4	16	4	4	8	48	4	2	4	6

(404)	**R**	Bk	R	Bk	G	Bk	G	Bk	**G**
	12	2	40	16	6	2	4	2	44

(405)	**W**	R	Bk	G	Bk	G	Bk	G	**R**
	4	48	12	2	2	4	2	12	24

(406)	**R**	Az	Bk	Y	Bk	W	Bk	G	R	Bk	R	**W**
	72	8	12	2	2	2	2	16	8	2	4	2

(407)	**R**	Az	Bk	Y	Bk	W	G	R	Bk	R	**W**
	128	24	32	4	8	6	64	16	8	6	4

(408)	**R**	Az	Bk	Y	Bk	W	Bk	G	R	Bk	R	**W**
	28	8	12	2	4	4	4	24	12	4	4	2

(409)	**R**	W	Az	W	Bk	Y	Bk	W	Bk	G	R	Bk	R	**W**
	4	48	6	6	12	2	2	2	2	16	8	2	4	2

(410)	**Bk**	R	Bk	Y	Bk	W	B	G	R	Bk	R	**W**
	6	48	8	2	4	2	8	12	6	2	4	2

(411)	**R**	G	R	G	R	Bk	Y	Bk	W	B	G	R	Bk	R	**W**
	6	2	4	2	36	8	2	4	2	8	12	6	2	4	2

(412)	**R**	W	K	W	K	W	G	R	K	R	**W**
	6	56	4	4	4	4	24	16	2	2	2

(413)	**W**	R	K	R	G	W	B	Y	B	K	W	R	W	R	**W**
	4	7	5	30	83	9	6	6	26	26	132	7	4	4	20

(414)	**G**	R	G	R	B	R	G	R	B	R	G	R	G	**R**
	12	4	4	36	18	6	6	6	18	6	48	4	4	8

(415)	**G**	R	B	R	K	Y	K	W	K	G	R	K	R	**W**
	4	60	8	8	12	2	2	2	2	20	8	2	2	2

(416)	**G**	R	A	K	Y	K	W	K	G	R	G	**Y**
	18	104	26	32	4	6	8	6	46	30	14	6

(417)	**B**	R	B	A	T	G	R	G	R	**G**
	12	6	56	6	14	52	10	6	6	16

(418)	G	K	G	K	G	R/Y	G	K	B	K	B	G		
	8	26	10	16	54	8	54	16	6	6	18	8		
(419)	G	K	G	K	G	R/Y	G	K	B	K	B	K	B	G
	4	12	4	6	22	4	22	6	2	2	2	2	14	4

Many different patterns appear among those tartans bearing the name of Stewart, or Stuart. Few of them are indisputably ancient. The most distinctive of these is the OLD STEWART (401). This is quite unlike any other tartan; it is subdued in colour, but rich in effect. Various settings of it are known to have existed, but the present one is that now in general use. It belongs rather to the Stewarts of the Western Highlands, but was early accepted as the Clan Stewart tartan.

The only other dark STEWART is the Hunting (402), and it is much more often seen than the former. It was first illustrated by James Grant, who refers to its wide popularity, it being then, as now, much worn by those having no claim to any other recognised tartan. He confesses ignorance of its history; but it is probably one of the large number of tartans that came into existence about the first or second quarter of the nineteenth century. It appears to be composite in its scheme, and as shown by Grant it has an unfortunate irregularity; the red and yellow lines are unevenly spaced. In this it violates the principle laid down by James Logan:

> All regular tartans are made, so that, in the folds of the kilt and plaid, which are formed in what is called quilled, or box plaiting, a particular stripe shall appear. Thus, in the Gordon sett, it s yellow, in the MacKenzie white, &c., and wherever one of these patterns cannot be formed in this way, the web is irregular ...

It is shown here with this irregularity rectified. Though universally called the HUNTING STEWART, there is no very good reason why it should be considered a Stewart tartan at all, and it is likely that it always was, as now, used indiscriminately.

What is possibly an old tartan, though it has only in recent times been widely put forward as STEWART OF APPIN (403), belongs to a pattern group that includes some MacDonald and several Clan Chattan designs. In this it resembles the MacColl (202).

The STEWART OF ATHOLL (404) has become more widely known in the last two generations. It is claimed for this design that it is found in a relic of 'the '45'. However that may be, it is one of a number of designs prepared for the *Vestiarium Scoticum*, but not published therein. It was first illustrated in *Old and Rare Scottish Tartans.* A closely related design (405), known as the STUART OF BUTE, was also among the illustrations withheld from the *Vestiarium.*

The remainder of the Stewart designs are all variants of the ROYAL STUART, and a few of them are shown here. The usual modern form of the ROYAL STUART is given first (406). An example of two hundred years ago, examined by the Author, shows that the design has been well maintained. In this example (407) one black line is absent. Although the colours have been made distinct in the present illustration, they are much less so in the original, which is a silk scarf; so faded is it, that it is difficult to decide what was previously dark green and what was black, and the missing black line may merely have become indistinguishable from the dark green. Here, as in the count given by Logan, the white line at the sides is appreciably wider than the nearby yellow, but this difference is not now observed. It appears also in the sett (408) given by the Smiths under the name of PRINCE CHARLES EDWARD (Plate 16 (j)). This is merely the ROYAL STUART with the red ground reduced in relative width; the tartan becomes richer to the point of congestion. It is stated to have been worn by the Prince at Holyrood.

What is sometimes called the DRESS STUART is the normal ROYAL STUART with the broad band of red changed to white. One variation of this is shown by James Grant (409), and named the 'VICTORIA', as having been favourably regarded by that Queen. It is similar to that given in the *Vestiarium* as ROYAL STUART.

The remaining two of our examples are the STEWART OF GALLOWAY (410) and the STEWART OF APPIN (411), both of which were among the drawings made for, but not published in, the *Vestiarium*. It will be noticed that in these the blue stripes, normally at the outside of the pattern band, have been transferred to an inner position — perhaps with the idea of tidying up the design. The text of the *Vestiarium* gives no more justification for including the yellow and the neighbouring white line of the ROYAL STUART in these two designs than it does in the other two, those of ATHOL and BUTE (404-5); but in the drawings prepared but not used for publication this difference is made. The drawings, not the text, were followed in weaving the specimens in D. W. Stewart's *Old and Rare Scottish Tartans*, and the use of these four designs was subsequent to their appearance in the latter work.

Royal Stuart is a kilt or plaid setting of Prince Charles Edward (Plate 16 (j) and (k) and probably owes its name — which seems to have been bestowed on it not much earlier than the end of the eighteenth century — to that relationship for the Prince Charles Edward tartan has many reputed associations with the Prince and The '45 and was known to Wilsons' as 'Prince Charles Stuart's tartan'.

Numerous versions have been recorded or invented of Royal Stuart on a white or other light-coloured ground; most of these either follow the 'Victoria' (409) or have the blue band conjoined to the black; the '*Tartaine Rioale*' described in the *Cromarty Ms* and the *Vestiarium* follows the former but the Royal tartan illustrated in the *Vestiarium* (412) differs somewhat. An example of one of these on show at the Smith Institute, Stirling was named as 'Victoria' but the blue was dark and the ground yellow as was the space between blue and black. Others at the same place were styled 'Dress Stewart' (413) and 'Stewart, (Galloway)' (416); all were of Wilson manufacture and are said to have arrived, unheralded and unexplained, in a brown paper parcel. They have the appearance of being non-standard webs and all are very large setts but nothing more is known about them.

For 'CLAN STEWART' the *Vestiarium* illustrates a tartan (415) not dissimilar to Royal Stuart but perhaps the most authentic looking of all the red Stewart tartans is STEWART OF URRARD (414), recorded by James McKinlay.

Variations upon Royal Stuart are many if not actually legion, from 'BLACK STEWART' — with black for the large red squares — and 'STEWART, BLACK AND WHITE', both of which made their first appearance in the Johnston work of 1906, to such modern confections as 'SILVER STEWART', 'MUTED BLUE STEWART' and 'AUTHENTIC GREY STEWART'.

Turning back to the dark Stewart tartans, 'STEWART OF APPIN' (417) — sometimes called 'hunting' — dates from early in the nineteenth century. Its resemblance to the dark MacDonald tartans speaks for its authenticity but the browns were probably black originally.

Stewart was wrong in 'balancing' the Hunting Stewart tartan which has always been unbalanced and appears to have given no trouble to kilt-makers despite what Logan had to say. In the earliest version (418) taken from the Key Pattern Book, the distance between the red and yellow overchecks is greater over the black stripes than over the blue section; in the version by James Grant (419) it is greater over the blue. We do not know who added the extra black lines; one seems to see a Sobieski finger in the pie. It has also been implied that the Hunting Stewart tartan is a 'jazzed up' version of the Black Watch. It is nothing of the kind and in fact the early pattern shows quite cunning use of the Mackintosh motif — in black on green and in blue on black.

420 STRATHEARN

Y	R	G	Y	R	G	R	Y	R	G	Y	G	R	G	R	Y
2	2	12	16	2	2	2	16	12	2	2	2	12	12	2	2

This flamboyant tartan is described by the Smiths as having been worn by the Duke of Kent, father of Queen Victoria. Though at first glance a complex pattern, it is made up of one simple element, rendered in three arrangements of the three colours employed; these three versions are then grouped into a symmetrical pattern. The name derives rather from a subsidiary title of the distinguished wearer than directly from the district, where it can hardly have been in general use at any time.

See Appendix F.

421, 422 SUTHERLAND

(421)	**B**	Bk	B	Bk	B	Bk	G	Bk	G	Bk	B	Bk	**B**
	22	2	2	2	2	16	16	2	16	16	16	2	2

(422)	G	W	G	Bk	B	Bk	B	Bk	B	R	B	**R**
	12	4	48	24	6	4	4	4	24	2	2	6

Two Sutherland tartans are recognised. The simpler of the two (421) is identical in scheme with the BLACK WATCH, though it is sometimes woven in slightly lighter colours. As worn by the Argyll and Sutherland Highlanders it is kilted to show the green, whereas the BLACK WATCH is kilted to show the blue. The design given in the *Vestiarium Scoticum* (422) has a foundation resembling the BLACK WATCH, with red and white lines superimposed. This second design is reproduced by Smibert indicating that it had come into use fairly promptly. There is evidence that an early Sutherland tartan contained red and white lines, but none that this is the tartan in question.

423 TAYLOR

G	K	G	Coral	G	P	G	**Y**
10	4	26	8	24	44	10	6

A modern family tartan loosely related to the Cameron of the *Vestiarium Scoticum*. It was designed by Lt. Col. Iain Cameron Taylor.

424 TEALL OF TEALLACH

T	A	T	Slate grey	G	W	T	R	**Y**
6	26	6	26	46	6	38	48	8

A modern family tartan of restrained and attractive style, though the colours are not entirely conventional. It was designed for Dr Gordon Teall in 1970.

425-427 URQUHART

(425)	G	Bk	G	Bk	B	R	B	Bk	G	Bk	G	Bk	**G**
	2	2	16	16	16	2	16	16	2	2	2	2	16

(426)	**Bk**	G	Bk	B	Bk	B	Bk	B	**R**
	4	18	12	2	2	2	2	12	6

(427)	**R**	G	Bk	G	Bk	B	Bk	B	Bk	B	W	**B**
	4	6	6	96	48	16	6	6	6	48	4	8

Logan records an Urquhart tartan (425), given also by Smibert, having a foundation similar to the BLACK WATCH, but with the pairs of black lines appearing in the green bands, not the blue. The foundation of the designs in the Smith work (426) and in the *Vestiarium Scoticum* (427) is identical with that in the latter's version of the SUTHERLAND (422). The Smiths write that their specimen was collected in the Highlands shortly before 1822 — presumably by George Hunter, the Army clothier.

Urquhart was the name of the reputed author of the MS on which the *Vestiarium* was claimed to be based. Whether Sir Richard Urquhart was an antiquarian with an expansive imagination, or was a fiction invented by a forger, we are not concerned to say. What we can say is that without him this book might have been shorter, the Author would have been saved a deal of often fruitless speculation — and many clans and families might have remained tartanless.

428 WALLACE

Bk	R	Bk	Y
2	16	16	2

Reproduced in the *Vestiarium Scoticum*, this tartan is known from examples in early collections of specimens (Plate 11 (b); D.W. Stewart states that Wallaces were known also to wear the MACLEAN OF DUART (271).

429 WAGGRALL SETT

C	W	R	C	W	P	A	W	A	P	W	LG	Y	W	P	W	Y
8	2	22	4	4	22	8	4	8	22	4	8	8	2	10	2	8
LG	W	G	LG	W	LG	G	W	A	P	W	P	A	W	C	R	W
8	4	20	8	4	8	20	4	4	12	2	12	4	4	4	22	2
C	W	R	C	W	A	P	W	P	A	W	G	LG	Y	W	Y	LG
8	2	22	4	4	4	12	2	12	4	4	12	4	4	2	4	4
G	W	C	R	W	**C**											
12	4	4	22	2	8											

One of the late nineteenth century Wilson plaid setts with three half setts to 19 inches in the 600 reed. It shows well how some of these early setts were made up from sub-setts, making it almost impossible to tell the positions of the true pivots from a small specimen.

430 WEMYSS

R	G	R	Bk	R	Bk	W	Bk	**R**
8	2	48	8	8	24	2	24	8

The tartan of this well-known Fifeshire family is found in the *Vestiarium*

Scoticum. It is similar in scheme to the HUNTING MACLEAN (272) and several other tartans.

431 JANET WILSON SETT

P	W	A	G	A	G	A	G	R	G	R	G	R	G	R	G	R
60	4	6	6	6	6	6	32	6	6	6	6	6	6	6	50	30
G	A	R	W	**R**												
8	8	16	4	30												

This pattern was named after Janet Paterson, William Wilson's wife, whom he married in 1775. There are three half setts to a width of 22 inches in the 28 reed.

432 'JACOBITE'

W	Cr	B	W	Orange	W	B	Cr	W	Cr	B	W	G	W	B	Cr	**W**
2	4	4	2	16	2	4	4	2	4	4	2	16	2	4	4	2

The tartans we have been considering have been such as might be supplied to anyone seeking a design appropriate to his own wear. But there are a few others that are nameless, or dubiously named, yet of great interest and genuine antiquity. Our first example (432) is that known as the 'JACOBITE' from a tradition that it was used early in the eighteenth century as a secret political badge. The Smiths were the first to illustrate it, and they say that the pattern was taken from a silk scarf made in 1712. In the Smith plate the colours are reasonably quiet; but subsequent reproductions from Grant's onward, have been in colours that were striking even beyond the indiscretion of the Jacobites.

There is a little-known fact about tartan-weaving in the past — that such articles as silk scarves were often actually woven at Barcelona. No doubt patterns were sent there to be copied; but it is possible that the Catalan weavers occasionally submitted ideas of their own, on similar lines, for the approval of likely customers, and that some innovations were thereby introduced. There is no reason to suppose that this trade was extensive, but it deserves to be borne in mind. It may be that the 'JACOBITE' had such an origin.

433 'MACKINTOSH'

R	Bk	R	Bk	R	G	R
72	4	4	4	6	24	150+

Instances have already been given of tartans reputed to have been worn during 'the '45' by Prince Charles Edward. We show three further examples. The first (433) represents a fragment copied by D. W. Stewart, who describes it as MACKINTOSH. Too little of it is shown to indicate a repeating pattern, but it is of special interest when compared with other tartans belonging to the same period. The green stripe is $\frac{7}{16}$th inch wide.

434 'ROBERTSON'

R	G	R	G	R	G	R	G	R	G	R	G	R	G
6	2	2	2	36	2	2	48	36	2	2	2	2	30+

The second example, a fragment of which now belongs to the Clan Donnachaidh Society, is given the name of Robertson. The plaid of which it was a part is said to have been presented by the Prince to a Robertson during 'the '45'. The original fragment is too small to show a repeat, but by collating the warp and the weft more of the design can be reconstructed than either alone will show. Our example gives the result. It is quite possible that the two ends of our colour-strip represent one and the same green stripe, similar in width to the other green stripes shown, but there is not the evidence that would permit us to make that conclusion with certainty. In the past, those who have been responsible for cutting up large pieces of tartan for distribution among relic-hunters have often failed to realise, or even to consider, how much is required to give an adequate representation of the design.

An almost identical design is given by McIan as MacDonell of Keppoch (214), and the matter is discussed in connection therewith; allowing that the McIan rendering contains a broad red band in error, our suspicion that the final green of our table constitutes the turning point of the design would be confirmed. Such an error would not be surprising in a McIan plate.

435 A PLAID FOUND AT CULLODEN

B	R	B	R	Y	R	B	R	Y	R	B	R	B	R	B	R	B
10	14	2	2	10	10	10	10	4	2	2	2	2	10	2	2	2
R	Y	R	B	R	Y	R	B	R	B	R	B	R	B	R	B	R
2	4	10	10	10	10	2	2	12	2	2	2	4	2	2	2	12
B	R	Y	R	B	R	B	R	**B**								
2	2	10	8	2	2	2	2	10								

At this point we introduce the pattern of a plaid found at Culloden and copied by D. W. Stewart, who asserts that the plaid was probably old even at that date. It is woven in blue, red, and yellow. We have here a scheme of which portions are identical with the scheme of the 'Robertson' (434).

The reproduction of the tartan given by D. W. Stewart unfortunately suffers from the defect that, owing to the large size of the complex design, it is not clear how the design repeats at one of the turns. The band of colour on which this turn occurs is probably the broad blue stripe enclosed by narrow blue lines, but may be the red stripe, of indeterminate width, at the extreme right of our drawing.

Subsequent to the publication of *The Setts,* the author was, by the kindness of the late Mackintosh of Mackintosh, given the opportunity of a thorough examination of several examples of tartan from the Moy Hall Collection. One of these has a close bearing on (435). The Moy Hall relic is a piece of hard tartan about 26 inches by 6 inches the length running from the selvedge towards the centre of the web. The scheme of the design is the same as that of (435), except that what is yellow in the latter is green in the Moy Hall fragment. The length of the piece is not sufficient to make clear at what point the sett reverses, but this difficulty is removed by the survival of a letter which puts the complete repeat beyond doubt.

Evidently the plaid from which the fragment was cut was intact in 1821, for the letter, from a dealer in tartans, contains a fully detailed count from which a number of plaids were to be woven by a firm in Jedburgh. The new plaids were to be in 'Prince Charles Stewart tartan, taken from a plaid worn by him, now in the possession of Lady Mackintosh, Moyhall'. The count, given below, is numerically less than that of the original, being scaled down in the proportion of about 3 : 2, but it gives the identical pattern, and shows exactly where it goes into reverse.

Bk	R	B	R	B	R	G	R	Bk	R	B	R	B	R	B	R	B
40	4	4	4	4	48	60	4	4	52	4	4	4	8	4	4	4
R	Bk	R	G	R	B	R	G	R	Bk	R	Bk	R	Bk	R	Bk	R
52	4	4	48	40	40	40	16	4	4	4	4	48	4	4	4	4
G	R	B	R	G	R	Bk	R	**B**								
16	40	40	40	48	4	4	52	56								

That a faithful rendering of the Moy Hall plaid was being sought is shown by the specification regarding the selvedge, which had to be in herring-bone weave — as it is in the fragment examined.

It is evident, then, that there were at least two ancient plaids showing the same scheme of stripes, the one with green at Moy Hall, and the other with yellow.

The (433) 'MACKINTOSH' is taken from *Old and Rare Scottish Tartans*; only enough of the pattern was exemplified in the original fragment to furnish our colour strip. One former owner of it affirmed that it was 'a piece of the kilt worn by Prince Charlie while in the Mackintosh country', and that the kilt had been cut up into fragments soon after, for distribution among relatives of The Mackintosh, of whom the owner was a descendant. Whether the Prince ever wore a kilt before Culloden is beside the point. What is remarkable is that the reproduction shown by D. W. Stewart, which he had had made to the dimensions of the original fragment, happens to coincide in pattern, colour and dimensions with a portion of the fragment still at Moy Hall. One may be forgiven for surmising that the 'Mackintosh' fragment (433) was in fact part of the plaid that had been cut up, and that the story of the royal kilt is an example of the building up of a myth on evidence too slender to support it, as so commonly happens. A single repeat of the pattern must have been 54 inches wide — admirable for a plaid, but quite unsuitable for a kilt, whether feilebeg or feilemor.

It is not intended to suggest that there is any immediate relation between the 'ROBERTSON'–'KEPPOCH' design and that of the plaid from Culloden; but the parallel portions of these designs show a connection that can hardly be one of pure chance. When a weaver wished to produce a variant on an existing design, he might turn first to a change in the colours, as in many Hunting tartans, rather than tamper with the basic scheme. Thus, he might reverse his red and green. With this in mind, we turn back to the 'MACKINTOSH' (433) This renders, in green and black, a portion of the Culloden plaid that is woven in red; in the ROYAL STUART (405), another very old design, it occurs in black.

We find, then, that the Culloden plaid, while itself to be regarded as of a 'Fancy' design, includes elements found in other tartans known to be of great age; that these elements may have been part of the common tradition of weavers over a wide territory; and that one of these elements provides the characteristic motif of the BLACK WATCH. The idea that weavers invented entirely original designs, however true latterly, is not true of the period before 'the '45'.

Apart from the Moy Hall fragment, at least four other pieces from the same web (or another identical to it) are extant. One is in private hands, two are at Blair Castle and one is in Inverness Museum; of the four, only the larger of the Blair Castle pieces is big enough to be of any help in reconstructing the very large sett. The Moy Hall fragment is 23½ inches long and stops just short of the plain selvage, leaving the rest of the pattern and the actual width of the web in doubt, but the Blair piece is from the full width of the web (24") and confirms that the sett of the 1821 copies is broadly correct, the discrepancies being attributable to adjustments needed to fit the count to the loom. The merchant who handled the 1821 copies was C. Blair, Jnr., Dunkeld and the weavers were John Hilson & Sons, Jedburgh.

Despite the correctness of the sett, I cannot agree with Stewart that the original plaid was complete in 1821. It is clear that accurate copies were intended, but the letter referred to says that it appears that a "scarf of three yards long will contain two complete sets (sic) and have (stripe) No. 2 (black herringbone) in the middle and at each end, or if you please, have (it) each end: if you have it in the middle have it only once there". Had the plaid been complete these options would not have been available; the black bars are, in any case, part of the selvage mark and this never appeared in the weft.

The count given below is from the original piece and for the whole width of the web; the blue bar at the plain selvage therefore has to be doubled at each pivot in the length. In setting up the loom threading begins at the plain selvage and continues as plain 2/2 twill for ten threads into the black selvage mark. The last seventy threads (K62, R8) are threaded 10 × 10 herringbone except for the last red thread; if this is threaded normally the weft will not pick it up and it is therefore put through the same heddle as its predecessor.

R	K	R	B	R	B	R	G	R	K	R	B	R	B	R*	B	R
8	72	4	4	4	4	72	90	4	4	72	4	4	4	12	4	4
B	R	G	R	G	R	B	R	G	R	K	R	K	R	K	R	K
4	72	4	4	90	80	68	78	20	4	4	4	4	72	4	4	4
R	G	R	B	R	G	R	K	R	B							
4	20	78	68	80	74	4	4	60	48							

With such relatively small pieces of material to work on there must be some uncertainty about the second pivot; that marked with the asterisk (R12) seems the most likely.

The red of the original is less bright than a true scarlet, the black is greenish and the blue approximates to French Navy; the green is dark and not at all yellow. Green can fade differentially and D. W. Stewart has shown himself to be unreliable on colour matching so there is a strong possibility that the plaid reported by him and illustrated in *Old & Rare Scottish Tartans* is the same as the Moy Hall fragment or at least another from the same web. See Note 3 at the end of Appendix F.

436 PLAID OF PRINCE CHARLES EDWARD

Bk	R	G	R	Bk	R	Bk	R	B	R	Bk	R	**Y**
4	4	14	14	2	6	2	14	18	4	10	6	6

Our third relic of Prince Charles is a design reconstructed by D. W. Stewart from fragments of a plaid given by the Prince to the Countess of Eglinton as a memento of his short period of residence at Holyrood Palace. It is quite unlike any other recorded tartan.

437 A COAT WORN AT CULLODEN

Y	Bk	DY	Bk	W	Heliotrope	Az	**R**
6	4	26	26	4	28	4	10

A Highland coat worn at Culloden by a member of the Prince's personal suite provides a fine specimen of old tartan. No clan or family name attaches to it. We have seen that highly complex tartans were in vogue at the time of the final crash of Jacobite hopes, and here we have one which shows that the Highland love of exuberant colour could express itself with admirable taste. It should be remembered that in all these colour-strips the colours are shown as they would appear in the warp alone, and that in the woven fabric they are for the most part blended one with another. In tartans no pure colour can appear beside another, but only beside a broken colour. It is to this fact that we owe much of the beauty of the tartans.

Some ten years ago I examined a plaid in the Forbes tartan which, at that time, was about the same age as was the Culloden coat when examined by D. W. Stewart. The blue and green of this plaid had faded to almost exactly the same shades as the heliotrope and dark yellow of the coat and we must therefore, his claims for colour accuracy notwithstanding, bear in mind that the coat may have been an ordinary blue, black and green tartan.

438 WEDDING DRESS: 1766

Bk	W	Bk	W	Az	R	G	W	G	W	B	Az	Beige	W	Beige	Az
8	4	4	2	12	12	12	2	54	2	8	8	6	2	6	8
B	W	R	B	Az	W	Az	**B**								
8	2	72	6	4	2	4	6								

The source of our concluding design is a fragment of silk tartan in the possession of John Ross, Esq., of High Wycombe, Bucks., by whose courtesy a description of it is here included. This fragment formed part of the dress, or possibly shawl, worn by Miss Middleton, of Mains of Logie, Angus, at her wedding in 1766 with George Ross, great-grandfather of the present owner. It may seem that 1766 is an improbable date for the wearing of any tartan, since the Proscription was then in force, and the Jacobite sympathies of the family were known; but such an infraction of the letter of the law might well escape serious notice.

In the original, the portion we give as red would be more correctly described as flame-colour. Fading is slight, though some strands of silk have perished. The design bears out what we have said of the complexity of some of the older tartans. It most nearly resembles in character the 'Jacobite' (432), which is first recorded as appearing in a silk scarf dating from 1712. So extended a design would be suitable for a fine fabric like silk, but not for the coarser woollen materials, and such tartans, though they may be Highland in inception, stand apart from the tartans of simpler design that are more appropriate for clan use.

439-445 MISCELLANEOUS JACOBITE RELICS

(439)

R	W	R	W	R	W	B	W	LR	W	LR	W	B	W	P	G	W
4	4	4	4	40	4	8	4	24	4	24	4	8	4	20	10	8
G	P	W	LR	R	W	R	LR	W	P	W	G	Y	G	W	A	W
10	20	4	20	22	4	22	20	4	24	4	4	6	4	4	10	8
A	W	G	Y	G	W	P	W	LR	R	W	R	LR	W	LR	B	W
10	4	4	6	4	4	24	4	16	16	4	16	16	4	20	8	4
Y	W	B	W	Y	W	B	LR	W	R	W	R	B	R	**W**		
6	4	8	4	6	4	8	20	4	40	12	8	4	8	4		

(440)

W	B	G	R	W	R	W	R	T	B	**W**
2	4	32	8	2	8	2	8	16	8	2

(441)

W	R	Y	G	Y	K	Y	G	**R**
4	12	8	48	16	8	16	12	48

(442)

G	K	R	G	R	G	R	A	R	G	R	K	**R**
4	2	24	24	8	8	8	4	8	24	24	2	4

(443)

G	R	G	R	A	B	R	B	R	B	A	R	G	**R**
12	4	4	48	2	2	4	24	4	2	2	4	48	4

(444)

R	W	T	W	A	G	Y	W	G	P	Y	A	P	R	**W**
12	4	80	4	28	28	6	4	12	12	4	12	60	24	4

(445)

C	K	C	W	C	K	C	DY	Y	W	K	W	Y	C	K	W	A	**W**
24	8	12	14	34	24	6	22	14	4	6	4	14	16	8	6	6	4

Fragments of tartan that are associated with the '45 in general and with Prince Charles Edward in particular are many and varied, but they have in common that they have been, for the most part, carefully preserved.

Prince Charles Edward's supporters were ardent in collecting fragments of garments he had worn, however briefly, and many of these have survived to add to our knowledge of the old patterns. Of particular interest, because of the size and complexity of the sett, is the pattern (439) of bedcurtains at Culloden House, from the bed in which the Prince slept the night before the battle. A portion of a silk plaid (440) worn by him is at Blair Castle. The patterns of a riding cloak (441), a plaid (442) and a coat (443) worn by the Prince during the campaign were collected by James MacKinlay; the last is in the West Highland Museum and has much in common with the red MacDonell of Glengarry tartan (217). Another plaid (444), from the Queen Street museum in Edinburgh, is said to have been worn by the Prince at Culloden; the white and yellow are silk and the brown probably began as black. From the Carmichael Collection in the same museum there comes an old Jacobite tartan (445). It is sometimes called 'STEWART' but more often 'ANCIENT JACOBITE'.

I have remarked earlier, in connection with the Moy Hall fragment, on the rarity of the survival of more than one piece of any of these 'souvenir' plaids. I find this rather surprising because a plaid can be cut into a great many pieces and although the material is perishable such pieces when connected with the Prince had, and retained, something of the status of holy relics. However, that is the way it is and such rarity certainly adds continuing spice to the hunt for specimens.

Two fragments in the Royal Ontario Museum are reputed to be parts of a kilt worn by the Prince when in a cave on Skye, and while the known itinerary of the Prince after Culloden makes it unlikely that the claim is strictly true, 'worn by' in this context has the loosest of meanings and there is nothing in the description of the specimens to suggest that they are not contemporary with those events.

The pieces are small, approximately $2\frac{1}{2}'' \times 1\frac{1}{3}''$ and $3\frac{1}{2}'' \times 1\frac{1}{3}''$ respectively and each gives two threadcounts, (a) horizontal and (b) vertical. The figures in brackets are cautious adjustments to the original counts made in order to balance the stripes.

1 (a)	W	R	Lav	W	B	W	Lav	Y	B	Y	B	Y	B	R	B
	4	8	8	4	10	4	8	(8)	(30)	6	30	8	6	8	4

1 (b)	W	R	W	R	B
	4	20	4	20	8

2 (a)	W	R	Lav	Y	B	Lav	B	Lav	B	Y	Lav	R	W	R	W
	4	(10)	8	8	(28)	(8)	30	8	28	8	8	10	4	10	4

2 (b)	Y	B	R	B	R	W	B	W	R	W
	8	8	8	8	20	4	8	4	20	4

Count 2a shows a well defined and plausible pivot at B30 from which it may be inferred that the pattern is a reversing one, but the apparent pivots at B30 Y6 B30 and W4 B10 W4 in 1a and at W4 B8 W4 in 2b are false, as can be seen from the count on either side of them, and so cannot give us the second limit of the pattern. The (b) counts, although apparently related to each other, show no relationship to the (a) counts and lavender, though present in both (a) counts is absent from both (b) counts, leaving a distinct possibility that the warp and weft patterns differ. It is clear that the pattern is large and diffuse but the existing data are insufficient for a reconstruction. (See Appendix E.)

By the early part of the eighteenth century tartan had become a highly developed art form and a surprisingly large number of pieces has survived to demonstrate this. Some are simple, some complex, but all are products of local artist-weavers making the best of what was available in the way of materials, dyes and apparatus.

(446)	**R**	A	B	R	G	T	**R**
	8	8	28	28	28	6	8

(447)	**R**	G	B	R	G	K	**R**
	4	8	16	18	18	4	4

(448)	**R**	A	B	R	Mid B	Dk T	**R**
	6	8	24	22	24	8	6

(449)	**W**	T	R	W	T	Fawn	R	T	**W**
	4	2	20	12	20	24	20	2	4

Typical simple designs are three related patterns, one from Glenmorriston (448), one in private hands (446) and one (447) in the West Highland Museum, where it is named 'Stewart'. Allowing that it is often not easy to differentiate between blue and green — light or dark — and remembering that brown often began as black, it is possible that all these counts are from the same piece of cloth. Even the discrepancies in the numbers of threads can be accounted for by the practice followed by some workers of making a table of measurements, Logan-style, and afterwards converting it to a thread count at some arbitrary number of threads per inch.

A rare combination of dyed yarn with natural colours is shown in No. 449. Provenance is unknown, but the earliest record of the count is by James MacKinlay. The white is described as 'creamy' and the brown is dark.

MacKinlay obtained many counts from A. W. Geddes, who appears to have specialised in eighteenth century patterns. Three patterns from this source follow; there is no record of where any of them was found.

(450)	**G**	R	B	K	B	R	G	R	B	R	G	R	K	B	R	B	K
	24	36	4	32	4	8	6	8	16	8	6	8	4	16	64	16	4
	G	R	**K**														
	24	4	32														

(451)	**K**	R	B	R	K	R	B	R	A	R	B	R	G	R	K	R	G
	2	12	24	2	24	12	2	2	2	2	2	12	24	12	2	12	24
	A	R	K	R	B	R	K	R	B	R	K	R	B	R	A	R	B
	2	12	24	2	24	12	2	12	24	2	24	12	2	2	2	2	2
	R	K	G	R	**K**												
	12	2	24	12	2												

(452)

NB	W	NB	RB	W	RB	NB	W	DG	MG	OG	W	NB	RB	W	OG
52	2	6	8	2	8	6	2	16	10	10	2	8	6	2	8
W	RB	NB	W	OG	MG	DG	W	NB	RB	W	RB	NB	W	NB	W
2	6	8	2	10	10	16	2	6	8	2	8	6	2	26	2
NB	R	**W**													
10	6	2													

The colours of the last are given as **N**avy blue, **R**oyal **B**lue, **D**ark **G**reen, **M**id **G**reen and **O**live **G**reen.

CURTAINS FOUND AT NETHYBRIDGE

(453)

B	R	B	R	W	R	G	R	**B**
4	98	102	18	4	18	102	98	4

In former times tartan was used for almost everything made from cloth and it cannot have been rare for an old plaid to be cut up for curtains or similar uses. This was a piece of hard tartan with dull red, dark blue and khaki green. The pattern is similar to the Gow tartan which looks much more like a local design of the Mackintosh type than that shown in the famous portrait of Neil Gow.

454 A PLAID FROM TOMATIN

B	R	G	R	B	**R**
8	112	52	8	52	8

This plaid is known to have belonged to James Dunbar, Edinchat, who died in 1859, but may have belonged to his father before him. It is a fairly coarse weave — about 40 ends per inch — and fairly typical of country made plaiding of the early nineteenth century. The pattern is that of the Fraser tartan (126) and lends some substance to D. W. Stewart's view that the design is properly a Grant one. In that event it would have travelled up the Spey and the Dulnain into Strathdearn to become, with much elaboration, 'Mackintosh' and, more recently 'Clan Chattan'.

455 A PLAID FROM GLEN TILT

W	G	R	G	R	B	R	G	R	**A**
4	4	4	56	4	24	44	4	4	4

Taken from a specimen in Perth Museum. It was woven at Clunes Farm and the pattern is a development of the red Mackintosh tartan. The date of manufacture is not given.

456, 458 TWO PLAIDS AT THE HIGHLAND FOLK MUSEUM

(456)	**R**	W	K	G	Y	G	**R**			
	192	12	12	8	24	8	24			
(457)	G	T	G	T	G	T	G	W	G	**W**
	64	4	4	4	4	24	44	2	2	6

The first example is taken from a plaid made at Banff in 1760 for Ferguson, the astronomer; the other, apparently using naturally coloured wool in conjunction with dyed yarn, owes much to ROTHESAY (378).

458 A PLAID FROM MORAYSHIRE

G	R	G	R	G	R	G	R	G	R	G	K	Y	K	B	K	R
56	2	4	6	2	32	2	6	4	2	28	6	6	6	6	6	96
W	R	**W**														
6	6	6														

A pattern from MacGregor Hastie, who ascribes it to the early nineteenth century.

Royal Stuart was used by Wilsons' as the basis of a number of their own designs. We have already met with Nos. 3, 43 and 155; some others are given below.

459 No. 4 (Plate 16 (m))

W	R	A	R	G	DP	W	DP	Y	DP	A	R
3	14	4	14	32	18	4	4	4	18	16	62

460 No. 156

R	K	R	W	R	G	Y	K	A	K	W	K	Y	K	A	W	**R**
16	4	8	8	28	40	6	30	32	4	12	4	4	8	8	4	60

461 No. 181

G	R	G	R	G	Y	K	W	K	Y	K	A	K	A	**R**
6	6	6	32	44	6	6	10	6	6	38	18	4	18	50

462 No. 227 (Plate 16 (l))

W	P	G	W	R	Y	P	A	**R**
4	20	40	6	6	6	16	14	52

The following patterns are taken from William Wilson & Son's 1819 Key Pattern Book as a change from ordinary tartans and as examples of the kind of pattern that was popular at the time. All are for the 24 reed (480 splits or 1920 warp ends to the Scotch Ell of 37 inches) and a nominal width of 25 inches.

Plain check patterns. These have a common thread count, only the colours being varied:

No. 93 or Small Rob Roy	R	K
No. 99 or Small MacLauchlan	R	G
No. 116	P	G
Light No. 116	Shade Green	P
No. 172	Sextian Blue	K
No. 210	A	G
No. 219	Shade Green	G
No. 224	K	G
	26	28
	12	14
	8	8

Not surprisingly, the black and green No. 224 was also known as 'Robin Hood'.

Unequal checks. Two of these also have a common count, the smaller square changing colour:

No. 134	G	R
No. 138	A	R
	14	42
No. 234	K	R
	6	16

Asymmetrical Patterns. The ringing of changes on these patterns is more complex; some are based on fixed counts and the colours changed to make new patterns, some have the colour of only one element changed and two have the colours constant and the count changed.

No. 52	G	K	A
No. 61	G	R	A
No. 198	K	R	A
No. 200	K	R	G
No. 202	G	K	R
	14	8	8

No. 174	G	P	A	Y
No. 189	G	P	W	R
No. 192	G	P	Y	R
No. 205	G	P	A	W
	20	8	2	2

No. 185	G	P	K
	18	20	22

No. 204 is as No. 185 but R for P

No. 55	A	P	G
	4	20	24

No. 81 is as No. 55 but Y for A
No. 84 is as No. 55 but R for A

No. 50	A	K	G
	4	24	20

No. 201	Y	P	G
	4	8	16

No. 79	W	G	A	K
	2	14	2	4

No. 140 is as No. 79 but Y for W

No. 159	G	R	P	K
	18	4	16	22

No. 220 is as No. 159 but W for R
No. 228 is as No. 159 but A for R

No. 203	G	R	A	Y
	20	16	8	4

No. 211	G	P	G	P
	16	16	4	4

	G	Orange	A	K
No. 195	28	20	4	8
No. 196	18	18	4	20

Reversing patterns

No. 188	**A**	G	**R**
	4	8	16

No. 207 is as No. 188 but has 8R

No. 53, or Mull or Glen Lyon	**A**	G	**K**
	4	8	10

No. 94 is as No. 53 but R for A
No. 203 is as No. 53 but P for K
No. 2/53 or Mull with yellow is as No. 53 but 2Y for 4A
No. 118 is as No. 2/53 but A for G in weft only

No. 212	**A**	R	**G**
	8	8	36

No. 113	**W**	P	G	**R**
	4	12	12	4

No. 62	**G**	R	**Officers' blue**
	26	4	26

No. 161 is as No. 62 but A for blue

No. 45	**G**	A	**K**
	16	4	8

No. 187	**K**	G	**R**
	8	8	8

No. 197	**G**	Y	**K**
	24	4	24

No. 208	**R**	A	**G**
	8	4	14

No. 55	**A**	P	**G**
	8	20	48

No. 95	**A**	G	R	P	**A**
	4	12	4	12	4

No. 75 or Austin	**K**	G	P	K	**P**
	4	12	6	6	6

No. 137 is as No. 75 but 4R for 4K

No. 137 is as No. 75 but 4Y for 4K

No. 179	G	Y	R	A	R	
	24	4	4	8	8	

No. 193 is as No. 179 but K for Y

No. 194	P	W	K	G	R	K
	6	2	6	10	2	6

'Fancy' tartans. All were made twenty-five inches wide.

No. 199 or MacNab	A	P	R	G			
Pattern	4	22	6	30			
No. 176	K	A	G	P	Y		
	8	6	26	24	4		22 half setts

A variation on the Douglas tartan, which was No. 148

No. 214	A	K	A	R	G		
	12	4	4	12	16		
No. 217	Y	G	K	A	P		
	4	20	20	4	22		24 half setts
No. 223	G	R	A	P	G		
	24	24	4	24	24		8 half setts
No. 111	P	W	G	A	K		
	38	4	24	6	4		24 half setts
No. 76	G	P	K	W	G	K	
	6	34	36	4	34	6	12 half setts
	4	22	22	4	24	4	18 half setts
	4	16	18	4	20	4	22 half setts

No. 100 is as No. 76 but Y for W
No. 231 is as No. 76 but A for W

No. 150 or	G	A	G	K	P	K	
'Cobourg Tartan'	36	4	8	28	24	6	16 half setts
	16	4	6	16	12	4	28 half setts

This has become the Graham of Menteith tartan.

No. 158	G	W	G	K	P	K	
	42	4	8	34	28	6	14 half setts
	18	4	6	14	14	4	28 half setts

No. 160 is as No. 158 but Y for W

No. 167	**K**	A	K	G	P	**K**	
	40	4	12	32	8	18	14 half setts

No. 183	G	R	G	P	A	**K**	
	4	4	24	24	4	8	22 half setts

No. 97	Y	P	K	G	K	G	**K**	
	6	24	24	24	4	24	22	12 half setts

No. 120 is as No. 97 but with R for Y and W4 for K4

No. 157 is as No. 97 but A for Y

No. 83	P	W	R	W	R	G	Y	**K**	
	28	4	6	4	30	36	6	28	12 half setts

No. 108	**K**	P	A	K	G	K	G	**K**	
	4	28	4	28	28	4	28	28	10 half setts

No. 33	**B**	G	A	R	A	K	Y	G	**R**	
	8	34	6	6	6	38	4	34	8	10 half setts
	8	26	6	6	6	30	4	28	8	12 half setts

No. 2/33 is as No. 33 but W for Y

No. 225	G	SG	P	A	K	Y	G	A	**K**	
	32	4	26	4	12	4	32	4	24	12 half setts

SG = Shade green, a very pale shade

No. 169	**G**	R	G	W	G	Y	G	R	**G**	
	10	18	20	4	4	4	20	18	10	14 half setts

No. 128	**A**	R	Y	R	A	G	A	R	K	R	**W**	
	8	6	4	18	6	48	6	18	6	6	4	11 half setts

No. 149	**G**	B	K	B	G	A	K	A	G	W	**K**	
	16	12	14	12	22	4	4	4	22	4	16	12 half setts

No. 30	**A**	K	A	B	K	Y	G	B	A	B	**K**	
	8	6	4	12	30	4	32	8	4	4	32	11 half setts

No. 60 is as No. 30 but with R for Y; another pattern, incorrectly numbered 157, has A in this place. All bear some resemblance to Logan's Cummin tartan.

The blue in Nos. 30, 60, 157 and 149 is Officers' blue.

No. 117	**G**	R	G	W	A	R	A	W	K	Y	K	A	W	P	**W**	
	8	8	8	4	24	10	24	4	10	4	10	8	4	10	8	10 half setts

Appendices

APPENDIX A

The Weight-Box Method of Tensioning the Warp

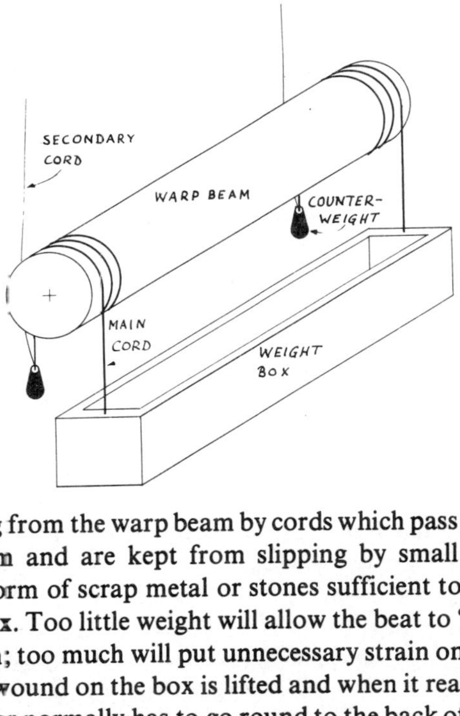

The box is hung from the warp beam by cords which pass four or five times round the beam and are kept from slipping by small counterweights; weight in the form of scrap metal or stones sufficient to resist the beat is added to the box. Too little weight will allow the beat to 'jerk' the box and it will slip down; too much will put unnecessary strain on the warp. As the woven cloth is wound on the box is lifted and when it reaches the top of its travel the weaver normally has to go round to the back of the loom and lift the counterweights by hand to allow the box to slide down to the beginning again. However, if the counterweights are slung from the loom frame by lengths of springy cord the whole action becomes automatic.

APPENDIX B

Fitting the Threadcount to the Loom

'Dark Logan sett' can supply an example of an adjustment to suit a thicker yarn with the same size of sett. The pattern was made with ten half-setts 19 inches wide. One half-sett was therefore 1.9 inches and using a 2/18s yarn *finishing* at 40 ends per inch would contain 76 warp ends.

Original count		*x76/132*	*adjusted (1)*	*(2)*
Black	2	1.15	2	1
Scarlet	16	9.2	10	8
Bottle green	60	34.55	30	36
Rose	16	9.2	10	8
Black	4	2.3	4	2
Rose	16	9.2	10	8
Black	18	10.36	10	10
	132	75.96	76	75

In order to maintain the narrow stripes at 4 threads the next size, 9.2 threads, has to be rounded up to 10, at which they are far short of correct proportions and this allows only 40 threads for the widest stripes which aggregate 44.91; 30 green and 10 black is the best that can be done. If the narrower lines are marked down to 2 and 8 — the correct proportions — 49 threads are left and 36 and 12 would be a suitable combination, giving 75 ends to the half-sett. The odd number of threads does not matter in this case as there is an even number of half-setts and means simply that the web will be ten threads narrower.

The counts given in *The Setts* are of the minimum size and will almost always have to be enlarged. Let us consider making the Hunting Barclay tartan to a 5″ sett (2½″ half-sett) at 40 threads per inch. A 27 inch web will contain 1080 ends and our half-sett will contain 100. Since 100 does not fit exactly into 1080 some concession must be made and we shall have to settle for either ten or eleven half-setts to the width. Let us try ten, which will give 108 ends.

Original count		*x 108/66*	*Adjusted*
R	1	1.63	2
G	32	52.36	52
B	32	52.36	52
G	1	1.63	2
	66	107.98	108

Remember to *halve* the pivot stripes before making these calculations from the counts given in this book.

A recent Lord Lyon, Sir Thomas Innes of Learney, maintained that adjusted counts should follow as exactly as possible the proportions of the originals. The result of this can be very clumsy but happily the rule has only to be applied to counts registered at the Lyon Court!

A typical selvage mark for 40 ends per inch would contain 64 threads and the twill threading of the main body of the cloth would extend eight threads into it, leaving 56 threads to be threaded as seven changes of 8 × 8 herringbone. The last two threads would be threaded in the same heddle.

APPENDIX C

The 'Sindex' System

Donald C. Stewart's note on its use

"The first thing to do is to draft a representative count. If a record is required of a *specific specimen,* the actual threads have to be counted over half a repeat, in a symmetrical sett; asymmetrical setts I shall deal with later."

"In laying out a colour strip, it is first decided how much of the sett will require to be shown, so that there is no doubt where it repeats. The pivots on which the sett reverses are marked with crosses. The approximate measurements of the stripes being determined, a suitable unit is chosen for the count. This unit may be a fraction of an inch or centimeter;"

"Near the top right corner (of the card) will be a code group of letters... This feature is the vital part of the system. Our early lists of these had a fanciful resemblance to log. tables, and acquired the handy name of

'Slogs.' Each letter represents a colour. Some tartans are rendered in various shades of colour, and to specify these would require such signs as Sc., Cr., Pk., for the reds, or Az., Mid-B, NB, for the blues. Experience showed that many colours could be grouped, and reduced to single letters. Those now in use are A, azure or light blue; B, mid-blue, dark blue, purple; G, any green; K, black; N, neutral grey; R, any red, whether scarlet, crimson, or pink; T (tan) for anything from beige to dark brown; W, white; Y, yellow or gold. Rarely used are O, orange, and M, maroon. A was differentiated from B, as in practice this is helpful, and the other blues are often interchangeable; and so with the other colours."

"The basic form of the Slog is 3 letters — colon — 3 letters. There are never more than 3 before the colon; after it the number may vary. To obtain the first three, look at the two pivotal stripes . . . Start with the one in earliest alphabetical order. For the next two letters, take the next two colours to one side . . . Now start from the other pivot and do the same."

"When there are less than six stripes, the first three must be maintained if possible." . . . "*No stripe may be* counted twice."

"In the case of asymmetric tartans, the principle is to select the colour with the earliest alphabetic initial, say A or B; then the adjoining colour next in alphabetic order, and continue *in the same direction* till 4 or 5 letters have been obtained".

The above is extracted from a letter that 'D.C.' wrote to a museum curator in October 1967; this letter also gave further elucidation which I have paraphrased below.

Six stripes is the minimum number required to give a full 3:3 Slog. Five stripes give 3:2, four give 3:1, three give 2:1 and a plain check 1:1. Should it occur that two tartans of six stripes or less give the same Slog, numbers are added to distinguish them. If two tartans of more than six stripes give the same Slog, the second group can be continued, either until the supply of stripes runs out, when the above remedy is applied, or until a difference occurs. I have found it best, however, to limit the second group to six letters, for Sindex cards are extraordinarily difficult to keep in the right order. The vast number of tartans based on the Black Watch sett call for slightly different treatment. Nearly all these are slogged BKB:BKB and so a third letter-group is added to indicate the distinguishing features. For example, the Gordon tartan is suffixed :YG, denoting a yellow stripe on green, Lamont has :WG and Forbes, with black guard lines to the white, has :KW.

APPENDIX D

A System for Classifying Tartans by Pattern

Many attempts have been made to devise a system by which tartans could be grouped by pattern and have usually foundered on either a too-narrow classification, leading to the forcing of nearly-square pegs into almost-round holes, with consequent uncertainties and ambiguities, or too much detail, resulting in a large number of almost indistinguishable classes. Although a great deal more work will be needed to prove it, some experiment has suggested that a system based on the three design groups already described would be practical, simple and effective, enabling the sorting of patterns into four groups and thence into families of closely related designs; the fourth group is needed both as a temporary resting place for setts that do not immediately fit into a group or family and as a final repository for those that do not fit anywhere. In this way the almost-round peg problem is overcome and if at the end of the day we are left with a bunch of patterns whose only mutual similarity is that they are different from all the others our end is still served.

Every pattern can be described, loosely but adequately, by using capital letters to indicate the colours and the basic design and small letters to give the colours, numbers and locations of overchecks. The resulting 'Slog' is used just as in 'Sindex' as the basis of a card index file.

The system uses the standard colour letters and the basic check is shown as in 'Sindex' by two capital letters with a colon between, for example, K:R (Rob Roy). Overchecked with black and yellow this becomes Wallace: $\frac{y}{K}:\frac{k}{R}$.

$\frac{2y}{K}:\frac{r}{Y}$ is a sufficient description of the yellow MacLeod tartan as is: $\frac{a}{G}$: ayya :$\frac{w}{R}$ of Buchanan; doubled pairs of overchecks, as in Home, are shown as such: $\frac{2g}{B}:\frac{2.2r}{K}$. It is preferable that fine accentling lines as in Buchanan and guard lines to overchecks generally should be omitted from the coding as inclusion of them tends to confuse the issue and to show up false differences as between Forbes and Lamont or the so-called Bean of Freeport and the green Shaw of Tordarroch.

Most of the patterns of the superimposed check type fall into one or another of a number of families such as Armstrong, Black Watch, Campbell, Mackintosh, MacDonald (which for our purposes is Campbell with a red line between B and K), MacDuff etc. Pattern now supersedes colour as a means of identification and it is only necessary to relate a pattern to the head of its family. The Campbell group, typified by Loudoun, is defined as a blue and black check with a green square superimposed on black (a convention adopted so that the colours can be expressed in alphabetical order as in 'Sindex' — see Appendix C) and answers to: $B : \frac{G}{K}$. Thereafter 'Campbell w/y' is a sufficient description of Campbell of Loudoun as is 'Campbell a:r' of Cawdor, the oblique stroke of the former showing that the colours alternate on one ground.

The third group makes only two families, the simple Ross and the MacRae 'Prince's Own' with extended pivot. Within the families differences are, with two exceptions, simple matters of overchecks dealt with as above. The exceptions are Wilsons' 'Rae tartan' and 'MacCrae tartan' woven in purple and green and so coded as 'Ross BG' and 'Ross BG(w)'. The same treatment is meted out to any tartan that is a complete colour change on another pattern as, for example, MacNab (Black Watch GRR) MacLachlan (Black Watch BKR) and Hunting Mackintosh (Mackintosh G(y)).

As in the case of 'Sindex' simplicity and flexibility are the keynotes of the system and some inconsistencies and anomalies must be expected as it develops. However, if the outline plan is followed there is no reason why these should make one worker's index incomprehensible to another.

APPENDIX E

Reconstructing Patterns from Fragments

It is always tempting to try to reconstruct a pattern from an incomplete fragment but the path is littered with pitfalls and only when a fragment is large enough to show an unequivocal repeat can it be said, hand on heart, that 'This is a true reconstruction'. In all other cases guesswork, intuition or general knowledge of patterns must be brought to bear on the problem and, although the importance of these must not be under-rated, a reconstruction based on all or any of them must remain in doubt.

As an extension to the mere mulling over of an incomplete thread count in the hope that light will dawn, colour strips, one for each count of the specimen, can be cut out of stiff paper and juggled with but a more useful aid is a set of drawings made by the 'Mauchline' method (page 56). Since it is a reasonable premise that a tartan pattern will be of the reversing type and that warp and weft patterns will be the same three drawings can be derived from a single specimen, using the warp and weft counts separately, each as warp *and* weft and then together as a representation of the specimen; these, fitted together and turned about like the remaining pieces of a lost jigsaw puzzle *may* call up some inspiration or fetch back from obscurity some half-forgotten pattern that completes the picture. Honesty and experience, however, have to admit that the chances are slim and that, even if a satisfactory and convincing result is obtained, we cannot be *sure* without further information; the best thing to do is to put it away and hope that this will turn up. Unfortunately, the tartan-seeking public greatly prefers a shadowy claim to a hard fact and if a doubtful reconstruction receives any publicity at all there can be no hope of substituting a correct one at a later date.

A type of pattern that it is impossible to reconstruct from anything much less than a full repeat is that which takes the form of a number of small setts distributed over a plain background. Each small sett has its own pivot and there is no means of telling which of these are the pivots of the pattern as a whole unless a full or almost full repeat is available.

APPENDIX F

Notes by William Wilson & Son, Bannockburn regarding *The Scottish Gaël*

For the purpose of compiling his tables of tartan patterns James Logan requested the weavers, William Wilson & Son, Bannockburn, to send him "patterns of all the *Clan and Family Tartans,* the authenticity of which is established." Our good fortune is that Wilsons kept a list of what was sent, made another of those that did not appear in the book and recorded their opinions of the patterns that were published. These throw some light on Logan's errors, real or supposed, though not as much as we might hope for since the remarks on the patterns are frequently couched in terms that suggest that the writer did not know what had gone before and quite often that he was not very good at relating the pattern table to the cloth. Possibilities are therefore indicated rather than questions answered but these particular notes are nevertheless an important part of the Logan story.

Patterns sent to Mr Logan in his work:

Abercromby — with silk.
Cameron — 2½ set Super.
Campbell — 2 Do. — Do.
Breadalbane — 2 Do. Com.
Colquhoun — 2 Do. — Do.
Chisholm — 3 Do. — Do.
Cummin — an imitation of this pattern made out of No. 155.[1]
Dalzell — our Com. George 4th with silk — no Pink.[2]
Douglas — Com. Douglas with silk.
Drummond — The Perth Super with silk.
Farquharson — 2 set Com.
Do. — 4 Do. — Do. 4 in yellow as certified by Monaltrie.
Forbes — 2 set Com. — only 8 in white.
Fraser — 3 set Do. — as generally sold.
Gordon — 2 set Super — officers 92nd.
Grahame — Com pattern.
Grant — 2 set as worn by Lord Gwydor.[3]
Gunn — 2 Do—.

Hay — 1 set Super Leith.
Lamont — 2 set-42nd with white.
Logan — as made for A. Logan Esqr.
McAlister — 1 set as bought from ( ) Arnot.
McDuff — 4 set Super.
McDonald — 2½ set Do. —
McDougal — 1 set & part — as we make it.[4]
McFarlane — 3 set Com.
McGillivray — as we make it.
McGregor — 4 set Super
McKintosh — 3 set Com — Chisholm no white.
Do.— Do.— Do.— shewy pattern with yellow
McKenzie — 2 set Super as worn by 78th.
McKay — 5 set as generally made.
Do.— Original Colours.
McKinnon — 3 set Super.
McLean — 4 set Com.
McNaughton — 3 set Do. — Montrose.
McNeil — 5 set — Do. —
McPherson — 3 set Com. Kidd — 27 inch.
Munro — 2 Do. — Do. — George 4th with yellow.[2]
Murray — 2 Do. — Super.
Ogilvie — 1 set Com. Green.
Ross — 1 Do. — Do. —
Sinclair — 3 set Super.
McTavish — 3 set Com.
Royal Stewart — 3 set Super.
42nd — 2 set Do. —
Lord McDonald — Scarlet & Green.
Earl of Inverness.

Patterns sent Mr Logan not in the Scottish Gaël:

Small Stewart, or Prince Charles Stewart's tartan, as worn by the officers of the 72nd Regt.
Earl of Strathearn. Tartan as worn by the Royals by order of the Duke of Kent.
McDonell of Glengarry Tartan — 3 set Super.
McDonald of Clanranald Do.— 2½ Do. — Com.
Do. — of Boisdale — doubtful.
McGregor of Glengyles Tartan.

Tartan of the Pipers of the 42nd Regt.
Small 42nd as worn by the officers of Do. —
McNab Tartan
Robertson — Do. —
Do. — with white stripe now generally sold as the Tartan of this Clan but thought to be a recent variation.
McCrae Tartan, generally sold in Ross-shire as the tartan of this Clan — 1 set with border — yellow silk
Cluny McPherson's Tartan — 2 set — 29 inch.

Remarks on the Clan Tartans given in Mr Logan's Scottish Gaël:

Abercrombie —

I am not aware that this is a Highland Clan or that I have ever seen the Pattern given as their tartan — From the idea I can form of it it is nearly the same as a pattern now generally known as the Abercrombie but which was so named after Sir Ralph Ab. end of last, or beginning of the present Century — a specimen of it is sent herewith — that scale is on the margin.[5]

)	Black	¼
)	Blue	3½
)	Black	3½
)	Green	3½
)	White	½
)	Green	3½
)	Black	3½
)	Green	3½
)	White	½
)	Green	3½
)	Black	3½
)	Blue	3½
)	Black	¼

Buchanan —
The scale given of this Tartan is very defective — a correct one is given — note this pattern is (sentence not completed)[6]
Cameron —
Campbell —
Breadalbane —
Chisholm —
Colquhoun —
Cummin — Have never seen this Tartan, but have every reason to believe it to be Fancy Pattern we have several of these description that resemble it and it is quite unlike a Clan Tartan — We have no Authentic Cummin Tartan — this we have sent is very generally in demand.[1]
Dalzell — We are not aware that this is a Highland Clan — the pattern you have given as the Tartan is quite well known to us as the 'George 4th' but

we never saw it before immediately after his Majesty's visit to Scotland. The pattern you give as the Munro is the same only yellow for the white stripes and we suppose the alteration was made about the time we ( ).[2]
Douglas — This we are quite aware is quite a Fancy Tartan — but for a considerable time has been sold under that name —
Drummond — We have long known this Tartan as the 'Perth' or Drummond — Lord Gwydor however wears the pattern you give as the Grant.
Farquharson — you give only the small Pattern as used for Trews —
Ferguson — Never saw this pattern before nor do we think the Fergusons a Clan.
Forbes — Defective
Fraser — This Pattern is generally sold as the Fraser — but there is some doubt as to its being the genuine Clan Tartan.
Graham — This is quite a Fictitious Tartan but is unreasonably sold as the Graham and a Pattern that has a great demand in the Tartan Trade — we are not acquainted with the Graham Clan Tartan — if it has one.
Grant —
Gunn —
Hay — Never (k)new this as the Hay Tartan but for some time as The Leith.
Lamont
Logan — Never saw this Pattern until we made it for A. Logan Esqr.
McAlistair —
McAulay —
McDonald —
McDuff —
McDougal — Very defective — the original of the Pattern sent us was more than a century old and perfectly genuine.[4]
McFarlane —
McGillivray —
McGregor —
McIntosh —

The following are additional notes which are filed with the foregoing but do not fit into the context:

Menzies Tartan — Scarlet and White 3 set
Rob Roy — Do. — 1 inch
New McNeil Tartan — whether this be the Tartan of the Clan or a variation of the other Pattern I cannot say

Cockburn Tartan — Authority D McAlpin 11 Broad Street Cheapside London.
Malc(l)olm —)
) no authority (deleted)
Mathieson —)
Davidson Tartan — worn by Davidson of Tulloch
Urquhart Tartan — The original of this pattern was sent us from Rosshire — it was a painting in which the checks half the size —
Buchanan — Small set — original as sent us
Do. — Large Do. —
Do. — sent from Dunkeld — thought to be the same pattern with variations[6]
Ramsay Tartan) from a M.S. dated 1571 in the
McKintosh — do.—) possession of Messrs Hay Stewart near Forres

NOTES

1 See Cummin
2 See Munro
3 Peter Robert Burrell, 2nd Lord Gwydyr, who married Clementina Sarah, daughter and heiress of James Drummond, Lord Perth, and took the name Drummond in addition to his own. It is clear that he wore as Drummond what we know as the Grant tartan but there is no evidence that he started the controversy.
4 The pattern referred to would seem to be that contained in the Key Pattern Book:

'MACDOUGAL TARTAN'

A	R	Pink	C	R	P	R	G	R	G	C	Pk	R	Pk	C	P	R	G
2	12	8	12	114	6	6	44	44	44	12	8	8	8	12	44	16	8
R	G	R	Pk	C	A												
16	120	8	4	16	2												

"The ... pattern is the real size of the Clan Tartan. To make 25 inches wide, it takes 2 half setts and a part of the third into the middle of the Scarlet Mark with 44 threads in it."
5 See Abercrombie
6 The only possible ending to the unfinished remark would be to the effect that the pattern is non-reversing and this would certainly make Logan's scale 'very defective'. A count from a reputed Wilson specimen gives the non-reversing sett and although it is undated and could therefore be post-McIan it does seem probable that this is the 'correct scale' mentioned:

A	K	G	A	G	K	A	K	R	W	R	K	A	K	Y	K	Y	K
8	4	10	6	10	4	8	4	16	4	16	4	8	4	10	4	10	4

NOTES

1 A recently-recognised fragment of 'George IV' pattern shows that the filling between the green lines of both DALZELL and MUNRO should be in scarlet, not rose, pink or crimson. Unfortunately, the fragment is not large enough to tell us if the sequence of three green lines should be doubled, as Logan's MUNRO, or single, as in DALZELL. However, having seen the pattern 'in the flesh', I incline to the belief that the latter is more likely.

2 The blue in the Cockburn Collection specimen is very dark and open to dispute but, having regard to the pattern, which is essentially MACKINTOSH with the green stripes divided into three and the blue stripes into two, and the tartan's origin in the Central Highlands, I am satisfied that the dark shade of blue that came to be called Purple is correct. Whether the old-time weavers used this shade in its own right or because no better 'black' was on offer is, of course, another question.

3 Yet another scrap of this plaid has now turned up. Though minute, it is attached to a note that gives the information that the plaid was cut up by Lady Margaret Mackintosh, widow of Sir Aeneas, the twenty-third Chief, to line the canopy of the State bed at Moy Hall. Lady Margaret died in 1835 and D. W. Stewart implies that the plaid that was lent for reproduction in his book was intact c.1890. If this is correct there can be no doubt that we can identify two plaids of the same pattern. This would be exciting enough but there is a strong possibility that the *Old and Rare* plaid has survived; discovery of this and comparison of the colours of the two specimens might reveal the existence of parts of two webs of the same patterns.

Bibliography

'Tartan in Books' deals only with the major books about tartan and there are many more that touch on the subject to a greater or less degree. I therefore make no apology for including the entire Bibliography from *The Setts* which is not only of value in itself but contains useful assessments of the worth of some of the less accessible material.

Constant reference has been made in these Notes to a small number of works that in the past have served as source-books for weavers of tartan. Some of these books are rare or not easy of access, and the reader may wonder what he will miss by not seeing them. A brief description of each will indicate its usefulness in regard to tartans. Most of them have been noted earlier in this book, but are listed here for ease of reference. The books have been listed in order of year of publication.

LOGAN, J. *The Scottish Gaël.* 1831. Smith, Elder & Co., London.

About the year 1826 James Logan wandered through Scotland, collecting information of antiquarian interest, and in 1831 he published his material in a two-volume work entitled *The Scottish Gaël.* In the course of the first volume he has a section dealing with tartans, particularly those used by the Highland regiments; but he says little about them that is not now generally known. As an appendix to the second volume he published a series of tables recording tartan designs, with instructions on how these tables were to be interpreted. Unfortunately the tables contain a number of palpable errors, and many of them must not be interpreted strictly. The whole work, with the exception of one illustration referring to his system of counting, was reprinted in 1876. For the benefit of those who have access to this reprint, we may say that the tables therein are exactly as in the first edition, errors included. M'Intyre North, in *The Book of the Club of True Highlanders* (1881), printed a series of tables, which he says was supplied by Logan. Compared with the earlier set, there are additions, omissions and alterations, and it is these later tables that were reprinted by Frank Adam. For the purpose of the present work Logan's original set has been used except where North's is mentioned.

STUART, J.S.S.; STUART, C.E. *Vestiarium Scoticum.* 1842. William Tait, Edinburgh.

The brothers John Sobieski Stolberg Stuart and Charles Edward Stuart (variously known by the names Allan Hay, Hay Allan, Stuart Hay, Hay, and Stuart), were responsible for this work, the former as editor, the latter preparing the drawings from which the illustrations were produced. These drawings were made from descriptions of tartans, found in a MS. the brothers claimed as belonging to the sixteenth century. Three copies of this old MS. were supposed to have existed, but all trace of them was lost before they could be brought to critical examination, though a transcript was printed in the *Vestiarium*. The work seems to have been planned and ready for publication by 1829, but publication was not achieved till 1842.

Seventy-five tartans are illustrated, and the reproductions leave little doubt as to colour and none as to pattern. Many of these tartans have since come into general use solely on the authority of this imposing work. That authority was from the first hotly impugned, but the tartans have remained. Less than a dozen of the seventy-five are supported by independent evidence of their previous existence.

LOGAN, J. and MCIAN, R. R. *The Clans of the Scottish Highlands.* 1845–47. Ackermann & Co., London.

The publication of the successive parts of this work extended over the years 1843 to 1849. It consists of a series of coloured plates, showing figures in Highland costume, with historical commentaries. Most of the plates show tartan, but they serve better to illustrate the forms of the costumes than the setts of the tartans. The drawings were the work of R. R. McIan, and the text was for the most part by Logan. There is usually some reference to the tartan where one is illustrated, but these references are not so helpful as they would have been had the drawings been more explicit. In his Introduction Logan says of the patterns: 'Those only will be given which are acknowledged by the present chiefs and clans, and which tradition and long prescriptive use have invested with a legitimate claim'. The opinion of the chiefs of the period was not a safe foundation on which to build claims of ancient usage, as Thomas Smibert a little later recognised. Though Logan had by this time seen the *Vestiarium*, the tartans therein are, with a few exceptions, ignored — a sufficient indication of Logan's opinion of the validity of that work.

STUART, J. S. S. and STUART, C. E. *The Costume of the Clans,* 1845. Menzies, Edinburgh. Reprinted 1892 by John Grant, Edinburgh, and others in London, Paris, Leipzig, and Prague.

Only the first volume of this work was published. Whatever its value in other respects, as a source-book for tartans it is almost worthless. From the illustrations about three dozen setts can be abstracted with some assurance, but they have little relation to the tartans known to have been in use before or since. D. W. Stewart checked many of the illustrations against the portraits from which it was claimed they had been copied, and found them not only inaccurate but quite misleading. The remainder seem to have been evolved out of the inner consciousness of the Sobieski brothers.

SMIBERT, T. *The Clans of the Highlands of Scotland.* 1850. James Hogg, Edinburgh.

Fifty-five tartans are shown. Smibert says: '... it was to ascertain and establish the genuine and oldest setts of the proper tartans of the Highland Clans, before the influx of such varieties rendered it impossible, that the present work was undertaken. The Highland chiefs themselves have of late thrown the most serious obstacles in the way, seeing that they have been too ready to adopt changes at the mere dictation of fancy, with the view of improving, no doubt, the look of their family setts'.

Smibert depended mainly on specimens obtained from Messrs Wilson & Son, of Bannockburn, who had been weavers of carpets and tartan possibly as far back as 'the '45'. Their name appears in the list of subscribers to Logan's *The Scottish Gaël,* and it is notable that Smibert's setts follow fairly closely those given by Logan. D. W. Stewart wrote that Smibert adopted some of his setts from the *Vestiarium*. Yet only three are found both in Smibert and in the *Vestiarium* but not in Logan, and these were probably being regularly manufactured by Messrs Wilson, who are known to have produced tartans for the Sobieski brothers as early as 1829.

SMITH, W. and A. *Authenticated Tartans of the Clans and Families of Scotland.* 1850. W. & A. Smith, Mauchline.

The Smiths gave various authorities for their sixty-nine tartans. It seems that, in preparation for the visit of George IV to Scotland in 1822, George Hunter, an Army clothier, toured the Highlands in search of old tartans. We cannot be certain of what he learned, but his report was passed on to Messrs Meyer & Mortimer, and the Smiths obtained many of their setts from this firm, and some from Messrs Wilson of Bannockburn. The Smiths had access also to the collection of W. F. Skene, the historian, and to the records of Messrs Romanes & Paterson, tartan merchants, of Edinburgh. A few setts are put forward on the authority of contemporary chiefs of clans, but Smibert's comment should be borne in mind. 'Use and wont' is the authority most often given.

GRANT, J. *The Tartans of the Clans of Scotland.* 1886. W. & A. K. Johnston, Edinburgh.

The greater part of the seventy-two tartans shown by Grant are to be found in the Smith work, sometimes with slight changes. Four others were previously given only in the *Vestiarium*, and for five we have to go to Smibert or Logan. The MACLAINE OF LOCHBUIE, the MACQUARRIE (305), and the HUNTING STEWART had not been previously illustrated or described, though the first is found in early collections. James Grant says that all his patterns were in use in his time, and that he took them from actual specimens. The plates are large, and were evidently intended to represent the specimens full size. Frequently they do not show sufficient of the pattern to reveal how it repeats.

STEWART, D.W. *Old and Rare Scottish Tartans.* 1893. Geo. P. Johnston, Edinburgh.

This does not profess to give a comprehensive list, but only a selection of tartans, chosen for special points of interest, for their unfamiliarity, or for their antiquity. Forty-five specimens, woven in silk, constitute the illustrations. Many of the designs, since become popular, had not been previously illustrated or extensively used. The Introduction gives a very full and interesting survey of the history of the Highland dress, and an account of the origin of the *Vestiarium Scoticum*, based on unpublished records, and of the controversy over its sponsors' claim that it represented a work of the sixteenth century. It has been said that D.W. Stewart supported the claim. From his presentation of the case this might reasonably be deduced, but several remarks made when he came to deal with specific tartans suggest he had an underlying doubt about the value of the *Vestiarium* as an authentic record.

WHYTE, H. *The Scottish Clans and their Tartans.* 1891. W. & A.K. Johnston, Edinburgh.

This was the first of a long series of pocket editions, of which the twenty-first was produced in 1929. They followed what had become the established scheme of a brief history of each of a large number of clans, accompanied by a plate showing a tartan. References to the tartans were conspicuous by their rarity, and the few lines allotted to the four or five that receive any notice were uninformative and apocryphal. We are told in the 1929 edition that 'The clan sketches in the original edition were prepared by the late Mr. Henry Whyte'; but there is evidence of considerable revision, as is shown by comparison with the edition of 1910.

WHYTE, H. and others. *The Tartans of the Clans and Septs of Scotland.* 1906. W. & A.K. Johnston, Edinburgh.

This handsome work, issued in two volumes and described as a 'library Edition', is in effect an enlargement of the above smaller work first produced in 1891. The clan histories and general chapters were written by the same Henry Whyte and several other contributors.

Each volume shows more than a hundred tartans. These include the earlier selection, supplemented by many that were new to the literature of tartans, such as the 'Dress' forms of the Black Watch, the Gordon, and the Campbell, into which a great deal of white ground had been introduced. Other tartans of the period first appear here, such as the Hope-Vere, the Lorne and the Louise, a Royal Stuart with black ground and a Stuart in black and white only. Many more such aberrations go to swell the total of tartans shown.

In an endeavour to give realism, the prints of the tartans had been passed through an embossing machine to give a fabric-like texture. This treatment, along with the very dark blues and greens used, tends to obscure the detail of the pattern, so that it is often difficult to separate the black and to distinguish one colour from another; this detracts from the usefulness of the work to the student by providing a mine of misinformation.

ADAM, F. *The Clans, Septs and Regiments of the Scottish Highlands.* 1908. W. & A. K. Johnston, Edinburgh.

This is an encyclopaedic work, touching on every aspect of its subject and far beyond. With the second edition it came under the influence of Thomas Innes of Learney (later Sir Thomas, and Lord Lyon King of Arms) until it has become what amounts to a joint work very much dominated by the latter writer. It was admittedly 'largely rewritten' by him, even to the extent of eliminating without apology Adam's account of the clan system after Culloden. Frank Adam wrote of its 'destruction'; Sir Thomas would have none of that, contending that it never expired, and still flourishes. There is no attempt to show how much of the original book survives and how much has been changed.

Of tartans, over a hundred are shown, many very indifferently. There is a chapter of comments on about half of them, at best harmless and at worst misleading.

INNES, T. *The Tartans of the Clans and Families of Scotland.* 1938. W. & A. K. Johnston, Edinburgh.

The main part of this work is a series of 112 plates of clan tartans, each with an outline history of the clan, and four of 'district' tartans without notes. The plates are based on those in James Grant's work of 1886, some errors in which are here perpetuated.

The extensive Introduction reflects the attitude of the late Lord Lyon King of Arms, which the author subsequently became, though his predecessor in that office, Sir Francis Grant, had little respect for many of the ideas on clan tartans here expressed, publicly describing the modern naming of tartans by clans as 'humbug'. Such differences characterize the literature of tartans. Though each clan history is faced by a clan tartan, there is an almost complete absence of any reference to that tartan as such.

BAIN, R. *The Clans and Tartans of Scotland.* 1938. Collins, London and Glasgow.

This was the first of our books to employ the photographic half-tone process to reproduce woven specimens of tartan, so gaining much in realism if not always much in precision. The book had what has become the established arrangement of a plate of a tartan faced by a brief history of the related clan. In the course of several editions and many reprints, revisions have been made, in particular those by the late Miss Margaret O. MacDougall, F.S.A.Scot., and it is currently (1974) under further revision both in text and plates.

McClintock, H. F. *Old Irish and Highland Dress.* 1943. W. Tempest, Dundalk, Eire.

A second edition of this scholarly work was produced, in two volumes — Old Highland Dress and Tartans, the Highland part of the first edition with an additional chapter on Early Tartans by J. Telfer Dunbar, F.S.A.Scot., in 1949; and Old Irish Dress, the Irish part, in 1950. The whole makes an impressive study, made by the author 'in order to find out what historical authority there was for the various adaptations of the Highland kilt and plaid that were being worn by the pipers of Irish regiments as a national Irish dress'.

The germinal theme of McClintock's studies was the question of 'The Irish Kilt'. His unequivocal conclusion was that there was nothing to justify the supposition that it had any place in the history of the Irish people, and that its adoption whether in tartan or in saffron, was no more than a piece of twentieth century myth-making, without historical or graphic evidence to support it.

Hesketh, C. *Tartans.* 1961. Weidenfeld & Nicolson, London.

No page in this book is without its illustration, very frequently in colour, and these add up to a remarkable gallery of portraits showing the variety of forms of Highland dress from the 17th century onwards. Three dozen postage-stamp-size representations of tartan patterns cover two of the pages; a third page is fully occupied by one tartan; and for the rest we depend on the portraits in colour. Lady Hesketh's 'Tartans' does not confine itself to the subject of its title. All the popular myths about tartan seem to come in for mention, and those myths are treated with a liberal measure of scepticism that is often refreshing, but the main theme of the text is the Highland dress, treated lightly but with understanding.

Dunbar, J. T. *The History of Highland Dress.* 1962. Oliver & Boyd, Edinburgh.

Though this handsome book is primarily concerned with the evolution of the dress and accoutrements of the Highlander, there is much in it of the greatest value to those interested mainly in the history of tartan. In particular, the story of the proliferation of clan tartans from the end of the 18th century to the second quarter of the 19th will be new to many. Though the idea of using tartans was a revival of a very old custom, nearly all the tartans we now use did not exist before the Jacobite Rising of 1745, nor indeed until after the ban on their use had been lifted in 1782. Mr. Dunbar relates in considerable detail how the Vestiarium Scoticum of 1842 was mistakenly accepted as authentic by many of the high-born friends of the Sobieski Brothers, so that clansmen still regard with veneration scores of tartans that had their origin only a dozen or so years before they were set before the unsuspecting public. Mr. Dunbar expresses our doubts of their authenticity; since he wrote of them, a deeper study of the evidence has proved beyond all reasonable doubt the fraudulent nature of these tartans.

SCARLETT, J. D. *Tartans of Scotland.* 1972. Lutterworth Press, London.

This book, though slight in bulk and price, is full of sound matter. It provides over seventy excellent illustrations of clan tartans, each with interesting notes on its clan. The clans are grouped geographically, and the notes are anecdotal rather than historical. The introductory matter is well adapted to the needs of anyone taking notice of tartans and Highland dress for the first time, and could help protect him from some of the over-romantic ideas with which he may otherwise be beset.

SCARLETT, J. D. *The Tartan-Spotter's Guide.* 1973. Shepheard-Walwyn (Publishers), London.

A book about tartans in general, for anyone prepared not only to admire tartans but to look at them with an analytic eye. What are the factors that go to make a pattern? What happens when these factors are blended? How much blending is and is not possible? Can a shorthand note be made when a tartan is seen for only a fraction of a minute, and used later in weaving a reproduction of it?

At a first glance one might take this book to be merely frivolous, but that would be entirely wrong. The author writes from a great fund of knowledge and practical experience; and, if he and his artist friend Angus McBride occasionally indulge in a smile, it is a welcome relief from the more usual portentous solemnity.

A small number of worth-while books has appeared since 1974, when the second edition of *The Setts* was published, and *The Setts* itself must take a place in any bibliography of tartan.

STEWART, DONALD C. *The Setts of the Scottish Tartans.* 1950. Oliver & Boyd, Edinburgh. Second Edition 1974. Shepheard-Walwyn (Publishers), London.

As a pioneer work on tartan *The Setts* is without peer and is the essential guide book to modern tartan research. It is covered in detail under 'Tartan in Books'.

Stewart, Donald C. and Thompson, J. Charles. *Scotland's Forged Tartans.* 1980. Paul Harris Publishing, Edinburgh.

The authors came together as a result of their independently held doubts as to the authenticity of the *Vestiarium Scoticum* and collaborated to produce a critical analysis of that work; their conclusions are summed up in the title of their book. This was the first and so far the only scholarly approach to the subject and whether you are convinced by the arguments or not it is a valuable book for it contains the texts of the Vestiarium, the Cromarty Ms. and the Lauder Transcript.

Scarlett, James D. *The Tartan Weaver's Guide.* 1985. Shepheard-Walwyn (Publishers), London.

Written around the publisher's *Guide to Scottish Tartans,* this book provides the would-be tartan weaver with 228 thread counts — each with a brief commentary — and a comprehensive guide to the specialized art of tartan weaving.

Munro, R. W. *Highland Clans & Tartans.* 1977. Octopus Books, London.

The author is a historian of note and tells the story factually of how the Clans were, how they lost their identities and how they revived as Clan Societies. The book is particularly useful for the large number of excellent coloured reproductions of paintings and old tartans.

Among sources yet untapped the Wilson records are by far the most extensive and so the most important. Most of them have now found their way to libraries and museums, where there is a lifetime of work waiting to be done in deciphering, transcribing and collating them before any serious study can begin.

Index

Figures in brackets refer to threadcounts, not page numbers.